WEED

the

PEOPLE

ALSO BY
BRUCE BARCOTT

The Last Flight of the
Scarlet Macaw
One Woman's Fight to Save the World's Most Beautiful Bird

The Measure of a Mountain
Beauty and Terror on Mount Rainier

Northwest Passages
*A Literary Anthology of the Pacific Northwest from
Coyote Tales to Roadside Attractions*

WEED
the
PEOPLE

THE FUTURE OF LEGAL
MARIJUANA IN AMERICA

BRUCE BARCOTT

TIME
Books

Published by Time Books, an imprint of Time Home Entertainment Inc.
1271 Avenue of the Americas, 6th floor • New York, NY 10020

ISBN 10: 1-61893-140-7
ISBN 13: 978-1-61893-140-5
Library of Congress Control Number: 2014952627

We welcome your comments and suggestions
about Time Books. Please write to us at:
Time Books
Attention: Book Editors
P.O. Box 361095
Des Moines, IA 50336-1095

If you would like to order any of our hardcover Collector's Edition books,
please call us at 800-327-6388, Monday through Friday, 7 a.m.–9 p.m.
Central Time.

For my parents, who encouraged me to explore without losing my head; and for my children, who carry out that practice every day.

AUTHOR'S NOTE

The English language contains more than 635 terms for marijuana. In this book I'll generally limit myself to four: *marijuana*, *cannabis*, *weed* and *pot*. They all mean the same thing.

Laws are changing, but in many circles marijuana remains a controversial substance and a taboo subject. It is also federally illegal. For those reasons, some people quoted in the book are referred to by first name only. A few have been given pseudonyms, as noted. My aim is to record and examine life as it's actually lived in a legalized state. The most telling comments can come in private conversation, and in some instances I've changed a name to protect a person's job, professional license, reputation or privacy.

CONTENTS

HARMONY IS PROPRIETARY

The first grow we saw that day was owned by a hard man named Mike. Mike had the look of a contract killer in a gangster film. He was a slim, compact gent who wore his jeans pressed and his silver hair trim. He spoke only when necessity demanded. His eyes held the warmth of steel pinballs.

Mike's head grower, a bro in his 20s all T-shirt and tats, snapped the first of two locks on a low industrial building near the highway. I hung back with Christian, Patrick and Jeff, three pot buyers with whom I'd embedded. They were scouting large quantities of product for their legal marijuana company. *Click* went the second lock. We all ducked through the door.

The smell hit me as I crossed the threshold. The glandular miasma of marijuana. Weed. *Cannabis sativa.* Most people of a certain age are familiar with the pungent signature of pot smoke. The living plant is something else. Its leaves and flower issue an enveloping aroma unlike any other vegetable matter. The smell of a grow room is the scent of transpiration, of fecund exertion. It's the trapped sweat of a high school locker room, the funk of a hockey jersey steaming on a radiator.

"This first room is all OG Kush," said the grower. The space, no bigger than half a tennis court, was flooded with marijuana. Each bushy waist-high plant grew out of its own 20-gallon bucket, with the buckets packed in tight rows. Thousand-watt grow lights dangled from the ceiling, so close to the plants they seemed poised to interrogate.

Jeff rubbed a bud between his thumb and forefinger. He pulled it close and smelled it like a rose. "Nice," he said.

A year earlier I'd known almost nothing about marijuana. I'd never even set eyes on a live pot plant. But now I knew a few things. I knew there were two marijuana species, *Cannabis sativa* and *Cannabis indica*. Sativas got you high; indicas got you stoned. OG Kush, the strain name, was a popular sativa-dominant hybrid. It was known for its earthy pine scent and its powers as an anxiety reliever. Mike's crop looked healthy, which meant Jeff and his partners would probably offer a bid.

Jeff, Christian and Patrick were legalizers. They worked for a government-registered company licensed to purchase, grow, process and sell marijuana. Mike was . . . well, Mike worked in a legal gray area. He was an independent operator. His grow was probably, possibly, theoretically and perhaps provably operating on the right side of the law. But also possibly not. That was Mike's business, not ours.

In the late spring of 2014, the two teams sat on either side of a historic pivot point. Marijuana was moving from illegality to legality. Christian, Patrick and Jeff were avatars of the new era: outsiders embracing marijuana not for its intoxicating powers or countercultural symbolism but for its profound economic potential. Christian was trained as a Silicon Valley investment banker. Jeff formerly ran logistics for a Texas steelmaker. Patrick was recently director of the U.S. Drug Enforcement Administration's field office in Portland, Oregon. A year earlier Patrick might have arrested Mike. Now the two were discussing contract terms.

Mike's gardener led us into a second room. This one held a different cannabis strain, with long spidery branches. I rubbed the flower on my thumb. I held it to my nose. *Zing!* Fragrance exploded in my brain. The plant smelled of lemon, but so much more than that; maybe lemon crossed with gardenias, night-blooming jasmine and one of those pheromones that arouse carnal desires.

I shot a look at Jeff. He was smelling it too.

"What . . . what is this?" I asked.

"This one's our special strain," said Mike. "We call it Harmony. Nice, eh?"

"Really nice," I said. I didn't tell him I was at that very moment suppressing a desire to disrobe and rub Harmony over every square inch of my body. I figured that would be bad form. Also, an expression of undue interest could undermine Patrick's negotiating position.

We moved on.

In another room, Mike showed me a collection of machines that looked like modified chainsaws. "This is my main business," he told me. "Years ago I invented a speed cincher. It tightens chains and winch lines on commercial vessels."

I have to confess that Mike's speed cinchers immediately brought to mind the bathtub chainsaw scene in *Scarface*. That's entirely unfair to Mike, who is not a gangster. But there it is. If you're a middle-aged American man and you wander through a marijuana grow and stumble upon a lineup of half a dozen chainsaw-size machines that could, conceivably, enact horrible twisting violence upon a human leg or forearm—well, some *Scarface* thoughts are going to bubble up. It can't be helped.

When it came time to negotiate, Mike and his lead grower chewed over terms with Christian, Patrick and Jeff.

Jeff inquired about the Harmony strain.

"We're open to selling that as a finished product," Mike said, "but not clones." Finished product meant dried and cured, ready to smoke. Clones are plant cuttings. Buying a clone would be like obtaining the engineering schematics and the patent. "That's proprietary."

Had I been negotiating for Jeff, my fist would have bruised the table. *We must have Harmony! Name your price, man!* But there was a reason that Jeff was a businessman and I was not. He shrugged off the loss.

"What about that Kush you got growing?" he said. "What are you thinking about a price?"

Before Mike could speak, his grower blurted, "Thirteen hundred."

Mike shot him a cold look.

"We could do that," said Patrick—$1,300 a pound was a steal.

Mike tried to salvage what he could. "We'll have to think about it," he said.

We shook hands and departed. I didn't want to think about what happened to Mike's grower after we left.

WELCOME

Welcome to dope year zero.

Welcome to the era of legal pot shops, cannabis farmers and brand-name marijuana. Welcome to the interregnum between criminal and customer. Welcome to a world where potency is calibrated in percentages and milligrams, which are measurements sort of like alcohol proof but really in so many ways not. Welcome to the end of stoner culture with its glorious tie-dyed shagginess and half-clever puns and propensity to turn any word, really any word at all, into a slang expression denoting cannabis or the ingestion of same. Welcome to the telltale odor of the skunk of the botanical world. Welcome to government pot inspectors and gainfully employed budtenders with health insurance and 401(k)s. Welcome to professional marijuana critics and cannabis connoisseurs who lord it over the rest of us with their insufferable haute-pot snobbishness. Welcome to ornery old men who were once outlaw pot growers but are now just cranky farmers. Welcome to marijuana millionaires; may they spend their winnings wisely and not squander them on jade-inlaid leaf-shaped swimming pools, although that would be kind of cool to see. Welcome to the beginning of the end of Mexican drug cartels, the War on Drugs, mandatory minimum sentences and 10 years in prison for a single joint. Welcome to the moment a political movement gives birth to an economic awakening. Welcome to unintended consequences and unforeseen problems and maybe, just maybe, welcome to common sense and sanity.

Welcome to the future.

———————

America is changing its mind about marijuana. For the past 80 years we've treated it as a ruinously dangerous drug, a public health menace, an addictive and illegal scourge. That is changing, and more quickly than many of us once thought possible. At the end of 2014 the U.S. reached a tipping point: for the first time ever, a majority of Americans lived in states with some form of marijuana legality. Four states and the District of Columbia embraced full legalization. More than 200 shops sold legal cannabis in Colorado. Eighty-nine operated in Washington State. Similar stores are expected to come online in Alaska, Oregon and D.C. by 2016. Twenty-three states now allow the use of marijuana for medical conditions.

The magnitude of the change in America's relationship to marijuana can't be measured by numbers alone. There are deeper shifts going on here. Cultural realignments. Social adjustments. The place of marijuana in our lives is being rethought, reconsidered and recalibrated. Four decades after Richard Nixon opened America's War on Drugs, that long campaign has reached a point of exhaustion and failure.

In the next few years, every American will face a moment of reckoning with marijuana. We owe it to ourselves, our country and future generations to be ready for it. The moment may arrive in any number of forms: a vote for or against legalization; a decision to purchase or decline a gram of legal weed; an agreement to allow it or banish it from the house; toking on an offered joint or passing it down the line.

My own reckoning came on Nov. 2, 2012.

It was a Friday night. We were four adults marking the end of the workweek. A bottle of red wine, a kitchen table, chat and jokes and laughter. My wife, Claire, and I had just shipped articles to editors in New York. We were feeling loose and boozy. Our friends Linda and Steve talked about their kids and their new Goldendoodle. We were middle-class parents in our 40s. Having survived four years of the Great Recession, we worried about making it through year five. Steve had a contracting business. He designed and built custom homes and remodels, the kind of work that mostly vanished in the crash of 2008. Linda practiced civil liberties law. Claire and I were writers; we made our way by hustling jobs.

For an hour we chewed over the upcoming election. President Obama's victory seemed assured, but as seasoned Democrats we imagined all the ways he might lose. We ticked through Mitt Romney's winnable scenarios. We soothed ourselves with Nate Silver's Electoral College projections. Then Linda shot me her serious-question look.

"How are you voting on Initiative 502?" she asked.

"Legalizing marijuana?" I shrugged. "No."

"Are you kidding me?" Linda said. "Come on."

"Pot. Eech. I can't stand the stuff."

Linda drilled a finger into my chest. "Listen," she said. "This is not about you. Nobody gives a shit whether you like pot or hate it. This is a race issue. It's a civil rights issue. It's about millions of people losing their liberty and their lives because of ridiculous drug laws that do not work. There are generations of black men in prison because they were caught with a substance that's less harmful than alcohol. You're a white guy, so you don't have to worry about it. Others do."

She really does talk like that.

"Fair enough," I said. "Still . . ."

"Still?" she said. "What are your reservations? I want to hear them."

Claire held up an empty wine glass. Steve reached for another bottle of Malbec.

I thought of our two children playing with our friends' kids. In the den our 11-year-old sons dueled at Magic: The Gathering, their wizards-and-weapons card game. In an upstairs bedroom our daughters, both 14, updated their Tumblr accounts and listened to Vampire Weekend.

"I don't want my kids to have easier access to it," I said.

Linda wasn't having it.

"Oh, you think they'll have easier access than they have now?" she said. "When they can buy pot every day at the high school or behind the Safeway? They've done studies on that. Do you know where most adults with teenagers get their dope? From their kids."

Did she just give me a *Bring it* wave? Like Keanu Reeves to Hugo Weaving in *The Matrix*?

"And in a couple years the girls are going to be out there driving with a bunch of stoned drivers on the road," I said.

Linda didn't flinch.

"As opposed to the drunks already out there? Ask a cop whether he'd rather pull over a person who's drunk or a person who's stoned."

Her argument assumed a zero-sum universe of impaired drivers who chose either alcohol or marijuana for their pleasure. I didn't think it was that simple.

"If we open up legal marijuana markets," I said, "aren't we just creating another corporate monster like Big Tobacco? Ten years from now pot companies are going to be lining the pockets of politicians."

That sent Linda back to her anti–War on Drugs stance. "The alternative we're living right now is to have for-profit prison corporations line the pockets of politicians and throw generation after generation of black men and Latinos in jail."

I sighed. "I just don't like marijuana," I confessed. "I don't want to smell it. I don't want to see it. I don't want to deal with it in my community and in my life."

She shot me a look of disappointment. *I expected more from you.* "You better not vote tonight," she said. In our county we vote by mail. Ballots weren't due for another four days. "You go home and you think about it."

And so I did.

A quick search led me to some startling statistics. Every year between

2001 and 2010, around 800,000 Americans were arrested on marijuana charges, most of them for small-time possession. That was nearly three times as many people as were arrested annually in the early 1990s. Pot use had been slowly on the rise, but pot arrests had gone through the roof. The data was especially dire if you weren't white. In California, arrests of nonwhite teenagers for pot possession surged from 3,100 in 1990 to 16,400 in 2010. A number of studies in the mid-2000s found that more than 40,000 people across the country languished in state or federal prisons on marijuana convictions. To put that in perspective, there are only 12 nations in the world whose entire prison populations exceed 40,000. The majority of those jailed on pot convictions were black men, who were four times as likely as white men to be arrested on marijuana charges.

Linda's words rattled around in my head. *This is not about you. This is a civil rights issue.* I couldn't deny it. The facts bore her out. My personal loathing of marijuana and my fear of a cannabis-legal future appeared to be petty complaints next to the injustice of the War on Drugs.

On a cold Sunday night in November, Claire and I considered our ballots. We were in bed. We often end up voting this way. I don't know why. It may be some sort of subconscious desire for privacy, or a way of acknowledging the intimate nature of ballot casting. It's not an erotic thing; we're not getting it on while we vote, for God's sake.

We worked our way through the voter's guide. President, Barack Obama, check. Senator, Maria Cantwell, check. Governor, Jay Inslee, check. Gay marriage? Hell to the check yeah.

"What's your call on 502?" asked Claire. I could see she had already darkened the YES bubble on her ballot.

"Eh, Linda's probably right," I said. I held my nose. I took a chance. I voted yes.

History changed.

2

HERE IS MY
PERMANENT RECORD

Before we go further, allow me to declare my true and complete marijuana history. It is, believe me, a slim dossier.

I was born in the mid-1960s. My family lived in a working-class Pacific Northwest mill town. Our neighbors manufactured Scott toilet paper and Boeing 747s. We lived within driving distance of Seattle, but Seattle back then bore no resemblance to the glamorous mirrorball it is today. There was no Microsoft, no Amazon, no Gates Foundation. Workers had titles like "carpenter," "fisherman" and "logger." When a bunch of motorheads dropped airplane engines into boats and raced them around Lake Washington, we considered it a major sporting event. People back East thought Seattle was located in Alaska.

I came of age in the late '70s and early '80s, just as the sex-and-drugs caravan plunged off the bridge. Not that I would have likely enjoyed much action in the '60s. My mother's clan adhered to a Minnesota-style commonsense liberalism. We experienced the radicalism of the '70s through *Godspell* and the groovy *Good News Bible*. The closest we ever got to a hippie was our cool uncle Jim, who drove a sweet '69 Camaro and wore his hair in a shoulder-length drape. Jim may have drawn on a joint in college (I don't know), but he never brought the stuff home. My grandparents were teetotalers, and my parents' drinking could be measured in Monopoly thimbles. The idea of marijuana entering our lives wasn't frightening so much as absurd. When you think of my family, think *The Best of Bread*, not *Houses of the Holy*.

The first time I saw it smoked by someone my age was in eighth grade. The dismissal bell had rung. I strolled across the outdoor basketball courts to retrieve my bicycle. Beside me, a ninth-grader with stringy hair withdrew a shiny device from his pocket. Without so much as a coast-clearing glance, he flicked a Bic and sucked the flame into a one-hitter. I know now that a small discreet pipe is known as a one-hitter. I did not possess that knowledge as an eighth-grade boy. All I knew was that something shocking was taking place next to me. My spine tingled. This was not a frisson of excitement and wonder. It was fear. My thought was, *Holy shit, this dude's gonna get busted and I'll be caught up in the net.* That's how it was with me. When mass rule-breakery occurred, I was always the first nabbed.

Also, there was this: I was a person who sought to rise above my station. Not that my station was intolerable. I grew up in a perfectly nice town among perfectly nice people. Whom I desperately wanted to escape. The contours of my culture were defined by ZZ Top, Def Leppard, Orange Julius, Chess King and Spencer's Gifts. I had the vague sense that other people in bigger cities were pursuing more sophisticated pleasures. Like, I don't know, listening to jazz. Riding subways. Living in apartments. Perhaps with Suzanne Pleshette.

So it was throughout my teenage years. I had zero interest in marijuana, in part because I worried a bust might ground my plans for flight. With my proven talent for getting caught, I figured I'd better wait and smoke pot in college.

My first try came during spring break of my freshman year at the University of Washington. We were at a friend's family cabin. Harold had some marijuana. Harold came from Berkeley, so we all bowed to his expertise in these matters. The five of us huddled around a small brass pipe in the garage. Why the garage? Beats me. Garages are kind of a thing with pot. We each inhaled and passed the pipe. As a newcomer to the ritual, I tried not to screw up. My friend Steve, also a rube, laughed in mid-toke, which had a blowpipe effect. Tiny green flakes sprinkled at our feet.

"Steve!" said Harold. "You blew the bowl, man."

What? the rest of us said. *No, no, no.* We dropped to our knees and swept the cannabis off the oil-blotched concrete.

We continued passing the pipe, which now contained cat hair and sawdust. Hilarity ensued. We all laughed for half an hour, then each retreated to quiet corners. I found the stereo, headphones and a copy of *Dark Side of the Moon.* As if driven to cliché by the drug. The next two hours were passed listening happily to Pink Floyd's mind-blowing exegesis on madness, greed and time.

The experience pleased me. And yet I didn't feel compelled to repeat the trip. I suspect it had something to do with the social context of pot. My friends just weren't into it. Neither were the girls. In the '80s, young women tended to congregate at gatherings juiced with alcohol, not marijuana. Everybody drank *a lot.* Also, pot had by this time acquired a bit of a has-been reputation. In the *Miami Vice* era, weed was a hippie drug, a relic of the '70s.

Pot resurfaced during my sophomore year, when I pledged a fraternity. This was not a well-considered decision. I was young. I gained experience. During spring quarter, the house master assigned me a bunk in a basement area known with typical frat-boy sensitivity as "the ghetto." The ghetto had a reputation. It was a place apart. Seven brothers, three rooms, one communal bong. Bobby was its name.

Bobby was constructed of sky-blue acrylic. Nobody knew where Bobby came from, who owned Bobby or where Bobby hung out during the day. But every night around 11:30 Bobby would make his nightly ghetto rounds. That funny bubble-making sound of a water bong . . . somebody else supplied the weed; we each chipped in 10 bucks now and then. We watched the end of Johnny Carson and the first half-hour of

Late Night with David Letterman. This was 1987, the heyday of early Letterman bits like Stupid Pet Tricks. Letterman was funny, but the weed made him funnier. We got baked a lot that spring. I got baked a lot that spring.

And then, at a certain point, I stopped. Oddly, I can still remember the moment. I was walking to class on a weekday morning. While waiting for the light at the corner of NE 45th and 19th Street, I found myself once again forgetting something—a book, a key, a class schedule. This forgetting seemed to be on the increase with me. I didn't like it. It was annoying and a little worrying. My mind immediately went to the pot. Whether the smoking caused these small memory malfunctions or merely made me paranoid about the possibility of a memory lapse, I didn't know. But marijuana seemed to be the major variable.

The light changed. I crossed the street and swore off the weed.

I didn't quit Bobby cold turkey. I took a little puff now and then. But my heavy-use days were over.

And then . . . that was pretty much it for cannabis and me. I'd hit the pipe once or twice a year during my 20s, when a friend offered a Friday-night toke. Sometimes it made me giddy. Mostly it put me to sleep.

I haven't tried many other drugs. I did LSD twice in my early 20s. Never did cocaine. I figured one of two things would happen with coke: I'd either love the stuff (bad) or explode my freakishly high-metabolism heart (worse). I like good bourbon and a robust Cabernet. When it comes to beer, the cheaper and colder the better.

Marijuana? I could take it or leave it. By my late 20s I'd abandoned it completely. And then in my late 40s something unexpected occurred. Marijuana returned.

POT'S CRONKITE
MOMENT

One of the things they don't tell you about life is that if you hang around long enough, you will see the once impossible come to pass. In my time on this earth I've seen Communism fall, apartheid collapse and capitalism roar through China. A black man was elected President of the United States. Gay marriage became accepted and legal.

The legalization of marijuana is the next great refutation of the impossible. It's happening in my own backyard. I live in Washington State. A few years ago I lived in Colorado. In both states my family and friends are serving as test subjects in one of the most unusual political and social experiments of the 21st century. If pot legalization works here, other states will legalize too.

This change is by no means permanent or assured. If legalization fails in Washington and Colorado, marijuana could return to the shadows for decades. President Obama has given the two states a three-year pass to see how things play out. If they go badly, the next president could enforce the federal ban and end legal pot during his or her first week in office.

Those of us living through legalization are enjoying new freedoms. We're also confronting unforeseen questions and awkward situations. The other day I found myself talking about marijuana with a friend while picking through the oranges at the local grocery store. Midway through the conversation I realized I was whispering. But why? I wouldn't talk about wine that way. Voice modulation had become a political act. My whispers implicitly shamed a legal commodity and all my neighbors who used it. I realized that speaking openly about marijuana was a step toward normalizing pot. Was that wrong?

There were tougher questions we were only beginning to confront. What constituted a single dose of pot? What should be the limit for drugged driving, and how quickly does the average adult reach it? Where and when was it acceptable to use? In what form? Treating pot like alcohol was all well and good when it came to sales and regulation, but the social niceties were more complicated. Was it OK to drink marijuana-infused soda or share cannabis bonbons at a cocktail party? What about an office party? Smoking, vaping, swallowing tinctures and consuming edibles: each contained its own unwritten rules of discretion. Were any of them OK to do in front of the kids? There were questions that dealt with the ethics of economics. Was it morally acceptable to get into the business? Were you a fool not to?

And then there was the organic act itself: How do you create a legal marijuana industry? Perhaps more than anything else, I wanted to watch the birth and baby-step days of the world's first legal marijuana market and see it with my own eyes. I wanted to know how it worked. If it succeeded, the rest of the world would want to know too.

On Nov. 6, 2012, I'd cast my vote in favor of radical change. In doing so, I helped close the chapter on America's disastrous War on Drugs and clear the path for a new cannabis economy. On Nov. 7, I wondered: What in the world did we just do?

This book is my attempt to answer that question.

The public perception of marijuana has been steadily shifting over the past decade, but it reached a turning point in 2013. Gallup polls in the early 2000s found that only about one third of Americans favored legalization. That climbed to 44 percent in 2009, to 48 percent in 2012—and then, boom! When Gallup asked the same question in 2013, 58 percent of Americans said marijuana should be legal.

What accounted for that swing? A host of factors, but none more important than medical marijuana. The steady expansion of medical marijuana (MMJ) laws—from one state in 1996 to 20 in 2013—changed the public face of cannabis. Word of mouth spread neighbor to neighbor and friend to friend. Millions of adults met an MMJ patient who turned their head and forced them to reconsider their assumptions. Many Americans remained cautious about full legalization, but by 2013 medical use had become a no-brainer. Seventy-seven percent of Americans believed marijuana had legitimate medical uses, and 83 percent thought doctors should be able to prescribe limited amounts for patients with serious illnesses. Seattle dispensary owner John Davis put it this way: "Medical marijuana polls slightly higher than apple pie."

If there was a single moment that crystallized the nation's new openness to marijuana, it arrived on Aug. 8, 2013. That was the day CNN chief medical correspondent Dr. Sanjay Gupta publicly changed his position on pot. Gupta, one of the nation's most trusted physicians, spent the early months of 2013 researching the science of medical marijuana for a documentary called *Weed*. An outspoken pot skeptic, Gupta had written a story four years earlier for TIME magazine headlined "Why I Would Vote No on Pot." The evidence he uncovered in *Weed*, though, forced him to reverse himself. He did so in a stunning mea culpa.

"I am here to apologize," he wrote on CNN's website. "I mistakenly believed the Drug Enforcement Agency listed marijuana as a schedule 1 substance because of sound scientific proof." In fact, Gupta wrote, the DEA had no such proof. Though the government continued to deny it, marijuana has "very legitimate medical applications," he wrote. "In fact, sometimes marijuana is the only thing that works."

It worked despite a continuing effort by the government to suppress medical marijuana research. "I calculate about 6% of the current U.S. marijuana studies investigate the benefits of medical marijuana," he wrote. "The rest are designed to investigate harm. That imbalance paints a highly distorted picture."

The CNN.com piece went viral. It was hard not to recall the night Walter Cronkite went on *CBS Evening News* and proclaimed that the U.S. could not win the war in Vietnam. "If I've lost Cronkite," Lyndon Johnson reportedly said after that 1968 broadcast, "I've lost the country." With the loss of Sanjay Gupta, the beginning of the end of the war on marijuana was upon us.

I found one of Gupta's phrases particularly haunting. "We have been terribly and systematically misled for 70 years in the United States," he wrote, "and I apologize for my own role in that."

Terribly and systematically misled. That's media code for *We have been fed the big lie*. Had the phrase come from another source, I might have brushed it off as a stoner conspiracy theory. Sanjay Gupta wasn't just another source. He was putting his job and professional reputation on the line.

With Gupta's phrase in my mind, I pushed aside the remnants of my aversion to the subject and took a deep dive into the history of marijuana in America. If we'd been misled—if—then somebody misled us. Mistakes don't make themselves. Deception doesn't occur through spontaneous generation. Someone creates it. I wanted to know who, when, how and why. I wanted to know how the hell we got ourselves into this mess.

4

HOW WE
GOT HERE

If you want to blame somebody for America's marijuana obsession, you might as well start with Pancho Villa.

In the early 1910s, thousands of Mexicans escaped the tumult of the Mexican Revolution by crossing into Texas border towns like El Paso and Laredo. They brought with them the wide-brimmed sombrero, a delicious menu of savory foods and an intoxicant known as marijuana. In 1914, El Paso became one of the first American cities to outlaw marijuana. Advocates of the ban warned that the city risked becoming a "hotbed of marijuana fiends." All sorts of low characters could be seen consuming the drug: Mexicans, Negroes, prostitutes, pimps, "and a criminal class of whites."

Pancho Villa drove marijuana north in two ways. By fomenting revolution, he drove refugees into the *Estados Unidos* and prompted President Woodrow Wilson to send Gen. John Pershing and 5,000 soldiers into Mexico to capture the elusive bandit. For nearly a year Pershing tramped across northern Mexico chasing Villa. What cigars were to Ulysses Grant, marijuana was to Villa—or at least to his troops, who often ended their days with an easeful smoke.

The attractions of marijuana, which flourished in the wild through-out northern Mexico, didn't go unnoticed by Pershing's men. During their time in Mexico, American soldiers gladly adopted the local custom. With the outbreak of World War I, Pershing's men returned home with a newfound taste for *mota*, the hand-rolled Mexican joint. "After the Guard went down to Mexico and came back," a U.S. Army doctor reported in the 1920s, "I saw the first white people who smoked the plant."

Caribbean sailors spread the practice via port towns like New Orleans, while Mexican immigrants carried marijuana into bunkhouses and labor camps throughout the American West. A number of states outlawed the drug—California in 1913, Utah in 1915, Texas in 1919, New Mexico in 1923 and Louisiana in 1924—but the evidence suggests they were more annoyed with the smokers than the smoke. States usually banned mari-juana, *Reefer Madness* author Larry Sloman noted, "when faced with significant numbers of Mexicans or Negroes utilizing the drug."

Those early laws treated marijuana as a minor nuisance, a snake oil that turned Mexicans silly on a Saturday night. So if it was true that Pancho Villa hastened marijuana's introduction to North America, it isn't quite fair to blame him for the government's extreme reaction. Which raises the question: How did a mild intoxicant turn into a deadly national scourge?

It really all boils down to the work of one man. His name was Harry Anslinger.

———

A Pennsylvania Dutchman born in 1892, Anslinger was a bright, ambi-tious go-getter. After attending Pennsylvania State University for two years, he entered the foreign service and enjoyed postings in Germany, Venezuela and the Bahamas. As a junior diplomat, he became an expert in smuggling issues, thanks to the Bahamian rum–smuggling trade during Prohibition. Anslinger liked the action. He quit the State Department and joined the Treasury Department's anti-smuggling effort. Within three years he rose to assistant commissioner of the Prohibition Bureau. When Treasury created the freestanding Federal Bureau of Narcotics in

1930, the 38-year-old Anslinger was tapped to run it.

The narcotics bureau policed illegal drugs, but in 1930 marijuana didn't fall under its purview. The Harrison Act of 1914, which established federal control over narcotics, dealt only with compounds related to opium or cocaine. When anti-pot crusaders asked Anslinger to take up the fight against marijuana, he initially demurred. The plant grew like dandelions in every roadside ditch, he said. You might as well try to stamp out crickets.

Years passed. Circumstances changed. In 1934, Anslinger found his agency in peril. Federal tax revenues collapsed under the weight of the Great Depression. Congress had to slash spending. There was talk of eliminating the narcotics bureau. Anslinger needed a compelling reason to justify his agency's existence. In his marijuana history *Smoke Signals*, author Martin Lee recalled how Anslinger "set out to convince Congress and the American public that a terrible new drug menace was threatening the country, one that required immediate action by a well-funded Federal Bureau of Narcotics." The menace was marijuana.

Fortunately for Anslinger, others had laid the groundwork for federal control of the drug. Chief among them was New Orleans District Attorney Eugene Stanley. In the 1930s, New Orleans voters were up in arms over a crime wave sweeping the city. Unable to contain the city's flourishing vice rackets, Stanley found a convenient scapegoat in marijuana. Wherever he found criminals, Stanley said, he also found the weed. He also found alcohol, of course, but what set marijuana apart, Stanley claimed, was its unique power of motivation. Marijuana wasn't merely an intoxicant used by criminals, he said. Marijuana *caused* crime. "Its use sweeps away all restraint, and to its influence may be attributed many of our present-day crimes," he wrote in the *American Journal of Police Science*.

Stanley's article spread the crime causation theory. Criminal attorneys began using "marijuana insanity" as a defense strategy. Judges and juries had no experience with or understanding of marijuana, so occasionally the strategy worked.

Marijuana scare stories became a staple of the yellow press. At the powerful Hearst newspaper chain, the Fox News Channel of its day, it was official policy to splash marijuana-tied horrors across the front page.

Hearst editors crafted howlers like "MARIJUANA MAKES FIENDS OF BOYS IN 30 DAYS; HASHEESH GOADS USERS TO BLOOD-LUST" and "MURDER WEED FOUND UP AND DOWN COAST—DEADLY MARIHUANA DOPE PLANT READY FOR HARVEST THAT MEANS ENSLAVEMENT OF CALIFORNIA CHILDREN."

Those stories padded Anslinger's famous gore file, a collection of news clips he drew from during speaking tours. Anslinger traveled the country offering demon-drug sermons to police agencies, civic clubs, religious groups, women's organizations and editorial boards. His listeners knew marijuana only through what they'd read in the Hearst papers. Anslinger appeared before them with the news that they hadn't read the worst of it. The nation's chief drug officer condemned cannabis as a substance that led to homicidal mania, race mixing and miscegenation. Marijuana unleashed a beast within ordinary men, spurred them to commit heinous crimes. Low ethnic types used the drug to seduce women above their station. And worse. "Marijuana causes white women to seek sexual relations with Negroes," he declared. As evidence, Anslinger cited unsourced reports from his own gore file. "Colored students at Univ. of Minn. partying with female students (white) smoking and getting their sympathy with stories of racial persecution," read one typical item. "Result pregnancy."

His campaign became a self-perpetuating machine. Anslinger's road show sowed fear among local thought leaders. They in turn published columns denouncing the marijuana menace. All of which added to Anslinger's gore file and increased pressure on Congress to halt the spread of the murder weed. His campaign inspired a whole genre of pulp fiction and exploitation films, including the notorious *Reefer Madness*. (That film, a classic of unintentional comedy, got its start as a cautionary tale about the evils of marijuana. A church group financed its production, then sold it to a grindhouse impresario named Dwain Esper. Esper recut the film, added some wacky freakout scenes and released it in 1936 under the now iconic title.) Anslinger's efforts achieved their intended effect. Assistant Treasury Secretary Stephen Gibbons, Anslinger's boss, began sending memos around the department calling for action against this "frighteningly devastating" drug that was receiving "rather considerable publicity."

The fact that hype so quickly hardened into accepted truth struck me as curious. Did we really know so little about marijuana in the 1930s? If it was such a frightening menace, surely somebody must have studied it.

As it turned out, a few people had.

In 1893 the British government commissioned a report on cannabis use in India. The Indian Hemp Drugs Commission spent years studying the issue before publishing an eight-volume report that found "the moderate use of hemp drugs is practically attended by no evil results at all."

In 1925 the U.S. Army investigated cannabis use by soldiers in the Panama Canal Zone. Marijuana was plentiful in the Central American nation. Concerned that the drug could lead to a breakdown in military discipline, the Army convened a committee of lawyers, military officers, public health officials and mental health experts. The committee found no evidence that marijuana "has any appreciably deleterious influence on the individuals using it."

Reports of soldiers and others flipping out after smoking the drug "appear to have little basis in fact," the committee said. "There is no medical evidence that it causes insanity."

In other words, marijuana had been investigated. But it was the 1930s. Information didn't travel. The Indian Hemp Drugs Commission study and the Canal Zone report were available at only a handful of research libraries. A few government officials knew of their existence but had every reason to keep quiet. Opposing Harry Anslinger and the Hearst papers would gain them nothing but grief.

Anslinger's relentless campaign led to the Marihuana Tax Act of 1937, one of the strangest pieces of legislation ever passed on Capitol Hill. To make sense of the whole thing, in fact, you've first got to understand the Harrison Act.

The Harrison Act. I know. Your lids droop even as you read the phrase. But stick with me. The deal with the Harrison Act, the federal government's first attempt to regulate narcotics, was that for much of its life it teetered on the edge of unconstitutionality. When it was enacted in 1914, most constitutional scholars believed that states alone had the power to regulate the practice of medicine, including prescriptions. Congress couldn't meddle with doctors, but it could impose taxes. So the Harrison Act was technically a tax act, even though its intent was to regulate narcotics. The Act squeaked past a 1919 Supreme Court review, 5–4, because it was cloaked as a tax law and not a drug regulation, much like the Supreme Court's Obamacare ruling nearly a century later.

Under the Harrison Act, pharmacists had to register and pay taxes on morphine and whatnot. The penalty for unregistered dealing was stiff, but the effective prohibition of street narcotics was deemed "incidental" to the tax, despite the fact that everybody knew the incidental was the intent. According to Richard Bonnie and Charles Whitebread, legal scholars and co-authors of *The Marijuana Conviction,* Treasury Department officials believed that folding marijuana into the Harrison Act "was illogical, possibly unconstitutional, and might even endanger the entire federal legislative scheme."

That's why Congress outlawed marijuana with a tax act. Instead of contaminating the Harrison Act, Anslinger and the Treasury Department quarantined marijuana in its own prohibitive taxing scheme. When I say prohibitive, I mean comically so. The Marihuana Tax Act of 1937 (Congress insisted on using the archaic *h* spelling) nicked registered cannabis handlers $1 an ounce at each transaction. Unregistered handlers were taxed $100 an ounce. To put that in context, in 1936 you could drive a brand-new Studebaker off the lot for $650.

During a series of legislative committee hearings in the spring of 1937, Congress heard from Anslinger, a handful of confused hemp farmers, a veterinarian, a pharmacist and an official from the American Medical Association (AMA). Anslinger presented his usual exhibition of drug-crazed killers. He described marijuana as "the most violence-causing drug in the history of mankind." Among other things.

Then came AMA legal counsel Dr. William Woodward. Cannabis, Woodward testified, was hardly the scourge Anslinger made it out to be. Members of the House Ways and Means Committee were dumbfounded. *Isn't this the fellow from the AMA?*

"We know that it is a habit that is spreading, particularly among young-sters," insisted Rep. John Dingell Sr., father of the longtime Michigan congressman. "The number of victims is increasing each year."

"There is no evidence of that," said Woodward.

Committee members scolded the doctor for not getting with the program. "The medical profession should be doing its utmost to aid in the suppression of this curse that is eating the very vitals of the nation," Dingell declared.

Woodward pondered Dingell's words. *Eating the nation's vitals.* "They are?" he said.

Dingell pressed on. "There is no question but that the drug habit has been increasing rapidly in recent years."

Woodward stood his ground. "There is no evidence to show whether or not it has been."

The exchange devolved from there. Members of the committee accused Woodward of obstructionism, evasiveness and bad faith. The final hearing on May 4 ended with committee chairman Robert L. Doughton lecturing Woodward on the necessity of the anti-marijuana law "to protect people from its insidious influence and effects." Without legislative control, Doughton thundered, "we would be at the mercy of the criminal class, and we would have no civilization whatever."

Five weeks later, the full House voted on the Marihuana Tax Act late in the afternoon of a humid summer day. Speaker Sam Rayburn introduced it by noting that the bill had received unanimous backing from the Ways and Means Committee. There is, he said, "nothing controversial about it."

"What is the bill?" asked Rep. Bertrand Snell of New York.

"It has something to do with something that is called marijuana," said Rayburn. "I believe it is a narcotic of some kind."

A question arose: "Did anyone consult the AMA and get their opinion?"

"Yes, we have," replied Rep. Fred Vinson. The Kentucky congressman, who would later become chief justice of the U.S. Supreme Court, had listened to Dr. Woodward's rancorous testimony before the House committee. "A Dr. Wharton and the AMA are in complete agreement," Vinson said.

The bill passed. The Marihuana Tax Act went into effect on Oct. 1, 1937. The following day, the FBI and local police raided the Lexington Hotel, a Denver flophouse, and arrested Samuel Caldwell and Moses Baca. Caldwell, a balding 58-year-old laborer, was charged with selling marijuana. Baca, his 26-year-old customer, was rung up on possession. Harry Anslinger himself turned up for the trial. Federal judge Foster Symes seemed to channel the narcotics bureau chief while pronouncing the sentence. "Marijuana destroys life itself," Symes said. "I have no sympathy with those who sell this weed."

Baca served 18 months. Caldwell was sentenced to four years of hard labor in the federal penitentiary in Leavenworth, Kansas. He died a year after his release.

———————

Despite Harry Anslinger's war on marijuana, some officials were willing to take an objective look at the drug. Most of them were in New York.

Walter Bromberg, the presiding psychiatrist at Bellevue Hospital, New York City's public mental health facility, acted as the psychiatric adviser to the Court of General Sessions of New York County. Marijuana users brought before the court or admitted to Bellevue came under his observation. He couldn't help but note the disparity between what he read in the Hearst papers and what he observed on his clinical rounds. That led Bromberg to look back through the hospital's records, which included examinations of 2,216 felons with at least a passing acquaintance with the drug. He concluded that marijuana lacked the addictive qualities of opium and other drugs. A marijuana user showed an interest in recapturing "the ecstatic, elated state into which the drug lifts him," Bromberg reported, but not an addictive compulsion to obtain it. Bromberg called marijuana habituation a "sensual addiction."

A few years later, New York mayor Fiorello La Guardia grew alarmed at rumors of weed peddlers moving the drug into the city's schools. Most mayors would have ordered the police to start cracking heads. But La Guardia was a different cat. Years earlier, he'd actually read the Army's report on marijuana. So he was skeptical of Harry Anslinger's spin. Instead of rounding up the city's hopheads, La Guardia went to the New York Academy of Medicine and said, *Tell me what's really going on with marijuana.*

Investigators quickly determined that schoolyard dealers were selling loose cigarettes, not joints. The Academy didn't stop there, though. Over the next five years its researchers undertook the most comprehensive study of marijuana since the Indian Hemp Drugs Commission.

After reviewing the records of 16,854 criminal offenders in the psychiatric clinic of New York's county court, the committee found only 67 marijuana users, six of whom had been charged with violent crimes. "No positive relation could be found between violent crime and the use of marijuana," the report concluded. "No cases of murder or sexual crimes due to marijuana were established."

The committee identified sex as the most blatantly overhyped concern. "Our investigators visited many 'tea-pads' in the Borough of Manhattan," the report stated. Often the walls of these establishments were adorned with lewd photographs. The researchers found it strange that the pot smokers paid no mind to the naughty snaps. "In fact one of the investigators who was concentrating his attention on the relation between marijuana and eroticism stated in his report that he found himself embarrassed that he was the only one who examined the pictures on the wall."

While reading the La Guardia report I have to say that I found myself developing a soft spot for the lost Manhattan tea pads of the '40s. They sounded like delightful social clubs. Smokers engaged in friendly conversation with strangers. They exhibited a tendency to philosophize on life in a manner "out of keeping with [their] intellectual level." Many displayed an unusual willingness to share their own reefer with total strangers. At a rooftop club in Harlem the clientele smoked their illegal cigarettes in private tents. "When the desired effect of the drug had been obtained," the investigator noted, "they all emerged into the open and engaged in a discussion of their admiration of the stars and the beauties of nature."

For 10 years Harry Anslinger had been telling the nation that marijuana turned men into monsters. The Academy of Medicine designed clinical studies to test that claim. Subjects were administered the drug in a variety of settings. In each group, the smoked marijuana cigarettes "produced a euphoric state with its feeling of well-being, contentment, sociability, mental and physical relaxation, which usually ended in a feeling of drowsiness." One subject unfamiliar with marijuana had a minor freak-out. Other than that, the volunteers generally laughed, talked, sang, listened to music or slept. In one session they carried on pleasant philosophical arguments and swapped jokes. At the end of the evening, "they all went to bed and reported the next day that they had slept very well."

The funny thing was that these weren't just any test subjects. The researchers got them from Rikers and Hart Islands and the House of Detention for Women. If anything, the results seemed to prove the opposite of Anslinger's claim. Marijuana took criminals and made them mellow.

The most curious experiment involved the Jack Benny radio show. On a Sunday evening, 32 volunteers gathered around a radio to hear Benny tell his jokes. One researcher noted the number of times the radio audience laughed, while another recorded the number of times the volunteers laughed. One week later, they all gathered again. This time the volunteers smoked marijuana prior to the show. Sober, the volunteers laughed about half as often as the radio audience. High, they matched the radio audience almost laugh for laugh. "Under marijuana," the researchers concluded, "the subject laughs more readily and for longer time intervals."

Here we have a moment in history. The anonymous researcher has just invented the stoner comedy. It's too bad the comedian wasn't made aware of the study. It would have made a killer album title. *Jack Benny: Funnier when High.*

If you're like me, at this point you're thinking that the La Guardia Committee should have put an end to marijuana prohibition. The committee concluded that smoking marijuana didn't lead to addiction; wasn't widespread among children; didn't lead to morphine, cocaine or heroin use; and didn't cause juvenile delinquency or the commission of crime. So why didn't marijuana prohibition fade away?

The problem was that it was 1944. Other events occupied public attention. World War II. The D-Day landings in Normandy. German V-1 bombs falling on London. MacArthur's return to the Philippines. President Roosevelt's re-election. People were busy.

La Guardia also faced more pressing matters. The city was running out of money. His popularity waned. To La Guardia, the committee's report meant only that he had one less issue to worry about.

In short, nobody cared. Well, almost nobody.

By 1944, marijuana enforcement had become Harry Anslinger's *raison d'être*. His power rested on the claim that marijuana was the worst of all narcotics, an untamable force, a threat to the very fabric of American society. Could he really have abandoned his great crusade?

In truth, he might have. The postwar years saw a spike in the abuse of amphetamines and heroin, not marijuana. Anslinger could easily have pivoted his bureau's attention from marijuana to heroin. He refused to do it.

Instead he doubled down on marijuana. Anslinger blasted the La Guardia Committee Report as a "government-printed invitation to youth and adults—above all teenagers—to go ahead and smoke all the reefers they feel like." Then he went further. Walter Bromberg, the Bellevue Hospital psychiatrist, had been a pain in Anslinger's ass for years. Bromberg's fingerprints were all over the La Guardia Committee Report. Anslinger needed to ensure that the Bureau of Narcotics remained the sole authority on marijuana. So he announced that anyone who carried out marijuana research unapproved by his bureau would be arrested and tried on federal charges. "As a direct result," wrote Richard Bonnie and Charles Whitebread, "the La Guardia report sank quietly into oblivion."

The more I investigated America's 20th-century marijuana history, the more I realized it could be read as a tale of two cities: New Orleans and New York. Time and again, the call for tougher drug laws originated in the Big Easy. With each new offensive came a counterattack of reform from the Big Apple.

In the early 1950s, the next wave of drug laws swept across America. They came from New Orleans. Congressman Hale Boggs, a Tulane-educated

Democrat, decided to tackle America's growing heroin problem. Heroin in the '50s was no imaginary menace. Data from the U.S. Public Health Service Hospital in Lexington, Kentucky, tracked an alarming increase in opiate addiction among young people. The Boggs Act, a package of tough new anti-drug laws, lumped marijuana in with heroin and other hard drugs. That alarmed Dr. Harris Isbell, research director at the Lexington "narcotics farm," as the Public Health Service Hospital was known. He told Boggs's committee that morphine and heroin were big problems. Marijuana, he said, was not. Cannabis smokers "generally are mildly intoxicated, giggle, laugh, bother no one and have a good time," he said.

Isbell's testimony forced the Act's sponsor to rethink marijuana's inclusion. It sounded like "only a small percentage of those marijuana cases was anything more than a temporary degree of exhilaration," Boggs said.

The words burned Harry Anslinger's ears. A few years earlier he'd quashed the La Guardia report by floating the "wrong signal to youth" theory. Now he could see Hale Boggs wavering. Anslinger had to think fast.

"The danger is this," Anslinger told Boggs. "Over 50 percent of those young addicts started on marijuana smoking. They started there and graduated to heroin. They took the thrill of the needle when the thrill of marijuana was gone."

Here was the gateway theory at its birth.

Anslinger's ploy succeeded. Congress approved the Boggs Act in 1951. By pounding on his gateway theory, Anslinger eventually molded it into the shape of accepted fact. By 1956, when Congress considered another draconian anti-drug law, one senator declared that marijuana use led inescapably "to the heroin habit and then to the final destruction of the persons addicted."

Why was there no pushback? By 1956 Dr. Isbell was no longer available to testify against the gateway theory. Perhaps he was advised to stay in Kentucky. Or maybe he was busy. Two years after the passage of the original Boggs Act, the Central Intelligence Agency recruited Isbell as a primary researcher in the agency's notorious MK-Ultra program, which secretly administered massive doses of LSD and other drugs to unwitting subjects in the hopes of finding a *Manchurian Candidate*-style mind-control drug. During one stretch, Isbell was reported to have dosed seven men with LSD for 77 straight days. So he might have been otherwise occupied.

Even as Congress adopted tougher sanctions against cannabis users, the first stirrings of two powerful counter-forces began to appear around the country. In the rich loam of the Mississippi Delta, the hustlers' alleys of Times Square, the nightclubs and pool halls of Chicago, Denver and Detroit, and the bohemian flats of San Francisco, buds and shoots emerged. They sprouted in jazz clubs, radio stations, art galleries and bookstores and along the nation's growing interstate highways. These first iterations appeared as ideas, attitudes, songs, novels, jokes and poems. They were the first stirrings of world-changing movements: rock and roll, and the counterculture.

The rough sketch of marijuana's midcentury movement goes like this. The jazzmen had it first. They bestowed it upon the beatniks, who passed it to the hippies and the rock stars. The reality is more complicated, and that makes for a better story.

Reefer spread through jazz clubs in the '20s and '30s largely through the efforts of horn player Milton "Mezz" Mezzrow, the Johnny Appleseed of weed in the hepcat demimonde. Mezz, a Jewish kid from Chicago, got his first taste in 1923 when some Orleans-sourced marijuana passed through Chicago's Martinique Club. He recalled that experience years later in his autobiography, *Really the Blues*:

> The first thing I noticed was that I began to hear my saxophone as though it were inside my head .... I found I was slurring much better and putting just the right feeling into my phrases—I was really coming on .... I felt like I could go on playing for years without running out of ideas and energy. There wasn't any struggle; it was all made-to-order and suddenly there wasn't a sour note, or a discord in the world that could bother me .... I began to preach my millenniums on my horn, leading all the sinners on to glory.

By the early 1930s Mezz had moved to Harlem, where he gigged with a pantheon of all-time greats: Louis Armstrong, Dizzy Gillespie, Fats Waller, Duke Ellington, Count Basie, Billie Holiday, Cab Calloway. In jazz clubs Mezz was as well known for his pot selling as his horn blowing, and he did a whole lot of both. Armstrong, an unabashed viper (as pot smokers were known), served as both Mezzrow's friend and celebrity endorser. "I loves me my muggles," he often quipped, using a slang term for pot. When others asked where they might find them some muggles too, they were referred to the Mighty Mezz. In the 1940s a new generation of bebop players came to Mezz for friendly conversation and a little product: Lester Young, John Coltrane, Charlie Parker, Miles Davis, Thelonious Monk. Here's where the crossover happened. At Minton's Playhouse, the Harlem club where Gillespie blew and Monk sketched the keys, one of the white guys digging the scene was a former Columbia University football player and aspiring writer named Jean-Louis Lebris de Kerouac. His friends called him Jack.

Kerouac had bailed on Columbia after a falling-out with the football coach, but he continued to lurk around Morningside Heights and Harlem with his new friend, "a spindly Jewish kid with horn-rimmed glasses and tremendous ears sticking out." That was Allen Ginsberg, age 18, as recalled by Kerouac. Blessed with a precocious mind, Ginsberg was hugely curious and oddly systematic. The first time he got drunk, the poet methodically recorded the loss of various mental functions with each drink. "He was fascinated with the experience of trying anything for the first time," Ginsberg biographer Bill Morgan later wrote, "and this was only one of countless experiments he conducted on his own mind during his life."

In late 1946, Ginsberg, short on cash, read Mezz Mezzrow's newly published autobiography in its entirety while standing in the Columbia University bookstore. The book wasn't so much a revelation as a confirmation. Mezz appeared as a younger version of himself, a bright Jewish kid who found authenticity, creative expression and moments of ecstasy by embracing the life of what Norman Mailer would later call, in his classic essay, "The White Negro."

Over the next decade Ginsberg, Kerouac and a growing set of writers, poets, musicians, queers, junkies, misfits, dropouts, idiots and geniuses would create an American bohemian scene to rival Paris in the '20s. Together with their older friend William Burroughs and a manic cat from Denver named Neal Cassady, Kerouac and Ginsberg spent their days chewing through Rimbaud, Cocteau, Baudelaire, Nietzsche and James M. Cain; at nights they caroused the Harlem bebop scene, the Eighth Avenue midtown bars, Times Square junkie-and-juicer joints and seedy coal-cellar haunts in the Village. Reefer and Benzedrine were their drugs of choice. They loved to get jagged and loose on bennies and pot, yakking nonstop about philosophy, literature, art, drugs and sex and laughing madly into the early morning of the night. The bebop blowing at Minton's expressed everything they sought but rarely found in postwar America: improvisation, freedom, creativity, surprise, nonconformity and discordance.

Ginsberg experimented with a variety of drugs in the '40s, but marijuana was the key that unlocked his consciousness. "It was the first time I ever had solid evidence in my own body that there was a difference between reality as I saw it myself and reality as it was described officially by the state, the government, the police and the media," Ginsberg told Larry Sloman during an interview in the 1970s. "To a few of us in the '40s, that experience of marijuana catalyzed a reexamination of all social ideas, because if one law was full of shit and error, then what of all those other laws?"

It's interesting to note that it wasn't the drug itself that led Ginsberg to question authority, but rather the discrepancy between official claim and experienced fact. The government's line on marijuana wasn't merely overstated. Ginsberg's mind and body revealed it as outright fraud.

Out of that questioning came revolutionary works of art. On an October night in 1955, Ginsberg debuted his poem "Howl" at a group reading in San Francisco's Six Gallery. In profane, raw and beautiful images, Ginsberg electrified the audience with a vision of America rarely seen. The poem blasted its readers with the famously apocalyptic opening:

I saw the best minds of my generation destroyed by madness,
    starving hysterical naked,
dragging themselves through the negro streets at dawn
    looking for an angry fix,

Ginsberg guided readers through a world filled with hipsters, pacifists, beggars and unshaven men riding boxcars through cities seeking "jazz or sex or soup," half-mad intellectuals getting off on bennies or "whoring through Colorado in myriad stolen night-cars," before building to an ecstatic finale:

Holy the groaning saxophone! Holy the bop apocalypse!
Holy the jazzbands marijuana hipsters peace peyote pipes & drums!

A year after "Howl" came *On the Road*, Jack Kerouac's madcap novel of an answer to Ginsberg, a sprawling road story about 20-something misfits going everywhere and nowhere in search of life, love and meaning in Eisenhower's America. At a time when the nation's culture was defined by Arthur Godfrey, Perry Como and other paragons of good taste and bland talent, Ginsberg and his beat generation offered a desperately needed alternative. They invented a counterculture.

———————

Meanwhile a wholly separate movement was growing out of the roots of rhythm and blues. It's hard to say exactly when R & B morphed into rock and roll, but 1954 seems to be the year when a kind of critical mass was attained. Big Joe Turner kicked off the year with "Shake, Rattle and Roll," a hit covered a few months later by Bill Haley and his Comets. Haley's band released "Rock Around the Clock" in May, and by July the radio waves were humming with "That's All Right," the debut single from a singer out of Memphis named Elvis Presley.

It seems odd in retrospect, but marijuana wasn't around for the birth of rock and roll. In the '50s pot was for jazzmen and poets. Booze and bennies were the drugs of choice among early rockers like Jerry Lee Lewis and Little Richard. It would be a decade before marijuana entered the scene, and it took two of the most powerful forces in music to introduce it: Bob Dylan and the Beatles.

Dylan's mind and music were nurtured by Minneapolis's Dinkytown bohemian scene in the late '50s, where marijuana mixed with folk music, jazz, radical politics, art films and coffeehouse intellectualism. By the time he moved to New York City in 1961, Dylan was well versed in the ways of weed. Ginsberg himself recognized a kindred soul in the young folk singer. According to Dylan biographer Sean Wilentz, after listening to "A Hard Rain's A-Gonna Fall" in 1963, Ginsberg "wept with illuminated joy at what he sensed was a passing of the bohemian tradition to a younger generation."

Dylan and Ginsberg met at a party in late '63 and hit it off immediately. The two spent much of the following summer hanging out, writing songs and poetry and smoking grass at the upstate New York retreat of Dylan's manager. At the end of August they turned up at New York's Hotel Delmonico to party with the Beatles. As legend has it, Dylan offered to share a smoke. The Fab Four and manager Brian Epstein blanched at the suggestion. Epstein told Dylan they'd never tried the stuff. (Not that they were teetotalers. The lads often used Benzedrine inhalers to get them through their grueling Cavern Club sets.) Peter Brown, Epstein's personal assistant, later recounted Dylan's perplexed reaction in *The Love You Make*, a memoir of Brown's time with the Beatles.

"But what about your song?" Dylan asked. "The one about getting high?"

He was referring to "I Want to Hold Your Hand": *And when I touch you I feel happy inside / It's such a feeling that my love / I get high / I get high / I get high . . .*

John Lennon corrected him. "The words are, 'I can't hide, I can't hide . . .'" he said.

Dylan handed a joint to Ringo, who smoked it to the nub. Dylan rolled another, and another. By and by, the Beatles were high. Lennon fell into Ginsberg's lap, laughing. McCartney told one and all he was "thinking for the first time, really thinking!" and asked the band's road manager to follow him and record his thoughts.

By the time the band filmed *Help!* in 1965 they were so high on pot—and occasionally LSD—that they often forgot their lines. The creativity, exploration and introspection fostered by cannabis and other hallucinogens sparked the band's evolution from peppy hand-holding tunes to experimental, boundary-pushing art.

Three years after Dylan rolled that joint in the Hotel Delmonico, marijuana had completely overtaken rock and roll. In early June 1967 the Beatles released their psychedelic masterpiece, *Sgt. Pepper's Lonely Hearts Club Band*. Two weeks later, thousands of proto-hippies descended on San Francisco for the Monterey Pop Festival—featuring the Jefferson Airplane, Jimi Hendrix and other musically gifted cannabis enthusiasts—and stuck around for the Summer of Love in the Haight.

Coverage of the emerging counterculture that year brought marijuana awareness into the mainstream, and pot smoking exploded as a generational phenomenon. Arrest statistics reflect the change. In 1965 police nationwide recorded only 18,815 marijuana violations. By 1967 that number had tripled to 61,843, and in 1969 it nearly doubled again to 118,903.

Something happened with marijuana in those years. From 1965 to 1969 cannabis evolved from its earlier role as a mild intoxicant and artistic stimulant into something far more profound: a catalyst for cultural and political change. The authority-questioning enlightenment Allen Ginsberg experienced on his own in the late 1940s spread to an entire generation of baby boomers in the late 1960s. "The kids were square, they believed in the war, and then they smoked some grass and everything was a little funny," Ginsberg told Larry Sloman. "The cops were after them, and they began to reexamine everything; they reexamined the war and reexamined capitalism, and I think that was a universal experience."

A widely shared experience, yes. Universal, no.

In 1966 Timothy Leary was arrested in Laredo, Texas, for trying to cross the border with less than an ounce of marijuana. He was tried, convicted and sentenced to 30 years in federal prison. The psychedelic guru and former Harvard professor fought the case all the way to the U.S. Supreme Court. He didn't dispute his commission of the act. He disputed the law itself.

Leary argued that the Marihuana Tax Act of 1937 violated his Fifth Amendment right against self-incrimination. To abide by the act, he reasoned, he'd have to register to obtain a marijuana tax stamp, thereby announcing his intention to commit a crime.

The Supreme Court agreed. On May 19, 1969, the court's unanimous verdict in *Leary v. United States* invalidated the law that had directly, by indirection, prohibited marijuana for 31 years.

President Richard Nixon would not let that stand. Nixon had been swept into office with the support of America's conservative "silent majority." He'd once called Timothy Leary the most dangerous man in America. The president wasn't about to let a Harvard longhair set off a legal reefer free-for-all.

To clean up the mess, Nixon worked with Congress to craft the Controlled Substances Act, part of a larger piece of legislation known as the Comprehensive Drug Abuse Prevention and Control Act.

The act separated drugs into five tiers, known as schedules. Drugs were lumped from least restricted (Schedule V) to most (Schedule I) according to their abuse potential, harmfulness, known effect and level of medical use. As the legislation made its way through Congress, one of the small but critical battles involved the power of scheduling. The Senate wanted the Department of Health, Education and Welfare (HEW) to control the list. The House, and President Nixon, wanted the attorney general to oversee it. (Nixon dismissed HEW officials as "a bunch of muddle-headed psychiatrists" whose "hearts run their brains." Boy, did Nixon hate psychiatrists.) To liberals, drugs were a public health issue. To conservatives, they were a crime issue. Here was the battle joined.

In the end, the Senate capitulated. Under the terms of the Controlled Substances Act the power to schedule a drug rested in the hands of America's top law-enforcement official. This single tweak in the law would have profound implications.

Most other drugs found their natural order within the schedule. Low-dose codeine: Schedule III. Cocaine and methamphetamine: Schedule II. Heroin, mescaline, peyote and LSD: Schedule I. The question remained: Where to schedule marijuana?

Medical authorities considered marijuana a mild hallucinogenic, not a narcotic. Congress reserved Schedule I for only the most dangerous drugs: those with no currently accepted medical use and a high potential for abuse. Anyone who'd seen Michael Wadleigh's *Woodstock* could see it was being abused. Yet there was some hesitancy about giving it "most dangerous" status, primarily out of concern that the children of the white middle and upper class—college kids—could face draconian prison sentences.

It's astonishing to see how fast marijuana use exploded on campus. In 1967, the year the Beatles released *Sgt. Pepper*, only 5 percent of college students had ever tried pot. Three years later, by the time of *Let It Be*, 43 percent of college students were experienced with cannabis. Nixon officials knew two things about college kids: most didn't vote, and the ones who did voted against Nixon. The administration pressed to put marijuana in Schedule I, "at least until the completion of certain studies" that were then under way. "Congress meekly deferred to this judgment," observed Richard Bonnie and Charles Whitebread, "but all of the participants seem to have anticipated a change after 'the facts were in.'"

In fact, the Controlled Substances Act created the Presidential Commission on Marihuana and Drug Abuse specifically to advise on the proper scheduling of pot. Thus was born a council that would become one of the most legendary fact-finding bodies ever conceived: the Shafer Commission.

In the annals of stacked decks, the Shafer Commission could have contributed a chapter laced with duplicity, obsequiousness and shame. Even before he appointed the panel members, President Nixon and his top lieutenants made it clear what they expected the commission to find. Attorney General John Mitchell, who now held the power to confirm or revise marijuana's Schedule I status, said he expected the panel to turn up enough negative evidence about marijuana "to allow youth to resist peer pressure to use the drug." Harry Anslinger wasn't around to throw haymakers (he retired in 1962 at age 70), but Mitchell paid the old man homage by pounding on his gateway-drug theory. "A kid gets into steady use of marijuana," Mitchell said. "After a while he gets less of a charge from it, and this psychological dependency causes him to move on to the harder stuff . . . we have to get proof that it does create this dependency."

That's an interesting sentence. Not "we have proof." We have to *get* proof.

Nixon's appointees were nearly all cut from solid Republican granite. They included John Howard, a college president who later founded a prominent neocon think tank; Charles Galvin, dean of Southern Methodist University's law school; Mitchell Ware, an Illinois Bureau of Investigation superintendent known for his law-and-order attitude toward drugs; and three high-ranking members of the American Medical Association. Joan Ganz Cooney, co-creator and executive producer of *Sesame Street*, was the board's token liberal. Michael Sonnenreich, a Nixon loyalist and former narcotics bureau official, was appointed executive director. Leading the commission was former Pennsylvania governor Raymond Shafer, a Nixon supporter and lifelong Republican. If all went well, Nixon expected to reward Shafer with an appointment to the federal bench. As if to underscore its conservative posture, the committee insisted upon using the old spelling of *marihuana*, with an *h*, which hadn't been in common use since the 1920s.

These were the days before dogma ruled the Republican Party. Shafer was an old-fashioned moderate who believed in facts, evidence and science. He threw himself into the work. Shafer commissioned more than 50 projects and studies. He held hearings in cities and towns around the country. He amassed thousands of pages of testimony. His committee sought input from professional experts, students, public officials and community leaders. He had 73 staff members working full and part time.

Keith Stroup, the lawyer who founded NORML (the National Organization for the Reform of Marijuana Laws), spent most of that year tracking the commission's work. According to Stroup, Shafer and his fellow commissioners went so far as to organize a private meeting at which marijuana smokers actually smoked marijuana, so the commissioners could see the effects for themselves. "Believe it or not, most of the commissioners had never actually seen anyone who was stoned," Stroup told me.

The Shafer Commission began working on March 22, 1971. Exactly one year later, the commission presented its findings to President Nixon. The 1,184-page report was so shocking that Signet books rushed a condensed 233-page paperback edition to press. I tracked down a faded, brittle copy of *Marihuana: A Signal of Misunderstanding.* THE MOST COMPREHENSIVE STUDY OF MARIHUANA EVER MADE IN THE UNITED STATES, the cover promised. A LANDMARK REPORT THAT CANNOT BE IGNORED!

The report debunked nearly everything the federal government had been claiming about marijuana for 40 years.

In 1972, half the American public believed it was possible to die from a marijuana overdose. The commission couldn't find a single fatality ever recorded. The dose required for death was so enormous, the report said, as to be "unachievable by humans." The commission found that some individuals were predisposed to marijuana-caused panic reactions and psychotic episodes. Adolescent pot smoking was an area of special concern. Chronic, heavy use of marijuana "may jeopardize social and economic adjustments" of the nation's youth. "Amotivational syndrome"—lethargy, loss of interest in school and achievement in general—topped the committee's worries. Amotivational syndrome was a technical way of saying *The kid's turning into a stoner.*

The gateway-drug theory took a beating. "The fact should be emphasized that the overwhelming majority of marihuana users do not progress to other drugs." In fact, the commission wrote, if any drug can be said to be a gateway, "it is tobacco, followed closely by alcohol."

Make no mistake. "Marihuana is not an innocuous drug," the commission reported. But its use "does not constitute a major threat to public health." Marijuana-related health problems generally occur only in heavy long-term users and "have been overgeneralized and overdramatized." Intermittent use of pot "carries minimal risk to the public health."

American society's opposition to indiscriminate drug use, Shafer & Co. argued, arose from public health concerns and "a preference for individual productivity." That is, we prefer our citizens to be sober individuals motivated to work for the benefit of themselves and society. We prefer them not to nod away the afternoon in a drugged stupor. In the early 1970s, half the American public believed marijuana legalization would turn ordinary people into drug addicts. That struck the commission as an alarming accounting of the American character. Were we really a weak-willed population, helpless to resist the allure of intoxication? This "suggests not that a restrictive policy is in order," Shafer's commission wrote, "but rather that a basic premise of our free society is in doubt."

The commission concluded that marijuana shouldn't merely be rescheduled. It should be decriminalized. Prohibition wasn't working. The threat of exorbitant prison sentences hadn't discouraged 24 million Americans from trying marijuana. Current anti-pot laws weren't merely costly to taxpayers and to society. They actually undermined the goal of discouraging marijuana use.

Decriminalization didn't mean legalization. Decrim was a politically palatable concept that, as Larry Sloman observed, allowed politicians "to deal with the deplorable fact that we were literally sending our own children to jail" for the use of a relatively harmless substance. The commission outlined a plan under which personal possession would carry no penalty under state and federal law. Growing and selling pot, however, would remain illegal.

The main thing was to cool down the rhetoric. "Considering the range of social concerns in contemporary America," the commission wrote, "marihuana does not, in our considered opinion, rank very high. We would *deemphasize* marihuana as a problem."

To say that Nixon resisted the advice of the Shafer Commission would be to say that water resists fire. By 1972, Nixon's bitterness toward those he called "goddamn longhairs" had reached epic proportions. The campus unrest originally incited by the Vietnam War turned on Nixon himself as a symbol of all that was wrong with America. *Right back at ya*, said Nixon.

Every now and then, I have the opportunity to plunge into the historical treasure known as the Nixon White House tapes, the secret recordings President Nixon made in the Oval Office and other White House rooms between February 1971 and July 1973. They contain more than 3,700 hours of conversations. The tapes are preserved in the National Archives, and there's so much material that less than 5 percent has been transcribed and published. Breathtaking in their candor, the recordings reveal Nixon as a greater plotter, schemer, paranoiac, racist, anti-Semite and delusional revenger than even his worst enemies imagined. He is a tragic Shakespearean king.

By a stroke of luck, it happens that the Nixon tapes span the years of the Shafer Commission. Which allows us some insight into the mind of the president vis-à-vis marijuana.

The first thing that stands out is Nixon's belief about who was pushing dope into the U.S. That would be the Communists. "Do you think the Russians allow dope?" Nixon asked his aides H.R. "Bob" Haldeman and John Ehrlichman in early May 1971. "Hell, no. Not if they can catch it. They send them up. You see, homosexuality, dope, immorality in general: these are the enemies of strong societies. That's why the Communists and the left-wingers are pushing the stuff—they're trying to destroy us."

It appears that Nixon obtained his primary intelligence about the drug issue from figures in the entertainment field. TV-show host Art Linkletter, for instance. When I was a kid I used to read Linkletter's book *Oops! Or, Life's Awful Moments*, a collection of church-friendly anecdotes that my parents shelved between *Kon-Tiki* and *The Best and the Brightest*. On May 18, 1971, President Nixon invited Linkletter into the Oval Office for a chat. Linkletter, a dyed-in-the-wool square, had embarked on an anti-drug crusade following the death of his 20-year-old daughter, Diane. In 1969 Diane Linkletter threw herself out the window of her sixth-floor apartment in West Hollywood. She was reportedly despondent and suicidal. Art Linkletter blamed her death on LSD. He insisted she was on a "bum trip" and that drug pushers caused her death. When the Los Angeles coroner found no drugs in her system, Linkletter said his daughter must have been experiencing an LSD flashback. Although her father's version of events was likely untrue, it resonated deeply with the silent majority. Linkletter suffered what at the time was every parent's worst nightmare. The story took on mythological significance in mainstream America. The first time my own father talked to me about the dangers of drugs, he used the example of Diane Linkletter on LSD, "thinking she could fly." I still have visions of a girl with wavy hair in a long nightgown swan-diving from a high window.

This was the background to Linkletter's chat with Nixon.

During the first week of May, thousands of activists converged on Washington to protest the Vietnam War. A small army of police and National Guard soldiers arrested more than 13,000 protesters. The arrests were later ruled unconstitutional.

Nixon told Linkletter that he blamed the protest not on the war but on marijuana. "These demonstrators that were here two weeks ago," he said, "they're all on drugs. Oh yeah, horrible. And just raising hell."

"That's right," said Linkletter. "And of course, one of the reasons you can beat them is that so many of them are on drugs."

Linkletter isn't saying "you can beat them" in the sense that you can defeat them. He means *You can assault them with clubs.*

Sensing a sympathetic audience, Nixon aired his theory of drugs and societal downfall. Drugs had retarded the progress of Eastern civilizations, he explained, while alcohol proved to be a character-building tonic to the Vikings, the Angles and the Saxons. "Asia and the Middle East, portions of Latin America, I have seen what drugs have done to those countries," Nixon said. "Everybody knows what it's done to the Chinese. The Indians are hopeless."

"That's right," said Linkletter.

"Look at the north countries," the president continued. "The Swedes drink too much, the Finns drink too much, the British have always been heavy boozers . . . and the Irish, of course, the most, but on the other hand they survive as strong races."

"That's right," said Linkletter.

"And your drug societies inevitably come apart," Nixon said.

"They lose motivation," agreed Linkletter. "No discipline."

"At least with liquor, I don't lose motivation," said Nixon.

"There's a great difference between alcohol and marijuana," said Linkletter.

Nixon turned serious. "What is it?"

"The worst that you can have when you're in with other alcoholics is more to drink, so you'll throw up more and get sicker and be drunker," Linkletter explained. "But when you are with druggers, you can go from marijuana to heroin. Big difference."

Nixon nodded. "I see."

"Another big difference between marijuana and alcohol is that when people smoke marijuana, they smoke it to get high," said Linkletter. "In every case, when most people drink, they drink to be sociable."

"That's right, that's right," said Nixon. "A person does not drink to get drunk."

"That's right," said Linkletter.

"A person drinks to have fun," said Nixon.

Linkletter agreed. "You smoke marijuana to get high."

"Smoke marijuana, you want to get a charge of some sort, and float, and this and that and the other thing," said Nixon.

A few days after his meeting with Linkletter, Nixon broached the topic of marijuana with Bob Haldeman.

"I want a goddamn strong statement on marijuana," Nixon said.

"Sure," said Haldeman.

"I mean one on marijuana that just tears the ass out of them." Nixon went silent for a moment, reflecting. "You know, it's a funny thing, every one of the bastards that are out for legalizing marijuana is Jewish," he said. "What the Christ is the matter with the Jews, Bob, what is the matter with them? I suppose it's because most of them are psychiatrists, you know. All the greatest psychiatrists are Jewish." It's always amazing to hear Nixon offend so many people in so few words. "By God we are going to hit the marijuana thing, and I want to hit it right square in the puss. I want to hit it, against legalization and all that sort of thing."

Days passed. June 2, 1971, Nixon to John Ehrlichman. Marijuana again. "Why in the name of God do these people take this stuff?"

"For the same reason they drink," Ehrlichman responded. "They're bored. It's a diversion."

Nixon corrected him. "Drinking is a different thing," he said. "Linkletter's point, I think, is well taken. He says, 'A person may drink to have a good time, but a person does not drink simply for the purpose of getting high.' You take drugs for the purpose of getting high."

A few weeks later, Nixon addressed the issue at a press conference. "America's public enemy number one is drug abuse," he said. "In order to fight and defeat this enemy, it is necessary to wage a new, all-out offensive." This June 17, 1971, comment is now considered the opening shot in America's war on drugs.

The White House received the Shafer Commission's report a few days prior to its release in early 1972. Nixon was not pleased.

On March 21, Nixon met with Bob Haldeman to discuss the president's response. The White House press office put together a draft that described drugs as a problem "that must be dealt with in a variety of ways." That struck the president as just a touch off-key.

"When I saw 'variety of ways,' I goddamned near puked," he told Haldeman. "And I thought, for pity's sake, we need, and I use the word 'all-out war,' on all fronts."

"You've got to attack it from every direction," agreed Haldeman.

"Just kick the hell out of it," said Nixon. "We enforce the law."

"Educating the kids, they talk about that, but that's a tough one to peddle," said Haldeman.

"Educate them, shit," said Nixon. "You've got to scare them."

———

Nixon gave his only public comments a few days after the report's release.

"I read it," he told the press, "and reading it did not change my mind." The White House round-filed the commission's work. The media moved on. Nixon trounced George McGovern and opened his second term with an expanded law-and-order agenda. His 1973 State of the Union speech bristled with tough new proposals. A federal death penalty. Life sentences for drug dealers. A powerful new law-enforcement division, the Drug Enforcement Administration, dedicated to the fight against drugs. No marijuana legalization of any kind. "The line against the use of dangerous drugs is now drawn on this side of marijuana," Nixon declared. "If we move the line to the other side and accept the use of this drug, how can we draw the line against other illegal drugs?"

The original purpose of the commission—to determine the scheduling of marijuana within the Controlled Substances Act—was buried and forgotten. Raymond Shafer never received that appointment to the federal bench.

———

Nixon disowned the Shafer Commission, but he couldn't prevent others from acting on its findings. *Decriminalization* became a bipartisan buzzword. Over the next six years Oregon, Ohio, Colorado, Maine, California, Alaska, Minnesota, Mississippi, New York, North Carolina and Nebraska passed laws that made the possession of small amounts of pot legal or, at worst, a minor infraction.

Around the same time, the first references to marijuana's medical potential began appearing in the press. Robert Randall, a college professor in Washington, D.C., sued the federal government for the right to use marijuana to treat his glaucoma. Smoking pot, Randall said, was the only thing that relieved the acute pressure in his eyes. His doctor testified that marijuana kept Randall from going blind. Science backed him up. Harry Anslinger's ban on marijuana research continued after his retirement, but now and then studies intended to establish marijuana's harm stumbled upon facts showing the opposite. In 1971 a UCLA ophthalmologist carried out research on marijuana and pupil dilation. The idea was to make it easier for police to spot pot smokers. The ophthalmologist discovered that marijuana significantly decreased eye pressure, one of the primary symptoms of glaucoma.

Randall won his case in 1978, but the government wouldn't allow him to grow his own cannabis. Instead the Food and Drug Administration established a protocol known as the Compassionate Investigational New Drug program to supply him with government-made joints.

The Randall case and the state decriminalization campaigns succeeded largely because of the emergence of NORML. Founded in 1970 by Georgetown Law graduate Keith Stroup, NORML brought together a cadre of young attorneys to fight for marijuana reform. What Nader's raiders did for American consumers, Stroup's troops hoped to do for the nation's pot smokers. Between 1973 and 1981 they racked up a remarkable string of victories. Eleven states decriminalized. Congress was giving serious consideration to a federal decrim bill. Robert DuPont, the Nixon-appointed head of the National Institute on Drug Abuse, favored decriminalization, as did the *Washington Post* and the American Bar Association. Democratic presidential nominee Jimmy Carter endorsed the idea during the 1976 campaign. With Carter's election, the end of marijuana prohibition seemed all but inevitable. In a 1977 interview with Larry Sloman, Stroup allowed himself an early victory lap. "To live through the end of prohibition is fascinating," he said. "How many times do you get to do that in your life?"

He had good reason to be confident. Nixon had resigned in disgrace. The Carter White House was famously pro-pot, in private use if not in public policy. But in three short years, Stroup and NORML suffered a devastating reversal of fortune. By late 1979, the once inevitable turned into the all but impossible.

It happened because of two men: Keith Stroup and Peter Bourne.

Bourne was Jimmy Carter's drug policy adviser, a smart, hip psychiatrist and mental health expert who was said to have the president's ear. Stroup, in turn, had the ear of Bourne. Together they planned to decriminalize marijuana in America.

Things went wrong from the start. Shortly after moving into the White House, President Carter had second thoughts about decriminalization. He worried that it would send the wrong signal. Bourne pushed back. In terms of personal and public health, he told the president, prison was far more harmful than pot smoking. They agreed to a compromise: Carter would call for replacing prison sentences with civil fines.

Then paraquat appeared. In late 1975, the Mexican government began secretly eradicating marijuana and opium poppy grows by using helicopters to spray them with the powerful herbicide. The U.S. State Department chipped in $35 million to fund the operation. Paraquat had a major drawback—it didn't work fast enough. Mexican pot growers dashed in and harvested their crops the minute the spraying stopped. Tons of tainted weed moved into the lungs of North America. Rumors spread. Paraquat was a known toxin. If swallowed as a liquid, a single teaspoon of the stuff could have a fatal effect. Millions of pot smokers wondered if they were poisoning themselves.

At a White House meeting on drug strategy in early 1977, Stroup asked

Bourne if the paraquat rumors were true. Bourne said he'd look into it.

Weeks passed. Finally Bourne reported back. He told Stroup the Mexicans were indeed crop dusting, but the U.S. wasn't involved in the program.

Bourne's seeming indifference infuriated Stroup. Carter had already begun to backpedal on decriminalization. Now, as Stroup saw it, the president and Bourne were turning a blind eye to the poisoning of America's pot smokers. He began to feel like Bourne was playing him for a fool.

In fact, Bourne was spending an inordinate amount of time on the paraquat issue. He flew to Mexico to investigate the pot fields first-hand. When the issue came up in meetings, other White House officials wondered why they should care. Bourne was the only one to speak up. "Because we have a responsibility," he said.

Keith Stroup didn't know any of this. All he saw was Peter Bourne selling out America's pot smokers.

———

As paraquat occupied Bourne and Stroup, a storm gathered over the horizon.

In the '60s marijuana moved from jazz clubs to college dorms. In the '70s it moved into the nation's high schools. In 1970, 4 percent of high school seniors smoked pot daily. By 1977, 11 percent of America's upper-classmen were toking up every day after school. Frustrated parents sought help. Some even rang up the NORML office. One mother, distraught at finding her 14-year-old son smoking a skull bong in his treehouse, phoned NORML and found herself talking to Keith Stroup. After hearing her plight, Stroup advised her to lighten up. It just wasn't a big deal, he said.

The parents finally turned to one another for support. They gathered in suburban dens and family rooms. They educated each other. *This is what a bong looks like.* Out of those support groups grew organizations like Families in Action and the National Federation for Drug-Free Kids. One of the most powerful forces in politics is the voice of an angry mother. And those mothers were angry. "They didn't want to hear about the Marijuana Commission report, or scientific findings that suggested marijuana was not harmful, or the arguments for decriminalization," Patrick Anderson wrote in his marijuana history *High in America*. "All they knew was that they didn't want their children smoking the stuff."

Stroup and his allies were too obsessed with paraquat to worry about a handful of uptight suburban moms. As 1977 drew to a close, NORML operated the hippest policy shop in Washington. Young Capitol Hill staffers and White House aides dropped by the group's office to hang out, swap gossip and share a toke. NORML's Christmas party was always the wildest bash in town. More than 600 people showed up for the '77 holiday fete, including *Playboy* CEO Christie Hefner, *Rolling Stone's* Hunter S. Thompson, a cadre of radical yippies, a few *Washington Post* reporters, members of the *High Times* staff, many of the nation's biggest pot dealers as well as the attorneys who kept them out of jail. Late that night, with the party at full roar, somebody sent word to Stroup that an unexpected guest had slipped past the door. It was Bourne.

Bourne's decision to attend the affair deserves an alcove of its own in the Poor Choices Hall of Fame. Then the error compounded. Later that night, in an upstairs bedroom, the White House drug policy adviser reportedly enjoyed a bump of cocaine. Years later Bourne would acknowledge that "there was no doubt cocaine was being used at that party," but he said he did not indulge.

The incident passed without notice in the press. But the rumor persisted.

Over the following months, Stroup and Bourne continued to bicker over paraquat. In July 1978 the strained alliance finally snapped. Bourne, who retained his medical privileges while serving in the White House, wrote a Quaalude prescription for a young staff member battling insomnia. 'Ludes were widely abused as a recreational drug, so to spare the young woman embarrassment, Bourne wrote the scrip, under his real name, to a fictitious patient. A friend tried to fill it for her and was arrested. Bourne's name hit the papers. A media frenzy ensued.

Patrick Anderson chronicled what happened next in *High in America*. Stroup got a call from Gary Cohn, a reporter who worked for Washington columnist Jack Anderson. Cohn had attended the NORML party where Bourne reportedly took the toot. He hadn't used the item out of professional courtesy. But circumstances had changed. "Somebody will break it," he told Stroup. "Can I go with it?"

Stroup could have denied Bourne's cocaine use. In the moment, though, his anger at Bourne over the paraquat issue overcame him. "I won't tell you not to use it," Stroup told Cohn. "But don't use me as a source."

The next morning, Anderson broke the story on *Good Morning America*: President Carter's drug policy adviser had been seen snorting cocaine at a NORML party. Bourne's resignation letter was on Carter's desk that afternoon.

A *Washington Post* reporter called Stroup for comment. Again Stroup refused to deny that Bourne snorted coke at the party. Then he twisted the knife. Of Bourne's demise, Stroup said, "I do not see it with any great sadness."

Federal decriminalization died that day. Stroup's allies abandoned him. NORML's reputation suffered a blow from which it took decades to recover. Bourne's successor, Lee Dogoloff, shunned the organization. During one of his first days on the job, Dogoloff was shocked to discover that 11 percent of America's high school seniors were getting stoned every day. He ordered his staff to set up a meeting with an expert who knew something about the problem. That call didn't go to Stroup. It rang in the kitchen of Marsha Keith Schuchard. She was a suburban Atlanta mother who had formed a local support group to help parents keep marijuana out of the hands of teenagers.

Did Keith Stroup and Peter Bourne blow America's best chance at legalization? Maybe. In truth, though, decriminalization stood a slim chance even without the Christmas cocaine fiasco. Jimmy Carter never loved the idea. Congressional support was weak. Public approval hovered around 30 percent. With White House backing, an extraordinary effort led by Bourne might have pushed decrim through Congress. But without Bourne it didn't stand a chance. When a Capitol Hill committee held a hearing on a last-gasp decriminalization bill in 1979, Schuchard and her fellow parents showed up to drive a stake through its heart.

There are those who wonder what might have been, who look back on the past 35 years and think about a different trajectory. "If Carter gets re-elected in 1980," NORML executive director Allen St. Pierre told me, "the War on Drugs never happens."

Maybe. But I doubt it. What the legalization movement lacked in the late '70s was a sense of differentiation. In the late '70s you saw a great lumping together of marijuana with all other drugs. Marijuana, cocaine, acid, pills—they constituted a panoply, and there wasn't a whole lot of distinction between them. Drugs were drugs. It's true that Stroup's organization was called NORML, not NORDL. He didn't want to change all drug laws, just marijuana laws. But at the time, cocaine was considered nearly as harmless as pot among many of the cognoscenti in Laurel Canyon, on the Upper West Side and around Dupont Circle. Successful and otherwise sensible adults popped uppers to party and downers to sleep. And why not? If nothing else, the previous decade taught the baby boom generation that the authorities, the official line, the government, The Man, had been spectacularly wrong. Their treatment of black people was wrong. They were wrong about the domino theory and the Vietnam War. Their assumptions about the capabilities of women and minorities were wrong. Their fear and hatred of homosexuals was wrong. Their attitude about sex was laughably wrong. Watergate revealed the president as a liar and a dangerous kook. On marijuana, the authorities had been wrong since the 1930s. Why on earth would anybody believe what the authorities said about cocaine, pills and all the other drugs in the pharmacopeia of the late '70s?

It would take years of hard experience to understand the differences. The glamorous cocaine users of the late '70s became the haggard coke addicts of the mid-'80s. Crack appeared and spread its destruction through America's cities. Meth and opioids culled the poor, rural and vulnerable in later generations. But that was all in the future. In the late '70s the destructive power of those drugs was too little known. When it came right down to it, the leader of the decriminalization movement couldn't bring himself to counsel a 14-year-old boy against firing up a skull bong in a treehouse. For the body politic, Stroup and his allies couldn't draw a bright line between cannabis and cocaine, pills and speed because they couldn't even draw the line in their own lives.

Then the Reagan administration came along and drew it for them.

———————

In the waning days of 1981, the Reagan administration had a problem. Her name was Nancy. While her husband's approval ratings soared, the First Lady found herself cast as the Marie Antoinette of the '80s. Michael Deaver, the Reagans' close friend and adviser, took on the First Lady as a turnaround project. He recalled how moved she'd been by a visit to a New York drug treatment center during the 1980 campaign. Deaver knew the anti-drug message played well with the Republican base, and especially well with suburban parents. He directed West Wing staffers to gin up a campaign.

In early 1982 the White House rolled out the new Nancy Reagan. The First Lady visited a series of drug abuse prevention and treatment programs with media in tow. "The hard statistics, not to mention the touching personal stories I've heard, make it clear to me that we must educate ourselves and others about drug abuse," said Mrs. Reagan. At a school in Oakland, a little girl asked her what to do if somebody offered her drugs. "Well, you just say no," Mrs. Reagan responded. A catchphrase was born.

Nixon saw drugs as a political issue and a police matter. The Reagans expanded it into an all-out cultural war. The First Lady favored universal drug testing. She encouraged children to call the police on their pot-smoking parents. She called casual users "accomplices to murder."

Leniency and tolerance were out. Shaming and arresting were in.

"Each of us has a responsibility to be intolerant of drug use anywhere, anytime, by anybody, and to force the drug issue to the point that it may make others uncomfortable and ourselves unpopular," she said. "We must create an atmosphere of intolerance for drug use in this country."

In the war on drugs, "there is no moral middle ground," she declared. "Indifference is not an option."

President Reagan backed up his wife's words with the power of the presidency. On June 24, 1982, he signed Executive Order 12368, the opening salvo in a radical escalation of the government's anti-drug efforts. In a Rose Garden ceremony, the president proclaimed, "We're taking down the surrender flag that has flown over so many drug efforts; we're running up a battle flag."

———

Over the next few years, President Reagan threw the full weight of the U.S. government behind the anti-drug movement. He waived the Posse Comitatus Act, an 1878 law prohibiting the military from enforcing state laws. That allowed soldiers to actually fight the War on Drugs. In five years the Pentagon's anti-drug spending went from $1 million to $196 million. Drug tests became mandatory for all federal employees. Federal funding moved away from drug treatment programs and toward surveillance and punishment operations. Congress and the Reagan administration abolished federal parole. New laws allowed the police to confiscate the assets of anyone suspected—just suspected, not convicted—of a drug crime. Between 1982 and 1991, $2.5 billion in assets were seized. Of those who lost a total of $500 million in property in 1991, 80 percent were never charged with a crime. Attorney General Edwin Meese began forcing defense lawyers to inform on their own drug-charged clients. "Constitutional freedoms," Meese said, "should not be used as a 'screen' to protect defendants who engaged in the evils of drugs."

Inside the White House, Reagan's drug policy was overseen by a curious character named Carlton Turner, a biochemist whose job prior to running the drug war was growing research-grade pot under federal contract at the University of Mississippi. No joke. Turner, a staunch conservative, grew pot, studied pot and hated pot smokers. Marijuana use, he once declared, "is a behavioral pattern that has sort of tagged along during the present young-adult generation's involvement in anti-military, anti–nuclear power, anti–big business, anti-authority demonstrations." Pot smoking, he said, went hand in hand with "people from a myriad of different racial, religious or otherwise persuasions demanding 'rights.' . . ." In other words, Turner believed that if you got rid of marijuana you might eradicate the civil rights movement and the counterculture in one fell swoop.

Turner carried out his war on marijuana for six years until his bizarre theories and big mouth finally tripped him up. In October 1986, he told a *Newsweek* reporter that he suspected pot smoking might lead to homosexuality. Turner said that during visits to rehab centers, he found that roughly 40 percent of the teenagers were gay. "It seems to be something that follows along from their marijuana use," he said. "The public needs to be thinking about how drugs alter people's lifestyles." Even in an administration infamous for its homophobic policies, Turner's statement elicited a groan. His welcome worn out, Turner stepped down a few weeks later and retreated to Florida, where he became head of a firm that offered drug-testing services to *Fortune* 500 companies.

The Reagan drug war continued on even after Reagan himself left office. George H.W. Bush carried on the "Just Say No" campaign even unto the close of the '80s.

Remember Robert Randall, the man who forced the government to supply him with pot for his glaucoma? Randall spent much of the '80s working with NORML to force the DEA to reschedule marijuana. In 1988 their work finally produced a victory. DEA administrative law judge Francis Young pronounced marijuana "one of the safest therapeutically active substances known to man" and said its Schedule I classification was "unreasonable, arbitrary and capricious." Bush administration officials sat on Young's ruling for nearly a year before quietly killing it on a day when nobody was watching. DEA administrator Jack Lawn officially rejected Young's decision on Saturday, Dec. 30, 1989, when newsrooms were empty and most Americans were out buying champagne.

THE LONG
CONVERSATION

In the 1990s, marijuana laws didn't change. Their enforcement did. The CompStat system adopted by the New York City Police Department rewarded cops for low-level pot busts. Between 1990 and 2002, arrests for possession increased 2,461 percent in New York City. Eight of every 10 New Yorkers arrested for pot were people of color. As other cities embraced CompStat, marijuana arrests shot up across the country. While the national arrest rate for all crimes decreased by 3 percent from 1990 to 2002, arrests for marijuana increased by 113 percent. The surge had zero effect on marijuana usage. In 1990 a little more than 10 percent of the American population used marijuana. By 2002 that figure had increased to 11 percent.

As more and more Americans found themselves arrested for smaller and smaller amounts of pot, two young mavericks began questioning the logic and justice behind it all.

———

In Virginia, a University of Richmond student named Mason Tvert found himself caught up in a grand jury investigation into the local marijuana market. "There was never any suspicion that I was using or selling," Tvert later recalled. "They questioned me simply because I was a college student." Meanwhile, all around him students were landing in the hospital with alcohol poisoning. But the authorities didn't care about that. "It was obvious to me that these laws were foolish," he said.

After college, Tvert moved to Denver and created a group to promote the proposition that marijuana was safer than alcohol. It was 2004. Tvert was 22. Colorado legalized medical marijuana in 2000, but dispensaries hadn't yet appeared. Polls indicated that the state's voters ran ahead of politicians in their support for legalization. "Colorado looked like fertile ground," he recalled.

In 2005, Tvert pushed a successful initiative to decriminalize small amounts of cannabis within Denver's city limits. The next year he took the "legal ounce" idea statewide and got trounced. "That was OK, because the point wasn't necessarily to win," Tvert told me. "Every time we put a marijuana issue on the ballot, it raised a discussion. My mission was to educate the public about the fact that marijuana is less harmful than alcohol. We knew the more people talked about it the more our support would grow. The facts were on our side."

Tvert had a natural gift for political theater. When Denver mayor John Hickenlooper refused to participate in an alcohol-vs.-pot debate, Tvert hired an actor to follow the mayor around in a chicken suit. "The Chickenlooper" won Tvert no friends among Democrats, but it got terrific media play. Weeks before the 2006 election, DEA agents made a splashy arrest of Colorado marijuana growers. Tvert responded with a press conference outside the DEA's Denver office, where he counted the number of liquor stores in the metro area: "more than 1,000 operations selling a more dangerous drug than marijuana throughout Denver."

Meanwhile, in Seattle, a young criminal-defense lawyer began making her own move on history. Alison Holcomb made her bones springing pot smokers. As a young lawyer in her 20s, she watched Seattle's drug culture parade through the offices of her employer, defense attorney Jeffrey Steinborn. An old-school '60s liberal, Steinborn operated the city's busiest drug-law practice. Seven years in Steinborn's office opened Holcomb's eyes to the injustice of the drug war. She saw lives ruined over a few ounces of marijuana.

In 2003 Holcomb helped implement Seattle's decriminalization law, which made marijuana offenses the Seattle Police Department's lowest law-enforcement priority. Soon after, ACLU of Washington executive director Kathleen Taylor hired her to head up the group's marijuana-reform project. One of Holcomb's early efforts required her to convince a famous travel writer to go on TV and talk about pot.

Like Tvert, Holcomb needed to open minds before she could change them. The first step was to raise marijuana reform as a grown-up, no-joke topic. Chicken suits would not be part of the plan. She wanted a one-time, one-hour, *Oprah*-style show about marijuana. And she wanted Rick Steves to host it.

Steves had a successful career as a good-natured American bumbling through Europe. His popular PBS travel show, *Rick Steves' Europe*, featured the amiable Steves grinning through cities like Florence, Amsterdam and Paris. Steves lived in Edmonds, a quaint Seattle suburb on the shores of Puget Sound. Holcomb knew two things about Steves: He was widely trusted by Middle America, and he firmly believed in marijuana legalization. Steves didn't touch the issue on his show (well, except during visits to Amsterdam), but he didn't hide his feelings. The guy was, after all, a member of NORML's advisory board.

To his own surprise, Steves agreed to host Holcomb's show. *Marijuana: It's Time for a Conversation* featured Steves talking cannabis policy with Holcomb, ex–Nixon aide Egil "Bud" Krogh, former U.S. Attorney John McKay and an audience that appeared to be recruited from a Lutheran estate-planning seminar. The show fairly dripped with rectitude. Nevertheless, the topic remained so taboo that few stations would air it. "The networks were too afraid," Steves told Nina Shapiro of the *Seattle Weekly*. "It ran after the *Girls Gone Wild* ads at two in the morning."

A funny thing happened with the *Conversation* special. Few people saw it, but everybody seemed to hear about it. What they noted was this: Rick Steves spoke publicly about legalizing marijuana and nobody fired him. Steves's modest media empire was built on a simple premise: if a big galoot like me can have fun in Europe, you can too. Foreign travel intimidated most Americans. Steves assured them there was nothing to be afraid of. After years of honing that message, he applied it to marijuana.

Come on in, he told the silent majority. The water's fine.

As Mason Tvert deployed bullhorns and chicken suits in Denver, a trim, mannerly lawyer remade Colorado's medical marijuana landscape.

Brian Vicente was the yin to Mason Tvert's yang. Tvert was the bomb thrower, Vicente the diplomat. Vicente's organization, Sensible Colorado, worked to secure safe access to marijuana for MMJ patients. In 2007 Vicente sued the state on behalf of Damien LaGoy, who suffered from AIDS and hepatitis C. At the time, Colorado prohibited any one caregiver from selling marijuana to more than five patients.

"The cap meant a lot of patients had to buy on the streets. A lot of guys were getting beat up in parks," Vicente said. He argued that the state's policy impeded LaGoy's access to medicine. On the witness stand, LaGoy painstakingly lined up each of his hep C and AIDS drugs on the wooden rail. "The only thing that allows me to keep these down," he said, "is marijuana." Vicente and LaGoy won the case.

That decision set off the Colorado green rush. With no limit to the number of patients, caregivers scaled up overnight. Hundreds of storefront dispensaries popped up across the state. "It was the Wild West," recalled Max Montrose, a pot activist who worked as a budtender during the early dispensary days. "We were moving thousands of dollars out of the store in brown paper bags every night." Banking was a problem. "We made a big deposit of cash on a Friday afternoon, and when they opened the vault on

Monday morning a cloud of cannabis fumes rolled out," Montrose told me. "The bank told us we had to wash the bills or they'd shut down our account."

Desperate to contain the chaos, Colorado legislators began drafting crackdown bills. The state's MMJ days looked to be numbered. Brian Vicente stepped in to save the industry.

Vicente convinced lawmakers the medical marijuana industry didn't have to be killed. It could be harnessed. All it needed was state regulation. Vicente and others negotiated a new system. The State Department of Revenue would license MMJ operations. Dispensaries had to track every plant, stem, bud and leaf with a sophisticated bar-code software system. Inspections would be made. Taxes would be paid.

It worked.

By 2011 Colorado had transformed its weed carnival into a safe, well-regulated medical marijuana industry. Lawmakers from other states flew to Denver to see what "cannabis best practices" actually looked like.

"Those state MMJ regulations were critical," Tvert told me. "They showed voters what would happen if we had marijuana stores. Because these dispensaries were, essentially, marijuana stores. That was no longer a scary abstract notion."

With the medical marijuana industry humming, Tvert and Vicente joined forces to overcome the final hurdle: full adult legalization. By this time, Tvert had been hired as a campaign manager by the Marijuana Policy Project, a national group looking to put serious money behind a legalization campaign. One that might finally win.

———

In September 2010, Alison Holcomb convinced America's marijuana brain trust to fly to Seattle and hear her pitch. She wanted to put legalization on the state ballot in 2012. To do that, she needed funding and support from the national players. NORML founder Keith Stroup was there. So was Graham Boyd, who directed political funding for Progressive Insurance founder Peter Lewis, a strong supporter of pot legalization. Joining them were Andy Ko, drug policy director for George

Soros's Open Society Foundation; Marijuana Policy Project founder Rob Kampia; and Drug Policy Alliance director Ethan Nadelmann.

Holcomb pitched her case like a start-up founder seeking venture capital. She bullet-pointed the state's pro-pot voting record. She flashed impressive poll numbers. She recapped the 20-year history of Hempfest, Seattle's summer pot festival. She previewed the campaign's talking points.

"It was pretty impressive," Kampia later recalled. "The polling was solid."

Solid but not convincing. Among political pros there was a rule of thumb about progressive initiatives: you didn't put one on the ballot with less than 60 percent polling support. The assumption was that 5 to 10 percent of supporters would get cold feet and switch at the last minute. The brain trust flew out of Sea-Tac without giving Holcomb a firm commitment.

"We weren't near 60 percent," Holcomb told me years later. "But we were starting to see a shift in the numbers. People were becoming less interested in the idea of decriminalization and more interested in regulation and taxation."

Holcomb moved forward. In 2011 she received an unexpected gift in the form of a veto. State legislators passed a bill to regulate Washington's booming medical marijuana industry with a scheme similar to Colorado's. Gov. Christine Gregoire vetoed the bill. Gregoire refused to force state employees to risk federal arrest, she said, for doing their jobs. Her concern seemed a little overblown. The feds were giving no trouble to Colorado's marijuana regulators. Nevertheless, the bill died. That left Washington with one of the largest and least controlled MMJ markets in the nation. There was no patient registry, no security codes, no tax requirements.

With Gregoire's veto, Holcomb's campaign became the state's best chance to bring the marijuana industry under control. She began gathering allies. One of her first hires at New Approach Washington, Initiative 502's backing group, was a former prosecutor named Tonia Winchester. A fierce, high-energy lawyer in her early 30s, Winchester had grown tired of hammering pot smokers with long prison stretches. When she spotted New Approach's help-wanted post on idealist.org, Winchester sent over her résumé. She was hired the next week.

Seattle City Attorney Pete Holmes, a good-government liberal, signed on as an early sponsor of the initiative. Holmes set about recruiting his longtime friend and colleague John McKay. A moderate Republican, McKay had been appointed U.S. Attorney for Western Washington by George W. Bush in 2001. Five years later McKay was fired as part of Attorney General Alberto Gonzales's campaign to purge prosecutors who hadn't proved to be "loyal Bushies." Holmes pressed McKay. "John, you need to sponsor this initiative with me," Holmes told him. "It's the right thing to do." When McKay agreed, I-502 gained its most important co-sponsor. He wasn't just a high-profile Republican. As a result of his firing at the hands of Gonzales, John McKay's name had become synonymous with integrity.

Meanwhile, Holcomb and Winchester tested media messages. Middle-aged women were the least receptive to pot legalization. So New Approach Washington tested an ad that featured a conservatively dressed woman in a coffee shop. "It's a multimillion-dollar industry in Washington State, and we get nothing from it," the mom said. "What if we regulate it?" Focus groups, including soccer moms, liked the ad. "It confirmed our top messages," recalled Holcomb. "Number one: people think law-enforcement resources should be focused on violent crime, not wasted on marijuana. Number two: people were becoming more aware of the horrific cartel violence in Mexico. They wanted to take money out of the hands of the bad guys and put it in the hands of the good guys, in the form of tax revenue."

What was shocking was the realization that one message had become superfluous: the drug war has failed.

On election day, President Obama's campaign rolled out one of the most effective get-out-the-vote programs in the history of American politics. The Colorado and Washington marijuana campaigns grabbed hold of the president's coattails and rode them all day long. The Obama campaign's savvy use of social media was especially effective at bringing out younger voters who would be critical to the chances of the legaliza-tion measures. In 2010 only one in four 18-to-29-year-old voters cast ballots. In 2012 that figure was one in two.

Colorado's Amendment 64 passed easily, 55 percent to 45 percent. The measure outpolled President Obama by nearly 200,000 votes. In Denver, pot proponents toasted one another with beer and discreetly passed joints at Casselman's Bar in the LoDo district. Then they pressed around flatscreens to watch the results from Washington State.

In Seattle, I-502 supporters gathered in a ballroom at the Andra, a boutique hotel at the edge of downtown. Alison Holcomb's voice had gone hoarse earlier in the day. Too many sound bites, too many rallying cries.

At a few minutes past 8 p.m. the Secretary of State's office released the first returns. Tonia Winchester called them up on her iPad. "Tonia handed it to me, and it showed us at 44 percent," Holcomb recalled. "And I thought, *Crap. It's going to be hard to come back from that.*"

Early results are notoriously unreliable. They often include only a few results from conservative rural counties. A campaign worker yelled at Holcomb from across the room.

"Alison!" he said. "Look at the King County results."

King County, which includes Seattle, contains so many voters that it dominates statewide elections. If you win King County, victory is in the bag.

Holcomb pulled up the King County numbers. I-502, yes: 63 percent.

"That's when I knew we'd won," she later told me.

———

Washington State voters adopted marijuana legalization by a wider margin than Colorado: 56 percent to 44 percent.

For Holcomb, the historic significance of the election didn't sink in until a few days after the vote. On Nov. 12, King County Prosecutor Dan Satterberg announced he was dismissing all of the county's current mari-juana cases. Effective immediately. More than 200 arrests and pending trials evaporated.

"When I heard that, it really hit me for the first time," Holcomb recalled. "I remembered representing those people."

"People think it's a chippy offense, a misdemeanor, nothing really happens," she said. "But it's not. It really does change people's lives, their families' lives, their job opportunities. In Washington State that happened to thousands of people every year. Those people went to jail. Convictions went on their records. When Dan announced he was dismissing all those cases, that was the first time I got tears in my eyes."

Later that afternoon, Holcomb returned to her office at the ACLU. More than a dozen voicemails awaited her. She put them on speakerphone while sorting through her mail. One of the messages stopped her cold. It was a man. He spoke with a Mexican accent. He said, "Alison, I just want you to know. I have family in Mexico. I have friends that have died in Mexico. What you have done is a very good thing."

The passage of I-502 raised a lot of questions. For a lot of people, "What do we tell the kids?" was at the top of the list.

Here's how I handled it. I'm not saying you should use me as a role model. I'm just saying this is what happened.

My son Willie was 12. One day, while laboring at his after-school job of eating Smart Puffs while on-demanding *The Colbert Report*, a segment came on about Toronto mayor Rob Ford. At the time, Ford seemed to be on a quest to move the city's entire cocaine supply up his nose. Willie turned to me. "So," he said, "I know cocaine's not marijuana. But what's crack?"

"OK," I said. I pressed pause. There are moments in every parent's life when fate calls upon you to stand and deliver. I drew a breath and gathered my wits.

"Here's the deal," I said. "There's an entire spectrum of drugs out there. From the least dangerous to the most." I made wide brackets with my hands. "Over here we've got things like Coke, coffee, aspirin, Red Bull. Things that energize you or tamp down a headache. Minor stuff. Then there are prescription drugs like antidepressants, and the pills your mother takes for her thyroid, kind of in the middle. Further along is alcohol, and the different types of alcohol: wine is stronger than beer, and liquor like whiskey and tequila is a lot stronger than wine. Over here at the far end," I said, waving my right bracket-hand, "are the most dangerous drugs, like cocaine, meth and heroin. They're dangerous both because of how intoxicated they get you and because they're hugely addictive and can pretty quickly ruin your life."

I paused. Willie looked at me wide-eyed.

"You asked about crack. Crack is a concentrated form of cocaine. You smoke just a tiny bit of it and it gets you really, really high."

High. A word, the implications of which my 12-year-old son did not necessarily know.

"In other words, it gets you loopy, like drunk, and makes you feel awesome for a while, and then you crash and feel lousy. And you want more, and then more, and that's addiction."

Now for the big finish.

"Marijuana's not cocaine, and it's not heroin," I said. "It affects the brain in a different way. If you take too much heroin, it can shut down your body and you die. That's a heroin overdose. With marijuana, you can't die from it. It just makes you loopy for a while. For about the past 75 years we've held marijuana way out here with heroin and cocaine," I said, waving my right hand. "But through research and experience, now we know it's not as dangerous as we once thought. In fact, it's more like alcohol. So in Washington and Colorado we're trying to see if we can legalize and regulate it like alcohol. Where only adults can buy it and use it. We're trying that. We don't know if it'll work."

I paused. "Does that make sense?"

Willie nodded in a way that communicated the words *Please, please stop talking.* He glanced at the TV remote.

"All right, then," I said. I pressed play, and *The Colbert Report* resumed.

————

For months after the election, state officials in Colorado and Washington

State waited for the federal response.

The supremacy of federal law is a founding principle of American democracy. It's written into our Constitution (Article VI, Clause 2) because our first try—the Articles of Confederation, which linked the states in a loose and leaderless coalition—proved to be a miserable failure. When state law rubs up against federal law, federal law prevails. The issue was supposed to be settled in Article VI, but then the whole states'-rights thing flared up again and touched off a little disagreement called the Civil War. So we settled it again.

There was no question that President Obama had the legal authority to send federal agents into the two states and arrest people for growing and selling marijuana. In fact, DEA agents continued to raid dispensaries and grows in both states. They just became more selective about their targets, shutting down dispensaries too close to schools and arresting growers who moved their product across state lines. Obama's ultimate response to the legalization votes remained an open question. When asked about it in late 2012, he deflected by saying the federal government had "bigger fish to fry."

Neither state's governor loved the new law. John Hickenlooper (D-Colorado) and Jay Inslee (D-Washington) opposed legalization during the campaign. But both agreed to carry out the will of the voters. Doing so required them to conduct a quiet campaign aimed at a single voter: U.S. Attorney General Eric Holder.

Starting in January 2013, Hickenlooper and Inslee fed Department of Justice officials a continuous stream of updates on security regulations, seed-to-sale tracking systems, background checks and leakage safeguards. The message they meant to send was clear: We believe we can handle this. Please let us try.

President Obama, a notorious pot smoker in high school and college, gave little thought to pot legalization as an adult. But he was well aware of the toll the War on Drugs had taken on black communities. So was Holder. During Obama's first term, the president and the attorney general left the issue up to local U.S. Attorneys, who became de facto drug czars within their jurisdictions.

In early 2013 Sen. Patrick Leahy (D-Vermont) offered Holder

political cover on the issue. "If you're going to be—because of budget cuts—prioritizing matters, I would suggest there are more serious things than minor possession of marijuana," he told Holder at a Senate hearing. Leahy joined Tea Party darling Rand Paul (R-Kentucky) to introduce legislation calling for an end to federal mandatory-minimum sentences in drug cases. The Leahy-Paul bill represented a signal moment in the beginning of the end of the War on Drugs: the alliance of drug-reform Democrats with libertarian Republicans.

Holder got the message. It took a while to work out the legal details, though. Finally, in August 2013, the attorney general made his first move. He instructed federal prosecutors to stand down on mandatory-minimum drug cases. Enough was enough. No more 10- and 20-year no-parole terms.

One week later, on Aug. 29, the attorney general held a conference call with Gov. Hickenlooper and Gov. Inslee. In Denver and Olympia, the governors and a coterie of staffers gathered around their speakerphones. Holder came on the line and read a carefully worded four-page memo prepared by Deputy Attorney General James Cole. The key passage: In states with "strong and effective regulatory and enforcement systems to control the cultivation, distribution, sale and possession of marijuana," federal officials would allow state and local law enforcement to address marijuana-related activity.

The operative word was *control*. States could now *control* the sale of marijuana. For the past 70 years, that word had been *prohibit*.

The feds didn't abandon their authority entirely. The Cole memo said that for now, federal law-enforcement agencies would step back and let state and local officials proceed with their pilot projects. This was permission, not a promise.

Inslee and Hickenlooper thanked Holder. Then they hung up.

Marijuana would be legal in Colorado and Washington State until President Obama left office in January 2017. After that, there were no guarantees. The two states would have three years and four months to show the rest of the nation that a safe and sane post-prohibition world was possible.

6

TWO SUITS IN A SEA OF HEMP PAJAMAS

"Bruce? You might want to have a look at this."

My wife Claire was checking her email at the kitchen table. I was fixing a sandwich. The kids were at school. It was lunchtime on a weekday in February 2013.

"What is it?"

"A tip about marijuana investors. You might be able to do something with it." She forwarded it.

The email mentioned an outfit called Privateer Holdings. They billed themselves as "a Seattle-based private equity fund focused on the cannabis industry." The founders were investment bankers with MBAs from Yale.

The weirdness intrigued me. Ivy League MBAs end up at Morgan Stanley, not Marijuana Inc. I followed up.

A few weeks later, Brendan Kennedy and Michael Blue settled into a conference room overlooking Lake Union to hear a pitch from a start-up seeking cash. Kennedy and Blue wore charcoal blazers and polished loafers. They conducted themselves with a regal confidence that bespoke an ease with the pairing of risk and large sums of money. Kennedy, 40, was the former chief operating officer of SVB Analytics, a division of Silicon Valley Bank. Blue, 35, learned his trade at the investment banking firm de Visscher & Co. in Greenwich, Connecticut. Two years earlier they and a third partner, Christian Groh, quit their comfortable posts to form Privateer Holdings, a firm that operated on the Kohlberg Kravis Roberts model: they bought companies using other people's money. What set them apart was the industry in which they intended to invest. Privateer Holdings was the first private equity firm to openly wager capital in the world of weed. Or as Kennedy and Blue preferred to call it, "the cannabis space."

The Privateer partners didn't court the media. Their natural inclinations were reflected in the appearance of the word *private* both in their firm's name and in its modus operandi. They weren't recluses, though, and after a series of phone conversations they invited me to watch them work. What intrigued me was the personal journey the founders had taken. I wanted to know how they moved from Point A, white-shoe investment bankers, to Point B, cannabis financiers. It seemed to me that they had already completed a transformation that much of America was considering.

On the morning I hung out with them, they were scheduled to hear a pitch from a company selling topicals, marijuana-infused lotions and creams.

Megan and Ben Schwarting were a married couple in their 30s. Their company, Kush Creams, produced cannabis lotions, eye creams, lip balms, shampoos and a pain-relieving product called Owie Wowie. Kennedy and Blue came into the meeting intrigued but wary. Their firm was predicated on the idea of making marijuana-related investments that didn't stray into illegal activity. In other words: don't touch the leaf. Infused lotions, which were federally illegal, seemed clearly over the line. The partners invited the pitch anyway. They wanted to know more about the market.

"Walk us through this like we're third-graders," said Kennedy.

Megan Schwarting led us through the theory behind topicals. "Through modern research it's been discovered that the body's euphoric CB1 receptors are found mainly in the brain, but CB2 receptors are in skin cells, spleen, stomach, liver, bones and immune cells," she said. "These non-psychoactive CB2 receptors are what respond to the anti-inflammatory, pain-relieving properties of cannabis."

"So if I rub this on my skin, I'm not going to get high," said Kennedy.

"That's right," said Megan. "But you may find relief for anxiety, stress, backaches and migraines."

What about the pot, Kennedy wondered. "Where does your supply come from?"

Ben Schwarting spoke. "Family-grown," he said.

"How do you extract it?" Kennedy said, referring to the cannabis oil mixed into the lotion.

"That's kind of our company secret," Ben said. "We work mostly with one strain. Others don't produce quite the same effect." Batch consistency and quality control: whether you're making Owie Wowie or Coca-Cola, the principles remain the same.

Then came the awkward question. "How'd you two get into this?" asked Kennedy.

Megan smiled and glanced at Ben. "We were private growers for a number of years," she said. "Then our three little girls came along, and we wanted to do something with a little less risk."

The Schwarting name actually carried quite a bit of weight in pharmacognosy, the study of the chemical and biological properties of drugs derived from natural plant sources. Arthur Schwarting, Ben's ancestor, co-founded the American Society of Pharmacognosy and was considered one of the fathers of the field, which today encompasses everything from naturopathic remedies to the billion-dollar search for new medicines by the world's largest pharmaceutical corporations. In his own craft-scale way, Ben was carrying on in the family business.

"What conditions do your topicals help alleviate?" asked Blue.

"Oh, these help with everything from fibromyalgia to toothache," said Megan. She passed around some material from the company's website. The list of ailments soothed by Kush Creams lotions and tinctures included rheumatoid arthritis, eczema, multiple sclerosis, restless leg syndrome, MRSA, gout, burn aftercare, scar restoration, skin rashes, bug bites, broken bones, artificial limbs and acne. At a certain point the length of the list became its own counterargument. How could one ointment simultaneously improve bug bites, broken bones, pimples and the Jimmy leg? Chris Rock's routine about Robitussin as a cure-all sprang to mind. *Broken leg? Pour some 'tussin on there.* I had to stifle a laugh.

Neither Kennedy nor Blue asked for evidence. Topicals like Kush Creams weren't regulated by the U.S. Food and Drug Administration—because products containing marijuana were inherently illegal—so they required no studies proving efficacy and safety. In the cannabis space, nearly all evidence was anecdotal.

"Where do you see Kush Creams in five years?" Kennedy asked.

"On the shelves in Whole Foods and progressive drugstores like Pharmaca," said Megan. "I can also see them in salons, spas and clinics. We're getting some strong interest from spas, but most of them aren't comfortable taking that step yet. So we're still exclusively in dispensaries."

After a while it became apparent that Privateer wouldn't be taking a stake in Kush Creams. Whipping together a small jar of the stuff violated all sorts of federal laws, and the market didn't seem mature enough to commit serious money to it.

Kennedy and Blue didn't betray any disappointment, though. "It's the nature of the job," Kennedy told me after seeing the Schwartings to the door. "You have to eliminate a lot of bad ideas before you find a good one."

———

Kennedy and Blue's entrance into the cannabis space began with a cold-call inquiry in 2010.

At the time, Kennedy directed the operations of SVB Analytics, a financial consulting subsidiary of Silicon Valley Bank, which specializes in entrepreneurial fields like high tech, genomics, medical devices and green energy. He split his time between Santa Clara, where the bank is headquartered, and Seattle, where his wife enjoyed a high-profile career as a dancer with the Pacific Northwest Ballet.

A call came in to the SVB office from an entrepreneur who sold inventory software to medical marijuana dispensaries. He wanted to know how to attract venture capital.

Kennedy shared a laugh over the call with Christian Groh, a colleague down the hall. Pot software? They knew their own firm wouldn't touch it. "Nobody wants to be known as the first banker or venture capitalist to make an investment in the cannabis industry," Kennedy later told me. "The risk to the firm's reputation is too great."

Just for fun, Kennedy and Groh drew up a list of Silicon Valley's boldest bankers, venture capitalists who might be open to the idea. "In the end, a couple of VCs listened," said Kennedy, "but they weren't ready for it. Not even close."

The idea stuck with Kennedy, though.

Later that week, as he sped between Silicon Valley's soft green hills on I-280, Kennedy happened to tune in to a radio show on marijuana legalization. He hadn't touched pot since he was 19. But the future proposed by one of the guests seemed to make sense: regulate marijuana like whiskey or vodka. Something fired in Kennedy's brain. He thought about the software developer. Maybe there was a way to get into the business without touching the leaf. Medical marijuana still wasn't legal, but ancillary products were. Insurance. Software. Lighting. "When everyone is looking for gold," Mark Twain once said, "it's a good time to be in the pick and shovel business."

Kennedy pulled off the highway and called Michael Blue, his old Yale School of Management classmate. "You know how we've always talked about starting something together?" he said. "I think I've found it. We need to start a venture capital firm in the cannabis space."

Silence.

At the time, Blue was happily ensconced at a sleepy financial firm in

Little Rock, Arkansas, where he and his wife had settled to raise their kids near her parents. Kennedy's pitch was outrageous. It was insane. And . . . it was interesting.

That night, lying in bed, Blue turned to his wife. "I'm going to tell you something about a conversation I just had with Brendan," he said. "No one knows about it yet. But here's what he's thinking."

They both laughed. Crazy Brendan.

Outlandish as it was, neither Kennedy nor Blue could shake the notion. Working during their off hours in Santa Clara and Little Rock, they dug into the existing research. They needed to know if marijuana truly helped medical patients or if that was just a story that characters like Turtle from *Entourage* cooked up to get their hands on some dope.

"The more research I did, the more I kept running into legitimate doctors prescribing it and people using it to positive effect," Kennedy told me. Blue, the more naturally cautious of the two, found his assumptions challenged by the volume of medical research pointing to the drug's therapeutic value. "One study after another pointed to its effectiveness for treating symptoms of multiple sclerosis, epilepsy and chemotherapy," he recalled. The research wasn't completely exculpatory, of course. Some studies indicated that chronic pot use could lead to long-term cognitive damage, especially among people who start in their teens. The key seemed to be, as with any drug, appropriate dosage.

The rise of medical marijuana lends itself to any number of narrative frames. It could be the cutting edge of a movement that leads to the nationwide acceptance of legal cannabis. Or we might be living through the Prague Spring of pot—a giddy moment of freedom doomed to be crushed by an intolerant federal government. Kennedy and Blue struck upon the analogy of Joseph Kennedy (no relation to Brendan) and the repeal of Prohibition.

It's a neat fit. In September 1933, as repeal of the 18th Amendment appeared all but inevitable, the father of the future president traveled to England, where he met with the managing director of the Distillers Company. By the time he returned home, Joseph Kennedy had locked up the import rights to Dewar's whiskey and Gordon's gin. According to Daniel Okrent, author of *Last Call: The Rise and Fall of Prohibition*, Kennedy had previously obtained medicinal liquor permits and bonded warehouse space. (As with marijuana today, "medical liquor" could be legally purchased with a doctor's note.) When Prohibition ceased on Dec. 6, 1933, Kennedy's Somerset Importers was already up and running.

The way Brendan Kennedy saw it, he and Blue had the chance to do what Joe Kennedy had done 80 years earlier.

Still, they worried. "We realized early on that the biggest risk wasn't legal," Kennedy told me. "It was the risk to our professional and personal reputations." Investing in the cannabis space would most likely burn their bridges to the traditional banking world. They wondered if they were feeding their Yale MBAs into a shredder.

Kennedy and Blue thought a lot about reputational risk, but it was a hard thing to quantify. The value of a reputation is often realized only when it's lost. Ask the folks at Philip Morris. In the 1990s, a series of damning revelations about the American tobacco industry turned Philip Morris into a symbol of venality and fraud. The company's reputation became so toxic that by 2001 it was forced to dump its world-famous name and recast itself as Altria. The reputational risk resulted in the destruction of hundreds of millions of dollars in brand value.

The Privateer partners faced a slightly different situation. At risk wasn't a corporation's name but their own personal reputations. They hadn't tarnished their names through any malfeasance of their own; they were embracing an entire industry synonymous with malfeasance. In essence, Kennedy, Blue and their third partner, Groh, were betting on marijuana as if it were a wildly undervalued stock. They believed the outlaw reputation of cannabis masked its true economic potential. The Privateer partners wagered that external beliefs and expectations about the drug would change for the better. If that happened, the value of their early investment would rise. If it didn't, they risked becoming the marijuana equivalent of mob lawyers.

This wasn't a hypothetical. At any cannabis industry gathering, you didn't have to look hard to find lawyers, bankers and others who had suffered a form of banishment for expressing an interest in the business of legal marijuana. Khurshid Khoja, a Bay Area business lawyer who is well known in the cannabis industry, was once a rising young attorney with the multinational firm Reed Smith. A few years ago he floated the idea of taking on a medical marijuana client. A senior partner dressed him down. "Son, do you really want to be known as the pot lawyer in the firm? Do you think anyone's going to want to work with you?'" Khoja resigned. He now operates Greenbridge Corporate Counsel, a firm specializing in medical marijuana. He's got more business than he can handle.

This was the puzzling part: It wasn't as if financiers shied away from risk, even criminal risk. Hedge fund managers and investment bankers were charged with insider trading all the time. In 2012 the banking giant HSBC agreed to pay $1.92 billion to settle charges that it illegally transferred or laundered billions of dollars for Iran and the Mexican drug cartels. Yet HSBC, like most banks, wouldn't touch state-legal medical marijuana companies. They couldn't handle the stigma.

Kennedy, Blue and Groh floated trial balloons to see how the idea played among friends and family. One of Kennedy's older brothers, a firefighter, was open to it. He told Kennedy about an old family friend, a rock-ribbed Republican fire captain, who used cannabis to fight the nausea from chemotherapy treatments when he battled cancer in the 1990s. Kennedy had no idea. "We heard stories like that almost every time we brought up the subject," Blue said.

Blue's elders at his Little Rock firm—old Southern country-club gents—reacted with interest, not disgust. Blue recalled James Atkins, the firm's 78-year-old managing director who was known as Bum, telling him, "You're talking about more risk than I've ever taken on. If you do it, do it the right way. Make sure everything's aboveboard and legal."

At the end of six months, Kennedy's idea had evolved from crazy to risky. "Where are you at with this?" he asked Blue. Blue thought about it. "I'm about 70 percent in," he said.

In January 2011 they reached a decision point: stay on the secure track or leap into the cannabis space. Kennedy laid out the upside. "This is an existing billion-dollar industry with immature companies run by unprofessional managers," he said. "There are no market leaders, no standards and poor branding. There's a taboo around the product that's rapidly changing. There's no involvement by Wall Street, venture capital or banks—yet. I've never seen an opportunity like it."

Blue needed to think it over. He and his wife dropped the kids off with her parents and took a day to map out the pros and cons. Pros: creating a new market; working with Brendan; financial returns potentially substantial. Cons: crazy idea; cannabis on your reputation and résumé; reaction of family and friends; legal concerns; start-ups often fail.

If Las Vegas gave odds on a pro/con list, this one would run 5 to 1 against the pro. But upsets happen.

Blue called Kennedy the next day. "One hundred percent," he said. "I'm in."

Entering an illegal industry as it transitions to legitimacy carries with it a number of challenges. There is, for instance, a lingering informality about things like accounting, security and management. In June 2011, more than 200 of the cannabis industry's top leaders met at a conference in San Francisco's Hotel Nikko. Kennedy and Blue showed up to scout for talent. They were two suits in a sea of hemp pajamas. "Most people thought we were DEA agents," Kennedy recalled.

They hoped to find investment-worthy companies and experienced executives. They found none. "It was a cavalcade of crazy," Kennedy recalled. One panel featured industry leaders discussing the benefits of taking a cannabis company public. To Kennedy and Blue, who had actually worked on IPOs, the notion was delusional. They eventually adopted a new tactic. Every time a panelist offered a crackpot assertion, the financiers scanned the audience to see who rolled their eyes or stifled a chuckle. "Those were the people we wanted to talk to."

They still believed the industry fundamentals were sound. Medical marijuana revenues grew 10 percent to 15 percent a year. Public acceptance of cannabis continued to rise. But the San Francisco conference forced them to reconsider their business model. "We're way too early,"

Kennedy said to Blue. Entrusting great sums of cash to Harold, Kumar and Jeff Spicoli seemed foolhardy.

This is where the fine details of a business model can make all the difference. Venture capitalists invest in start-up companies, but they generally don't exert much day-to-day influence in the business. By switching to a private-equity model, Kennedy and Blue realized they might be able to make the whole thing work. Private-equity firms don't invest; they purchase entire companies and often install their own management teams.

In September 2011 they founded Privateer Holdings. Blue relocated his family from Little Rock to Seattle a few months later. Kennedy and Christian Groh, the SVB colleague who had taken that initial phone call from the pot programmer, commuted to Seattle from the Bay Area for a few months before moving to Puget Sound.

The private-equity model proved popular with investors, who began sending Privateer Holdings chunks of money in November 2011. By the middle of 2012, the firm had enough cash on hand to purchase Leafly.com, a Yelp-like website that offered crowdsourced reviews of cannabis strains and dispensaries. Privateer bought the website partly for what it lacked. "It didn't have any of the old clichés," Kennedy said. "The site wasn't plastered with pot leaves."

If Privateer Holdings had one point of arbitrage over the rest of the investing world, it was this: everybody else thought Cheech and Chong; the Privateer partners thought soccer moms. Even edgy cultural representations like Mary-Louise Parker's middle-class dealer in *Weeds* lagged behind reality.

"Eighty-one percent of Americans believe medical cannabis should be legal," Kennedy told potential investors. "We've passed the tipping point. The end of cannabis prohibition is going to happen."

———

A couple of hours after the Kush Creams meeting, Kennedy and I drove across town to McCaw Hall, home of the Pacific Northwest Ballet. "Quick errand," he told me. He led me deeper and deeper into the recesses of the auditorium, up front stairs and down back stairs, around curtains and stage props, and just about the time I was thinking *Should we be back here?* we came to an unmarked dressing room. He knocked. "Maria!" he called out. "It's me."

Maria Chapman, PNB's principal dancer, opened the door.

"Bruce, this is my wife, Maria," Kennedy said.

A bit starstruck, I offered my hand and a goofy smile. Dressed in toe shoes, a leotard and a cardigan, she'd just finished an afternoon rehearsal of *Swan Lake*. She was dancing Odette, the lead. Later that night she'd be performing Balanchine's *Concerto Barocco* before a sold-out house.

"I brought you some samples," Kennedy told her. He handed her two jars of Kush Cream.

She eyed the label. "Oh, this is the one I like!" she said.

She rubbed some cream into her ankle and offered the jar to her colleague Lesley Rausch, who had also returned from the *Swan Lake* run-through.

"You both use this stuff?" I asked. Frankly, I was kind of shocked.

"Yes, I got my MMJ card a while back," Chapman said. "With all the stress our joints and muscles are under, you've got to watch it or you'll be popping ibuprofen all day long and do some serious damage to your liver."

Rausch had a dispensary card too. "When we're doing a classical ballet like *Swan Lake*, my calves get really tight because there's so much pointe work," she said. "So at night I'll rub this in to calm them down."

Chapman told me she used the balm mainly for her joints. "Last year we did a ballet that always jammed my ankle in the first section," she said, "so I'd rub a little of this on to loosen the joint. That allowed me to finish the ballet without any more problems."

As we chatted in their dressing room, it occurred to me that Chapman and Rausch were professional athletes as much as artists. The demands on their leg muscles and ankle joints were at least equal to the stresses of an NBA point guard or a defenseman for the Canucks. Like all pro athletes, they were constantly on the lookout for new ways to strengthen their bodies, heal their wounds and improve their performance. The dancers weren't disturbed about the historical stigma of marijuana. They only cared that it allowed them to dance for one more day.

The challenge for Kennedy and Blue was to reach more ballet dancers and soccer moms, more accountants and middle managers and IT specialists. To do that, they needed to clean up and mainstream a product with a seriously seamy reputation. Fortunately for Kennedy and Blue, there's an entire profession devoted to that process. It's called advertising.

On a sunny afternoon I accompanied Kennedy, Blue and Tonia Winchester as they traveled to Heckler Associates, a Seattle ad agency. Winchester, the outreach director for the I-502 campaign, was hired on as Privateer's marketing director and legal counsel a couple of months after the election. In early 2013 she was overseeing the rebranding of Leafly, the cannabis website bought by Privateer. The first step was to convince an ad agency to accept them as clients. "We had to pitch the Heckler partners for six hours to get them to take us on," Kennedy told me on the way over.

In the Heckler office, account director Scott Lowry greeted the Privateer team in the lobby. On the walls were famous logos that Heckler Associates had designed for Starbucks, K2, New Balance and other brands. Heckler was known for taking small companies and breaking them nationwide.

Lowry led the Privateer team into a back office where he laid out the contents of a Leafly.com marketing kit being readied for shipment to 500 medical marijuana dispensaries.

"Have you seen the new stickers?" asked Lowry. "The white ones?"

Everything about the Leafly logo, from the rounded typeface to the red, green and purple rectangles, had been designed to be as mainstream and friendly as Amazon.com or Target.

Blue nodded, pleased with the stickers. An earlier version had featured a light green background. This the Privateer partners abhorred. They believed the medical marijuana industry had grown saturated with the color green. Everywhere you looked there were green crosses, green leaves, green logos, green doors. Green had been shoddily used, reduced to an embarrassing calling-all-stoners signifier. Green was downmarket, grotty, unclean. Enough! No green.

"Yes," said Kennedy. "I definitely like the white better."

Lowry ticked through the marketing box. "We've got T-shirts, hats, stickers, magnets, window clings, dispensary bags, posters and a brochure display," he said. The dispensary bags were especially clever. To reinforce the medicinal aspect of a dispensary, the Heckler team had printed up thousands of Leafly-branded bags just like the ones handed out at the pharmacy counter at Walgreens or Rite Aid.

One item on the contents sheet caught Kennedy's eye.

"Where we list the hat, it says *skull cap*," he said. "*Skull cap* is skater. It's aggressive. What about *beanie*? *Beanie*'s happy."

Toward the end of the meeting Lowry revealed a Leafly.com ad aimed at a mainstream print publication. The ad featured two upscale professionals in a residential New York City neighborhood. A dapper businessman exited his brownstone. "While beating cancer, Ian used Blue Dream," the copy said, referring to a specific cannabis strain. A woman on her morning run passed nearby. "Molly prefers Kali Mist to relieve pain." The tagline: "WHAT'S YOUR STRAIN?" It was styled to look like a pharmaceutical ad, implying that these clean-cut citizens each used a specific strain of cannabis to address a specific need—and they used it like an antidepressant or a statin.

Lowry later explained the thinking. "In the early '60s, Honda wanted to sell motorcycles to Middle America," he said. The problem was the motorcycle's reputation. Hoodlums and outlaws rode motorcycles. Think of Brando in *The Wild One*. "So Honda came out with a campaign: 'You meet the nicest people on a Honda.'" The ads featured mothers and daughters, wealthy dowagers, even Santa Claus, all riding Hondas.

Cannabis, Lowry said, is the new motorcycle. The Privateer team loved it.

"This ad could run in the *Wall Street Journal* or an AARP publication," said Kennedy. Whether the publications would accept it was another question.

"It works," added Blue. "We're conveying the idea that the main consumer base is mainstream."

Scrub the product, erase the stigma; normalize, normalize, normalize. "Ultimately we're trying to create reliable, trusted products that are attractively packaged," Kennedy said. "What this industry needs is a clean American brand."

7

YOU MIGHT WANT
TO TRY THE
JOINT NEXT DOOR

At the end of my time with the Privateer Holdings partners, I found myself holding a jar of pot cream. Megan Schwarting, co-founder of Kush Creams, left behind a few samples, and Brendan Kennedy suggested I take one home. So I did. I tossed it in the back of the Subaru, where it settled under a drift of jackets, library books and ferry receipts. A few months later I rediscovered the jar while searching for my phone. At the time, my knees had been giving me trouble. I coach in a summer roller-hockey league. This involves lacing up inline skates and moving with great vigor. The wear and tear on my hinges is extensive.

One day after practice, I decided to rub some Kush Cream into my aching knees. The pain went away. *Whattaya know*, I thought. *The ballerinas were right.* When I rubbed it in before practice, I found I could avoid the pain altogether. I used a little before yoga class. Suddenly I could do that cat-cow maneuver without knee pain.

By the end of summer I had nearly used up the jar. I needed more. There was only one way to get it. I would have to get a medical marijuana card.

A few months earlier the thought would never have crossed my mind. What changed was my brief encounter with the ballet dancers. Something about the incongruity between their elite profession and marijuana's low reputation cracked the shell of my worldview. Their openness and their unapologetic, matter-of-fact attitude toward "the pot cream," as my wife had taken to calling it, opened me to the possibility that there might be many different kinds of medical marijuana patients. Not just late-stage cancer patients or pain-faking stoners but a wide variety of others in between. If the pot cream allowed professional ballet dancers to work without pain or liver damage, I couldn't see the harm. For that matter, what was the harm in using it to skate pain-free?

So began my quest for the card.

———

Within the city limits of Seattle there were more than 300 medical marijuana dispensaries, clinics and delivery services. Though there was no official list, city officials estimated that at least 5 percent of the population, or 25,000 people, were card-carrying medical marijuana users.

Obtaining medical pot was a two-step process. You first had to go to an MMJ clinic to get qualified and certified. Then you could shop at a dispensary.

I went to THCfinder.com and zeroed in on three likely clinics.

Green Wellness positioned itself as the Mercedes-Benz of the industry. Its clinic featured expensive low-pile carpeting, modern chairs and hushed lighting. Its motto: "You Get What You Pay For." You paid a lot: $175 for a sit-down with a pot doc.

Was Green Wellness the clinic for me? I clicked "Let's Chat!" on the clinic's website. A photo of a woman named Miranda appeared.

"Hello Bruce Barcott. How may I help you?"

"Hi, Miranda. I'm interested in talking with someone at Green Wellness about anxiety, stress and lower back pain."

I waited for Miranda's reply. "Your condition must be a physical disability, chronic physical illness, or debilitating disease," she wrote. I would need to present my medical records with my doctor's signature.

I didn't like the sound of that. Our Seattle physician, the beloved Dr. Erickson (not his real name), was a grandfatherly gent with a keen medical mind and a comforting bedside manner. He approached maladies like a lepidopterist discovering a new butterfly. Presented with the most disgusting suppuration, he'd lean in with delight: "Oooh! Whattaya got there?" The idea of Dr. Erickson receiving a records request from an outfit called the Green Wellness Clinic filled me with dread. It felt like a backhanded rejection: *Enough of your fancy book learning, Doc. I'm putting my health in the hands of the weed peddlers.*

Clearly I needed to lower my sights. Find someone who wasn't so picky about medical records. A clinic like . . . ah! Here we are. Seattle Selective. A cannabis clinic ensconced in a head shop.

"We are located inside Piece of Mind which is pound for pound the dopest shop around," said the clinic's website. Piece of Mind had been serving the paraphernalia needs of University of Washington students since the 1990s. Its website featured a disturbing chart of a toking hippie with his organs exposed. Mercifully, not all of his organs, but still.

Seattle Selective's hours were consistent with its name. Tuesdays, 3-6. I called. The counter guy at the head shop answered.

"Oh . . . yeah . . . hold on," he said. After a long wait, he returned. "You know, the best thing would be to call back during their hours," he said.

"I thought these were their hours."

"Mmm. Yeah. Don't know what to tell you."

If Green Wellness was too upscale and Seattle Selective too sketchy, the Hope Clinic looked to be my just-right bowl of porridge. Seventy-five-dollar exams. Regular weekday hours. I booked an appointment for noon the following Friday.

To save myself and Dr. Erickson the embarrassment, I used a vague pretense to obtain a copy of my medical records.

———

The Hope Clinic was located along a quiet stretch of University Way, two blocks south of my daughter's old kindergarten. At 12:04 the waiting room was nearly full. The place felt like a day-labor hiring hall: plastic tables, folding chairs, a lonely ficus by the window. The desk clerk noted my arrival and invited me to settle in. At that moment I heard a gaggle of children pass by the clinic's open door. *Zounds!* I scuttled to a far chair before Lucy's kindergarten teacher could catch sight of me. Not like walking out of a porn shop, but not exactly waving through a library window, either.

I relaxed and had a look around. My fellow patients were an eclectic group: WASPy matrons; stringy-haired beanpole stoners; a couple *vatos* in black flat-brims; a hipster girl, mid-20s; and an African-American Navy veteran oversharing about his glaucoma. A marijuana documentary looped on a flat-screen TV, which bathed us all in the somnolent tones of Peter Coyote: "*. . . and yet almost every government in the world restricts or bans its use. . . .*" For nearly an hour I thumbed through the waiting-room magazines—*Dope, Northwest Leaf* and *Culture: The Medical Cannabis Lifestyle Magazine*—while a bearded man in khakis summoned patients, one by one, behind a door marked "Doctors Office." (What kind of doctor has a door like that? Aside from Harvey Korman in a *Carol Burnett Show* sketch, I mean.) A number of patients were dealing with serious maladies. One woman bore the hairless head of chemotherapy. Others . . . well, if you bring your skateboard into a clinic, you're not doing yourself any favors, image-wise.

"Bruce?"

Next patient up.

I was pointed to the "Doctors Office."

Dr. Daniel Dixon presented as a kindly chap in his mid-60s: reading glasses, brown chinos, green shirt. Dixon was an old-school homeopath. He'd been practicing alternative medicine since the mid-'70s, when there were only a few hundred homeopathic physicians in the entire country. "What brings you in today?" he asked.

I told him about my knee discomfort and about the shooting lower-back pain brought on by stress and anxiety. "I'm taking ibuprofen now and then, but I wonder if there's a way to supplement with something"—what was the word—"more natural."

I displayed the empty jar of Kush Cream.

The doctor brightened. "Well, there are some very good products that can help with the anxiety," he said.

"Really?"

I remembered the sheaf of paper in my hands. "I've got my medical records if you'd like to see them."

"Sure." He examined the file. We talked about the meniscus damage in my left knee. At this point we had a confidential doctor-patient conversation about my qualifying conditions.

I asked about various forms of . . . er . . . medication. "I'm not really a smoker."

Dr. Dixon suggested trying edibles, tinctures and balms.

"Tinctures?" Such a ye olde term.

"Concentrated liquid," said the doctor. "Take it in a dropper under the tongue." He mimicked the action.

And then we were done.

While a clerk prepared my MMJ card, the old sailor chatted me up. "Did you bring your medical records with you?" he asked.

"Yes," I said. "You?"

He nodded. "Got mine from the VA." He made like a vise with his fingers. "I got this pressure in my eyes."

"And this helps?"

"Sure does."

"How?" I said. "Does it relieve the pressure, or the pain?"

"Both."

He offered his hand. "Spencer." (I've changed his real name.)

"Bruce."

"I used to drink," Spencer said. "But it made me feel so terrible the next day."

"I know, right?" I said. "You could drink every night in your 20s. But now it kills you the next day."

Spencer nodded. "But with this, I'm fine the next day."

The clerk waved me to the front. She held out my MMJ card. There were a number of dispensaries in the neighborhood, she said. "You might want to try the joint next door."

This struck me as a bit informal, even for a cannabis clinic. I exited furtively, hoping not to be seen by my daughter's kindergarten teacher. Immediately south of the Hope Clinic there was indeed a medical marijuana dispensary. I looked up at the sign. The dispensary was called The Joint.

———————

It wasn't easy to enter The Joint.

After being buzzed through the street door, I found myself in a man trap dolled up as a waiting room. One couch, two locked doors. Behind a thick pane of glass, a young woman asked if I was a member.

"Of what?" I said.

She shrugged and slid a form through a cracker-thin slot. "Fill this out and we'll get you admitted."

My paperwork complete, I submitted my driver's license and freshly minted MMJ card. An unseen force buzzed the inner door. I stepped through.

The Joint's inner sanctum exhibited an aesthetic of plush shabbiness. A fellow patient lounged on a black leather couch. The same old issues of *Dope* were strewn on a glass-top coffee table. I felt unsure about how to proceed.

"You're welcome to relax, have some bottled water, read a magazine," said the woman who checked me in.

I have to admit I was utterly confused. Was I expected to play it cool, be mellow, hang for a while before casually making my purchase? It seemed like maybe this was the MMJ equivalent of making small talk with your pot dealer about his pet cockatoo. Or perhaps I was waiting to be called by—a nurse? A pharmacist? I perched nervously on the leather couch.

"Bruce, are you ready?"

I nearly pissed myself. "Yeah . . ." I said, adopting a *no big thang* pose, ". . . sure."

The young woman, my budtender, had come to work that day clad in a Seahawks jersey. She could not have been more than eight years older than my own daughter. I felt like a creepy old pervert.

"My name's Amanda," she said. (I've changed it.) "I'll be helping you today."

"Hi, Amanda," I croaked.

Bullets of sweat seeped out of my arms and forehead. The floor began to tilt.

"This is our dry medicine case," Amanda told me, indicating 12 strains of marijuana kept in glass canning jars. The buds, fat as August blackberries, glowed Heineken green. "Top shelf is 12 dollars a gram. Middle is 10. And the bottom is eight."

I forced myself to breathe. *Maintain, dude. Maintain.* My rational mind kept repeating *legal, legal, legal,* while my hypothalamus sent my sympathetic nervous system into full scramble. My shirt dampened. I steadied myself on the glass product case.

"We've got concentrates over here, bubble hash, hash oil, waxes and shatter," Amanda said. I nodded and understood nothing. What the hell was a shatter? "And we've got single-dose edibles for five dollars. In the fridge are medicated butters, soda, capsules and ice cream."

Wow. In the medical world, a prescription for amoxicillin allowed you to obtain a precise dose of amoxicillin. It didn't give you access to Demerol and Valium too. In the medical marijuana world, a green card apparently gave you the run of the entire pharmacy.

I scratched my chin discerningly. "Today," I said, as if there had been other days, "I'm looking for a tincture to help with anxiety and insomnia."

Amanda brightened. "My favorite ones are the Sativa Valley ones. Those are going to be indica-heavy, more mellow, more chill. We also have one that's really CBD-heavy. It relaxes your whole body."

"I'll take it. The CBD one."

CBD was all the rage that fall. CBD is an acronym for cannabidiol, one of 66 cannabinoids found in marijuana. Cannabinoids are natural compounds that interact with specific receptors within parts of the central nervous system. THC is the psychoactive cannabinoid that gets you high. CBD isn't psychoactive, but researchers have found that it can reduce anxiety and calm certain types of seizures. About the time I visited The Joint, the news was full of stories about Charlotte's Web, a special high-CBD, low-THC strain of marijuana that had cured a 5-year-old girl who'd been suffering more than 300 grand mal seizures a week. CBD was the Lorenzo's Oil of 2013.

Whoops—don't forget the pot cream. I had Amanda add a jar. Toss in some medicated chocolate-covered gummy bears too. What the heck.

The bill came out to $74.34.

"And today is 'free joint Friday,' so you can grab a free one from the jar there if you like," Amanda said. "They're, like, a house blend, a nice mix of indica and sativa."

I dropped one into the bag.

Back in the safety of my Subaru, I closed my eyes and took stock. The back of my shirt was sopping wet. My head was still a little woozy. What the hell was that about? The only thing I could think of was this. When you absorb more than 40 years of messages about the horrors of marijuana, walking into a dispensary where it's all on display, without shame or fear, can be an utterly disorienting experience.

I texted my wife. "First purchase," I wrote. "Rolling dirty."

At the ferry terminal, a Washington State Patrol canine team trotted past my car. I gave a start. *Could the dog smell the pot? Were they even trained to find it anymore?* Free joint Friday didn't seem like such a great idea anymore.

My children greeted me at the door. "Dad's got pot stuff!" they cried. The idea of their uptight father scoring weed sent them into gales of laughter.

"It's not for you," I said, and stormed off.

―――――――

My reaction surprised and embarrassed me. Clearly my children had handled the situation with appropriate good humor. I had not. My own hang-up was my own hang-up.

There are times in life when you are forced to stop pretending that your own psyche defines normality and examine clearly the weirder ridges and runnels that form the topography of your mind. That evening I realized that I had absorbed four decades of social messages and official teachings about marijuana. Nearly every word, phrase and photo had been pitched with the intent of making me fear and loathe the substance. As a teenager, and later as an adult, I defined myself as the kind of person who did not smoke pot. And I certainly wasn't the kind of father whose children knew he smoked pot.

Now I was.

The worst part of it was recalling how I once viewed my friends who smoked dope. None of them were stoners. They were smart, creative and profoundly decent people who showed up for work on time. They paid their dues at school plays, parent nights and science fairs. They held positions of trust in the community. They just enjoyed a little evening toke in the garage now and then. Not long ago—hell, last year!—those people disappointed me. I read the act of partaking as a sign of moral weakness. Don't ask me why. Sometimes my internal rules of probity don't make sense even to me. Now that I was one of the partakers (and I hadn't even *partaken* yet), the beliefs and judgments of Past Bruce struck me as arbitrary and silly. Would others be disappointed in me? That thought was there. But so was this one: Past Bruce, you were a real jerk.

The psychology of the whole situation was plainly screwed up. It made me appreciate the evolution my own parents had undergone on other issues. When they grew up in the 1950s and early '60s, mainstream society defined homosexuality as an unmentionable moral abomination. My folks heard little but revulsion, shame and pity about the subject. Society's mores didn't change until the 1970s and '80s, when gay men and lesbians came out and claimed their rightful due as legal and socially accepted citizens. My parents, bless them, kept their minds open and their hearts full. I wouldn't call them early adopters of the rainbow flag. But they were able to consider new evidence, different ideas, and come around to a more complex and tolerant view of sexuality and identity.

My generation came of age in the '80s. I had friends who struggled to come out. It was a tough and courageous thing to do. I know it gave my parents a jolt when I mentioned it to them back then. They filtered the information through 40 years of social messages and official teachings about homosexuality. Or rather, the evils of same. My friends and I had fresh minds. We could say: They're gay. So what?

On the subject of marijuana I did not possess a petal-fresh mind. As pot began turning legal in the mid-2010s, those of us in our 40s functioned with brains encrusted with dogma and tortured by our developmental history. If I was going to find a new way to think about cannabis, I would have to remember my parents. A change in their outlook wasn't cast upon them by some magic wand. As they considered new evidence, they didn't blithely remove all social and legal constructs surrounding sexuality. They exercised good sense and discernment. Their generation might have done it a damn sight faster, for sure, but eventually gay and lesbian couples began to be treated as normal people exercising basic civil rights.

This is where I see my generation in our endeavor to reframe marijuana. We—well, OK, I—am open to a new look at the drug. That doesn't mean I'm ready to remove all legal strictures against all drugs. It means I'm open to the effort and struggle of change.

I USE IT
BEFORE CHURCH

Over the following weeks I received a steady stream of emails from The Joint. The dispensary's staff kept me on my toes with their daily specials.

"Swing on by The Joint for HASH WEDNESDAY!"

"Tomorrow is VAPOR THURSDAY at The Joint!"

"SUNDAY FUNDAY SPECIALS at The Joint!"

The messages may have boosted sales, but they did nothing to raise my own estimation of the medical marijuana industry. Frankly, the whole enterprise smelled like fraud. A minority of truly needy patients seemed to serve as a beard for a majority of "patients" who had simply found a legal way to score recreational weed.

Then I met Perry Parks.

Parks was an Army officer.

I use the past tense, but Parks is a soldier like I am a writer. When

I stop tapping on a keyboard, I don't cease to be a writer. Occupation and identity are one. Perry Parks won't stop being a soldier until they bury him in his full dress blues.

I met him at a drug policy conference in Denver in the fall of 2013. I'd flown to Colorado to learn more about drug laws and the emerging marijuana industry. Parks was the most unlikely character at the conference: a 71-year-old silver-haired Southern gentleman displaying a matrix of ribbons on a dress uniform. He held his carriage so erect that I wondered if he wore a back brace.

I stopped him. "Pardon me for asking," I said, "but what's your role here?"

This was my way of asking, What the hell is a guy like you doing in a place like this?

Parks described himself as a son of North Carolina, a loving husband, a doting grandfather and an usher at the First Baptist Church of Rockingham. He was also a decorated Vietnam combat veteran and a medical marijuana user.

"I take it every day," he told me. "I'm not ashamed to say it. Because it works."

"Let's talk further," I said.

We found a quiet corner.

"I served as a pilot for the 101st Airborne in Vietnam," he told me. I asked about the ribbons. One was the Distinguished Flying Cross, he said. Others were Army commendations. After 11 years of active duty, Parks spent 30 years training helicopter pilots in the National Guard. He retired when he turned 60, in 2003.

Age began catching up to him. Doctors prescribed a cocktail of opiates and muscle relaxants for a degenerative disc condition. He took sleeping pills to get through the night. "I had nightmares," he said. "I'd be flying a helicopter and see a radio tower with guide wires up ahead. I'd fly too close to the wires and there'd be no way to turn. When you're a helicopter pilot, wires scare the hell out of you."

His doctor told him the nightmares were a symptom of post-traumatic stress disorder. He'd probably been suppressing it since Vietnam.

"I didn't see myself as disabled," Parks told me. "That was somebody in a wheelchair." But the doctors kept prescribing more pills. That bothered him. "Somebody told me that cannabis worked on PTSD. So I tried it."

The nightmares went away. Parks began sleeping soundly through the night. He stopped taking sleeping pills. He ratcheted down the pain meds.

"Now I use the bong two or three times a day," he said.

I have to tell you that hearing "the bong" coming out the mouth of a spit-shined Southern military man is like catching your grandmother rapping some Wu-Tang Clan. It's a moment.

"How do you get through the day?" I asked. In my head I imagined a stoned 71-year-old watching *Jeopardy!* reruns all afternoon.

"Just fine," he said. By fine-tuning his dosage, Parks said, his regimen kept him relaxed and alert, not high. "I'm healthy. I run 5K races. I use it in the mornings even before I go to church. Do you see me acting crazy? No. My wife and I are the perfect example of a Christian couple."

We talked some more. As we ended the conversation, a woman with long curly black hair walked past. "Have you spoken with Dr. Sisley?" Parks said. "You should talk to her."

Suzanne Sisley was an assistant professor of psychiatry at the University of Arizona. For the past three years she'd been trying to get federal approval to study the effects of cannabis on veterans with PTSD.

"It's extremely difficult to get the OK from federal agencies to do marijuana studies," Sisley told me. "They're fine with studying its negative effects on teenagers, but anything else usually gets rejected."

Sisley's study had been authorized by the university's research ethics board and by the U.S. Food and Drug Administration. Now she had to get permission from the U.S. Public Health Service and the DEA.

"We have about 50 veterans with PTSD signed up as subjects," Sisley told me over a cup of coffee. "If we get approval, we'll break them up into three groups. Some will be administered a high-CBD strain with 12 percent THC, others a 6 percent THC strain, and a control group will get a placebo."

Veterans around the country kept a close eye on Sisley's progress. Among America's wounded warriors there were few more pressing issues than PTSD and its treatment. By some estimates, at least 20 percent of the 2.3 million American veterans of the Afghanistan and Iraq wars suffered from PTSD. Half didn't seek treatment. Of those who did, only half received adequate treatment. For too many, the pain and depression became unbearable. The Department of Veterans Affairs (VA) reported that between 2005 and 2011, an average of 22 young veterans committed suicide every day—that's more than 8,000 a year.

Doctors at the nation's VA clinics often sent PTSD patients home with a mixture of antidepressants, opioids and other drugs. That led to an alarming increase in opioid addiction. Veterans tend to keep in touch with one another, so when guys like Perry Parks found relief with cannabis, word spread. By 2013, thousands of PTSD veterans had ditched their opioid prescriptions in favor of medical marijuana. But those thousands of stories were just that—stories. They didn't constitute the kind of scientific evidence that might allow VA doctors to talk openly and legally about cannabis with their PTSD patients. Or, one day, actually prescribe it.

"They've been stonewalling us for three years," Sisley told me. She sometimes thought about giving up. "I have plenty of other research I'd like to be doing," she said. What kept her going were the letters and emails she received from veterans all over the country. They ask her to keep going. Hang in there. Don't give up.

I liked Sisley, but I found her story a little suspect. Why would the government stonewall a legitimate scientific study? Tens of thousands of studies got approved every year. Researchers studied anthrax, pluto-nium and the Ebola virus. Surely a little weed study wouldn't be worth anyone's time and effort to quash.

A few days later, back home, I received an urgent message from The Joint.

> Hello Bruce,
>
> We need as many patients as possible to show up at tomorrows Snohomish County Council meeting to show your support so we can keep our local access points open.
>
> The Joint will be giving a credit to all patients that show up at tomorrows meeting. After the meeting Kylan will be taking your name down so you will be able to redeem your credit at The Joint anytime.

Ah, the old extra-credit-for-showing-up-at-the-council-meeting ploy. Was The Joint run by high school civics teachers?

In the council chambers the next morning, a gallery of dispensary owners, patients and aspiring pot farmers confronted six skeptical county selectmen. Snohomish County sat directly north of Seattle. It encompassed the mill town of Everett, shire of my birth. The council wanted to ban all marijuana operations countywide for six months. Nobody could say exactly why.

One by one, aspiring marijuana farmers argued against the ban. If the county banned pot, they would be denied the chance to obtain a state pot-growing license. These weren't black-market pot growers. They owned commercial nurseries, horse farms and alfalfa acreage. "Finally a crop comes along that threatens to make farming profitable, and you want to shut it down," one farmer said. "That just makes no sense."

Then came the dispensary owners and their clients. One young woman appeared with a bald head that told you all you needed to know about her struggle. An older gent said that a year ago he'd been so stiff he couldn't walk. And now look at him! Medical marijuana.

A number of patients told compelling stories. One made time stand still. Her name was Jessamyn Way. She was 38 years old. She stood straight and tall with an athletic build. She lived near Lake Stevens with her two young boys.

"Five years ago I was diagnosed with glioblastoma, an extremely aggressive brain tumor," she said. "It almost killed me. The doctors said I had a 5 percent chance of survival. I had surgery and I lived. But the surgery left me pretty messed up. It left me with severe epilepsy. I had 15 to 20 seizures a day. Some of them lasted 20 minutes or more.

"You name it, I tried it. I tried 20 different prescriptions from Swedish Hospital. I went to a doctor at Overlake Hospital. He gave up after three different medications didn't work. The seizures just kept getting worse. So finally I tried medical marijuana. I went to a dispensary. And it worked. That week my seizures went to near zero. My head stopped hurting. People say this isn't medicine. All I know is that I can hold my boys without shaking with seizures. Yesterday I ran five miles at the gym. Tomorrow I'll go do a 30-mile bike ride. People are like, *How do you do that?* But I've figured out the dosage that works for me."

She pleaded with the council members to allow medical marijuana to continue. "I'd probably be dead right now without it."

At the end of the session, votes had changed. The council dropped the six-month moratorium. The dispensaries of Snohomish County remained open, and the farmers were free to apply for the state's first grow licenses.

———

I spent some time looking into Suzanne Sisley's complaints about the government's blocking marijuana research. It wasn't that hard. It just took some slogging through the swamp of federal drug policy and parsing titles like *21 U.S.C. 801 et seq.* Pleasure reading, truly.

I didn't find it surprising that the government maintained strict rules for the study of Schedule I drugs like heroin, cocaine, LSD and marijuana. It did strike me as unusual that the rules for the scientific study of marijuana went above and beyond the strictures for heroin and cocaine, though.

Here's how research-grade drugs work. Pharmaceutical companies like Pfizer and Bayer are licensed by the Drug Enforcement Administration to manufacture a tightly controlled supply of heroin, cocaine, methamphetamine, LSD and other Schedule I compounds for use in research. Federal law not only allows it, it demands it. The Controlled Substances Act calls on the head of the DEA to maintain "an adequate and uninterrupted supply of these substances under adequately competitive conditions." By and large, the system works. There's a caveat, though. The DEA administrator can register a Schedule I drug producer only if it's deemed "in the public interest."

That leaves the DEA with enormous wiggle room. What the agency has done with that power lends credence to Sisley's complaint.

Pharmaceutical companies don't grow pot. In fact, there's only one legal source for research-grade cannabis. It's a single marijuana greenhouse at the University of Mississippi that operates under contract to the National Institute on Drug Abuse (NIDA), an arm of the federal National Institutes of Health (NIH). There is no "competitive condition" for research-grade pot because the DEA has deemed it not in the public interest. To obtain research pot, a scientist must submit to extra reviews by NIDA and the U.S. Public Health Service in addition to the usual FDA and DEA scrutiny. The FDA and the DEA have to respond to research requests within 90 days, but NIDA and the Public Health Service have no response deadline. The upshot is that studies unlikely to show negative health effects from marijuana use are nearly always denied or delayed to death by NIDA and the Public Health Service.

There's more. In 1996, California passed the nation's first medical marijuana law. That scared the bejeezus out of federal drug officials. Bill Clinton's drug czar, Barry McCaffrey, asked the Institute of Medicine, the medical research arm of the National Academy of Sciences, to undertake a comprehensive review of the science on medical marijuana. McCaffrey expected it to be exposed as bunk. That didn't happen.

"Scientific data indicate the potential therapeutic value of cannabinoid drugs, primarily THC, for pain relief, control of nausea and vomiting, and appetite stimulation," the review's authors wrote. Marijuana also proved to be effective in some people for the relief of chronic pain, as an epileptic-seizure suppressant and as a drug to reduce intraocular pressure in glaucoma patients. In other words: it actually worked.

The only real drawback to medical marijuana, in fact, was its mode of delivery. Smoked marijuana, the authors found, "is a crude THC delivery system that also delivers harmful substances" including benzene, toluene, naphthalene, carbon monoxide and tar, the same inhaled nasties that came with tobacco cigarettes.

The Institute of Medicine report displeased Barry McCaffrey. "I think what the IOM report said is that smoked marijuana is harmful, particularly for those with chronic conditions," he said. Which is kind of not what the report said at all. Nevertheless, he and Attorney General Janet Reno vowed to prosecute medical marijuana patients and any doctors who prescribed the drug.

It's worth noting that at the time the institute issued its report, two other things were happening with regard to marijuana within the government.

At an NIH lab in Bethesda, Maryland, a team of federal researchers was studying the use of cannabinoids as neuroprotectants. The lead researcher was Aiden Hampson, guided by his mentor Julius Axelrod, a Nobel Prize–winning pharmacologist and neuroscientist. Axelrod founded the NIH's pharmacology department in the 1950s, and his work on neurotransmitters led to the development of antidepressants like Prozac. (Also, he was kind of a badass. Axelrod lost his left eye in a lab accident, so he wore eyeglasses with one side blacked out. Seriously, the guy looked like something out of *X-Men*.) Cannabinoids, Hampson and Axelrod discovered, "are found to have particular application" for limiting neurological damage following stroke and trauma, or in the treatment of diseases like Alzheimer's, Parkinson's and HIV dementia. NIH scientists found cannabidiol (CBD) to be "particularly advantageous" because it produced results without THC's psychotropic side effects. Their research was so promising, in fact, that the NIH applied for and was granted a patent on the medical use of CBD. You can look it up: it's U.S. Patent No. 6630507.

Meanwhile, at the White House Office of National Drug Control Policy, McCaffrey, its director, was funneling millions of dollars into a

clandestine program to insert anti-drug messages into popular television shows. Between 1998 and 2000, McCaffrey's office spent upward
of $25 million to make sure marijuana users were portrayed as losers
on *Beverly Hills 90210, Chicago Hope, 7th Heaven* and *The Drew Carey
Show*. When reporter Daniel Forbes's expose was published in Salon,
McCaffrey responded with a contemptuous non-apology.

"We plead guilty to using every lawful means to save America's children," he said.

The Institute of Medicine report was the most rigorous review of medical
marijuana ever conducted. And it changed nothing. Instead of adjusting
federal guidelines to fit the scientific evidence, McCaffrey suppressed
the science to fit the policy. He and other officials at the Department of
Health and Human Services (HHS) quietly enacted a constraint unique
to marijuana. They made it against HHS policy to conduct any research
that could lead to the development of smoked marijuana as a licensed
drug. That may sound like a stoner's conspiracy theory. It's not. The
agency's "Guidance on Procedures for the Provision of Cannabis for
Medical Research" was released on May 21, 1999. It remains in effect
to this day.

The upshot is this. It's not merely difficult to obtain permission to study
marijuana. It's federally illegal to engage in science that could, in theory,
lead to the permissible use of smoked marijuana for any medical condition.

On those grounds, Suzanne Sisley's research on PTSD and cannabis
appeared illegal on its face. Technically, though, it wasn't. Her subjects
wouldn't be smoking cannabis. They would inhale the drug using a
vaporizer. So her study had a chance.

Her complaints also had my sympathy. One of the main arguments
against medical marijuana and the legalization of recreational pot has
been the lack of scientific information about marijuana and its effects on
human health. *It's too risky. We just don't know enough.* I've spoken those
words myself.

At the same time, it appeared that the federal government was actively blocking the effort to fill in those knowledge gaps, to the point where federal agencies had done something truly Orwellian. They had made scientific inquiry illegal.

———————

That autumn I thought a lot about Perry Parks and Jessamyn Way. The evidence of my own eyes and my email inbox confirmed some of my suspicions about MMJ dispensaries. There were, in fact, a lot of healthy stoners using dispensaries to obtain pot. But that wasn't the end of the story. The Joint catered to plenty of 20-something bros with flat-brimmed caps. It also served the Perry Parkses and Jessamyn Ways of the world.

The full picture was made clearer to me during a visit to a dispensary in Washington, D.C. The nation's capital was an early adopter of medical marijuana. The District legalized it in 1998, but Congress blocked its implementation for 15 years. In 2013, House Republicans finally relented. Two dispensaries opened that year. It wasn't as easy to get a green card in Washington, D.C., as it was in Denver or Seattle, though. There were an estimated 32,000 registered MMJ patients in Denver and at least 25,000 in Seattle. In Washington, D.C., there were 59.

Takoma Wellness Center, one of D.C.'s two operating dispensaries, occupied a discreet storefront next to a Chinese restaurant one block south of the Takoma Metro Station. When I stopped by in October 2013, it had been open for about six weeks. In addition to being D.C.'s first medical marijuana shop, Takoma Wellness was the nation's only dispensary operated by a man of the cloth. Rabbi Jeffrey Kahn spent 30 years as a congregational rabbi prior to opening the shop with his wife Stephanie, a nurse at a long-term acute care center.

The Kahns' experience with medical marijuana stretched back to the 1970s, when Stephanie Kahn's father used it to control spasms brought on by multiple sclerosis. "He'd gone from doctor to doctor trying to find relief, and nothing worked," Kahn told me. Finally a physician suggested he try marijuana. "It helped him immediately," she recalled. "You could see the difference in minutes."

They considered the dispensary a continuation of their life's work: caregiving. "The day I was ordained as a rabbi, June 5, 1981, was the day the CDC's *Morbidity and Mortality Weekly Report* published the first AIDS cases," Rabbi Kahn said. "Through the mid-'90s, a good portion of my rabbinate was tied up in families and people who were living with AIDS." Jeffrey offered emotional and spiritual support while Stephanie tended to their physical needs in her hospital career. "I lived through the time when physicians could offer just about nothing to people living with AIDS," Rabbi Kahn said. "I saw firsthand how cannabis brought relief. In some cases not just relief but great benefits."

The Kahns ran a professional clinic. There were no budtenders rocking Redskins gamers, no issues of *Dope* in the waiting room. The Kahns had locked up the actual weed after the departure of the day's only patient, so they had nothing out on display. About the only thing Takoma Wellness had in common with The Joint was its selection of glass pipes, which even at a place as classy as this were as striped and goofy as clown trousers.

"How many patients do you expect this week?" I asked.

"Maybe seven," said Rabbi Kahn.

I did the math in my head. Seven, multiplied by, what, $300 per patient? "We hope one day we might draw a salary from the Wellness Center," Rabbi Kahn told me. Until then, "it's a labor of love." The Kahns weren't operating a profitable business. They were administering a philanthropy.

My visit with the Kahns put a thought in my head. My suspicion was that a few legitimate patients acted as cover for an army of stoners seeking weed. What if I had it backward? Takoma Wellness Center served only the most severe cases. If things continued this way, the Kahns would run through their life savings and the clinic would go out of business.

It might just be, I thought, that weed-seeking stoners provided the economic foundation to keep dispensaries open and available to serve those for whom marijuana was a critical medicine.

THE WASHINGTON
STATE SCRAMBLE

Throughout the fall of 2013, people across Colorado and Washington who had never smoked, touched or spoken of cannabis suddenly began dreaming of becoming marijuana millionaires.

In the river valleys between Seattle and the Canadian border, hundreds of farmers began calculating the cost of a cannabis grow against the financial returns. Weed fever. Some called it a sickness, a delusion, a fool's fantasy. But the fact could not be denied: a lot of people were going to spend serious coin on legal marijuana. *Somebody* had to grow it.

In Colorado, the first retail marijuana licenses went to those already operating within the state's well-regulated medical marijuana system. Washington State, by contrast, was setting up to be a free-for-all. The Liquor Control Board announced it would issue 334 retail marijuana sales licenses spread throughout the state according to population. Seattle, for instance, would be allotted 21 store licenses; the burg of Washougal would get one. Existing medical dispensaries were given no advantage. Me and you and your old Aunt Sue would have just as much chance of winning a pot license as the owners of The Joint.

The rules were long, complicated and confusing. Only Washington residents could own or invest in a license. Retailers had to secure a storefront lease before applying for a license. All pot operations had to comply with the 1,000-foot rule, which required a 1,000-foot distance from the nearest school, day care or park. There were rules about computer tracking software, packaging, THC limits, advertising, store signage, and on and on. To cut through the confusion, the Liquor Control Board held a series of public seminars throughout the state. On a Tuesday in October I attended one at a Best Western conference room in Mount Vernon, a farm town 60 miles north of Seattle. The joint was SRO.

———

"We're full up!" one of the organizers shouted. "If you haven't pre-registered you'll have to go on the wait list." The farmers cattle-chuting the door didn't like the sound of that.

"What the hell do I do if I'm not signed up?" said a farmer standing next to me. In his rubber boots and filthy Carhartt jacket, he looked like he came straight from the morning milking. Panic flashed in his eyes. Dude was not going to get shut out of this meeting.

I gave him a stage glance toward the open conference room door. "Sneak in," I said.

And so he did.

Farmer Sneak and I found a couple of empty chairs. An overhead screen read, "What to Expect When Applying for a Marijuana License." The room buzzed. Would-be growers and storefront retailers exchanged greetings.

"Where you looking?"

"Bellingham. What about you? You going retail?"

A guy behind them cracked a *Midnight Express* joke.

A family of horse breeders sat eight strong one row ahead of me. One of the horsemen, an early-30s fellow I'll call Jaden, looked like a young Levon Helm. He wore a hoodie, jeans and a Seahawks cap. Jaden raised horses and worked for an industrial supply company, but he was hot with pot fever. "I just don't want to look back and say, 'I wish we woulda,' " he said.

A doughy "marijuana licensing specialist" guided us through the rules. Farmers, processors (those who package the bud or convert it into hash oil) and retailers each had to apply for separate licenses. Colorado insisted on vertical integration: you grow it, you package it, you sell it. Washington State wanted separation. A grower couldn't open a retail shop. Farmers could grow no more than 30,000 square feet of plant canopy. That's not much, about two thirds of an acre. Processors had to be at least 1,000 feet from schools, just like retailers.

A question from the 10th row: "Where does producer end and processor begin?"

The specialist thought it over. "Producers can grow, harvest, trim and cure. But curing—that's the line. Anything past that is the processor's job."

When the specialist said applicants had to be paid up on their state taxes, you could practically hear 20 percent of the room bail.

"What about federal taxes?" somebody asked.

"That's between you and the IRS," said the specialist.

"You're not going to turn us in, are you?"

That got a laugh.

The specialist looked to his boss. "It is not our job to be proactive," said the boss, "but we must cooperate with the federal government when requested."

That didn't get a laugh.

By the end of the seminar, it became apparent that most of the conventional farmers hoping to grow pot had no clue about how to produce top-quality cannabis. But by God they were eager to learn.

Washington had no shortage of alfalfa growers looking to jump into the cannabis space. Legalization was sold on the promise of bringing black-market operators into a state-regulated system, though. I went looking for an old-school pot grower to see if that was actually happening. It didn't take long to find one.

"My name is Jeff Gilmore. That's G-I-L-M-O-R-E. I have been growing this region's finest dope for most of my adult life. If you smoked pot in the Pacific Northwest, you more'n likely sampled my crop."

Gilmore was a 59-year-old gentleman with flowing white hair, and that's how he introduced himself to the Liquor Control Board at a public meeting in Seattle.

A few weeks after that meeting I drove to southern Thurston County, 75 miles south of Seattle, where Puget Sound's urban corridor gave way to Douglas fir forests and lonely county roads. I pulled into Jeff Gilmore's driveway and found the old man in his garage, trimming marijuana with a pair of nail scissors. His jeans and flannel shirt were covered with flecked leaves. He looked content.

"I'm trimming this up for some guys who live out in the woods," he told me. "They're a bunch of unmedicated schizophrenics who make a living foraging. Dropped these off with me a couple days ago." He paused to examine a ripe bud. "Yep. Unmedicated schizophrenics. Nice guys, though."

With his white beard and folksy baritone, Gilmore looked like a mandolin strummer in a bluegrass band. He invited me to have a seat.

"This stuff here," he said, *snip snip snip,* "is really low-market stuff. A little mildewy. They left it out in the woods too long."

"Out in the woods," I said. "You mean they just picked a spot in the woods and planted some seeds?"

"No, they use these garbage cans as planters," he said, pointing to a marijuana shrub rooted in a 64-gallon plastic can behind him. "They've got a spot up in the. . . ."

I tuned him out because at that moment it occurred to me I had never actually been in the presence of a live marijuana plant. What an odd thing. I'd been living for nearly half a century in a nation obsessed with marijuana, desiring it like sex and destroying it like the pox, and had never, ever come face to face with the actual living plant itself. That struck me as completely insane. Because you know what? It's not a nuclear warhead. It's not a deadly virus. It's a plant.

". . . let 'em grow all summer, then haul 'em over here for me to gut like a mess of fish."

Gilmore shrugged. *Ah well, what are you gonna do.* His nonchalance puzzled me. Were I a marijuana grower, I don't know that I'd throw open my house to a band of schizophrenic scavengers who'd fallen off their meds.

The kitchen phone rang. Gilmore excused himself.

Seizing the moment, I got up close and personal with the plant. It looked stronger than I expected. Sturdy. Like if you went diving for a loose basketball, a hedge of cannabis might support your weight. Its leaves, on the other hand, were long, thin and delicate, like the fingers of a beautiful princess.

Gilmore returned.

"It's weird now when I'm talking on the phone," he said. "People are still wanting to talk in code and stuff. Saying they're coming by with 'four beers.' I tell 'em, 'Dude! We're not selling meth here. Quit talking like that. It's legal.'"

Snip snip snip.

Gilmore had been growing illegal weed since the late '70s. He learned his trade in Humboldt County, Northern California's marijuana breadbasket. "A grower staked me to some seeds and told me to plant 'em next to a stream," he recalled. In one summer he made $20,000.

In 1982 Gilmore returned to the Northwest, where he'd been raised, and started growing indoors. "I could buy a house for $2,500 down, grow a crop in the basement and have the house paid off in a year." At one time he owned and operated 13 grow houses around the south Sound.

"How'd you offload your product?" I asked.

"I had a buyer come to my house Sunday mornings at seven o'clock," he said. "He'd take everything I had. By five past seven every Sunday I'd made a king's ransom."

"Why Sunday morning?"

He smiled. "Nobody expects a pot dealer to be up and moving that early on a Sunday, let alone hauling some serious weight. All the cops are in bed or at church. So if you're going to be hauling 10 pounds of pot across the county, seven o'clock Sunday morning is a pretty good time to do it."

"And you never got caught?"

He paused.

"In 1992 I got a knock on the door," he said. Thanks to a good lawyer, Gilmore copped to a lesser charge and did 30 days in county. He started growing for the medical marijuana market, and he gave away a fair amount of pot to patients in need. "Getting busted was the best thing that happened to my life," he told me. "And the worst thing that happened to my financial life."

I asked if he was going legal now.

He nodded. "I'll be one of the first in line with my paperwork once the application window opens."

"You going to grow or sell?"

"That's going to be my grow house," he said, pointing across the driveway where two-by-four studs rose from a poured concrete foundation. "I'll have four grow rooms and a drying loft. But hey, take a look at this," Gilmore said. He held up a coffin-shaped box made of blonde maple. It was the size of a fat cigar. A script logo had been burned into it: *JD Cannabis*.

"Nobody's going to sell pot in a little quarter-ounce baggie anymore," he said. "It's going to be a high-value product. They say the cost of packaging is usually 5 percent of the retail value. So if an eighth sells for 40 bucks, packaging should cost about two bucks. That's what I'm targeting. This," he said, holding up the box, "is exactly designed to hold an eighth."

"Are you going to put THC content on the box?" I asked.

"The Liquor Control Board wants me to, so I'll do it," he said. "But that number gives you nothing. When you're comparing a $40 bottle of wine to a $14 bottle of wine, they're both 12 to 14 percent alcohol. Why the difference in price? Quality and packaging. You don't buy a Stradivarius because it's been tested to produce sound at a certain volume. You buy it because it's a fucking Stradivarius!"

Jeff Gilmore was going legal not because he was afraid of the cops. He was going legal because he believed he grew the finest marijuana in the Pacific Northwest, and he wanted to prove it in the open market.

———————

Meanwhile, in Seattle a citywide scavenger hunt was under way. Schools, day care centers and parks were so evenly salted through the city that finding a 502-legal storefront, with a 1,000-foot buffer zone, an available lease and a landlord willing to host a pot shop was like finding a penguin in a sandstorm. Some quick thinkers made money by selling maps that demarcated parcel-by-parcel marijuana legality. All over the city, real estate agents and clients spread the maps across their laps as they dashed from site to site.

I spent a day with one of these hopeful hustlers. His name was Pete O'Neil.

O'Neil was nebbishy and hyperactive. His mouth never stopped moving. A 49-year-old father of a teenage son, he and his family had recently moved to Seattle from Fort Lauderdale, where O'Neil managed a comedy club. Before that he'd run a professional bicycle league, a small television station and three upscale dog-grooming salons in Manhattan. O'Neil combined the savvy of a serial entrepreneur with a mask of guilelessness. His ability to barge in and ask impertinent questions had gotten him far in life.

"OK, the name," O'Neil told me. "I decided to name my business C&C Cannabis out of respect for Cheech and Chong, you know, the godfathers of marijuana." We were wheeling down Aurora Avenue in his Acura on a late Tuesday afternoon.

"Did you get the OK from them?" I asked.

He nodded. "We're in talks with their management team," O'Neil said. "We're trying to figure out a licensing deal that works within the state's regulations." He swerved. "Whoa!" he said. "People in Seattle don't know how to drive."

I asked where we were headed.

"I got a tip on an existing medical dispensary that's for sale on Lake City Way," he said. Lake City was a used-cars-and-nail-salons strip in north Seattle. "The guy's asking for $100,000," he said. "My realtor says it's 502-legal. But why would a dispensary owner sell out now?"

I shrugged. "Uncertainty?"

Washington's new pot law made no mention of medical dispensaries, and it was widely assumed that the state would force the MMJs out of business. Some dispensary owners were selling out while the selling was good.

The address of the Seattle MMJ Coop vibed a little scruffy. A tire store, a gun shop and a martial arts studio operated nearby. The sign on the door said KNOCK LOUDLY. O'Neil did. When it swung open, the building exhaled a breath of weed funk.

The owner, whom I'll call James, greeted us warmly.

"So you're looking for a 502, huh?" he said.

James was a teddy bear of a guy, Italian, 50s, thick mustache, sad eyes. His wife had recently passed, he said, and he was looking to get out of the business. "She kept the books and kept me in line." He glanced at a flyer on the wall that announced her memorial service later that week. O'Neil and I glanced at each other, sharing the awkwardness.

James showed us the space. Upstairs was a one-room dispensary with 20 strains of weed neatly shelved in glass jars. Downstairs were two grow rooms with a handful of spindly plants.

"I'm asking $175,000," said James.

O'Neil pokered his expression. That price bought neither the building nor the land, only the right to take over James's $2,800 monthly lease for a storefront in a 502-legal zone. It was a $175K ticket to the Seattle pot license lottery.

"The listing said $100,000," said O'Neil.

James nodded. "The guy down the road just sold his MMJ for $125,000," he said. "And he's not even zoned 502-legal. So I figured . . ."

"Why would anyone buy it if it's not zoned legal?" O'Neil asked.

James shrugged. "The buyer didn't do his homework."

———

Over the following months I continued to check in with Pete O'Neil. He and his company struck me as a type specimen of *Cannabis boomicus*, those fast-evolving enterprises struggling for survival in a highly dynamic environment. Plus, his phone calls were always entertaining.

"Lynnwood is screwing us over," he told me one day. This is how he began the phone call. In fact, he began all his phone calls in medias res.

"Who?"

"Lynnwood. The city."

"How so?"

"They're putting a moratorium on marijuana businesses." O'Neil had leased a Lynnwood storefront in order to apply for a retail license there. "So now I'm paying $2,000 a month for an empty storefront."

I asked what his lawyer thought.

"He says we can't fight it. He says pot shops are like porn shops. Cities can zone them however they please."

"Well—"

"But what would happen if a city said, 'We don't want cigarettes or alcohol sold here'?" O'Neil said. "This is like towns outlawing rock and roll in the '50s!"

He called again a few days later.

"I didn't bid on that Lake City Way dispensary," he said. "But I've got a line on another storefront on First Avenue South. And I'm working on that Cheech and Chong deal," he said.

"What's happening with it?"

"They're considering it. Cheech isn't so much into pot. He's got his acting thing going. Tommy Chong, though, he really believes in cannabis for cancer and pain. He's working on a whole medicinal cannabis line he wants to launch in Washington and Colorado."

"Is that kind of branding allowed—"

"Whoops, that's Mr. Cohen, Tommy's manager, on the other line. Gotta go!"

Click.

Another week, another call.

"I'm meeting on Tuesday with a grower named James Dean—yeah, like the movie star, but he's actually a former drug task force agent and the last five years he's been a dispensary grower," O'Neil said. "I'm hoping maybe he'll be one of our Tommy Chong brand growers."

"So the Tommy deal is a go?"

"We're getting there."

Hmm.

"I really like the way the Tommy licensing deal is going," O'Neil said. "But we still need a store. All we need is one. One store and we can build out the C&C Cannabis brand. Every great supermarket started as an apple cart."

There was honking in the background.

"Gotta run!" he said.

Click.

———

Another Pete O'Neil call.

"We've got a meeting with Tommy Chong's manager next week. Tommy and Cheech are doing a show at the Emerald Queen Casino. We're meeting up backstage. You want to come?"

Which is how I found myself talking marijuana history and watching the USC-Stanford football game at an Indian casino with Cheech and Chong on a Saturday night in Tacoma, Washington.

"Stop that fucker!"

A Stanford running back shredded the Trojan line. Cheech Marin was displeased.

Marin was a big USC fan. The Trojans were taking on the fourth-ranked Cardinal. In the front of the house, 1,400 comedy fans filed into the Emerald Queen Casino event center. Backstage, Cheech exhorted his team and chowed on a plate of rice.

A generation before *Pineapple Express* and *Harold and Kumar Go to White Castle*, Cheech Marin and Tommy Chong invented stoner comedy. Their classic routine "Dave," from their 1971 debut album, became a cultural touchstone for any kid who lived through the '70s. A string of hit movies—*Up in Smoke*, *Nice Dreams* and *Things Are Tough All Over*—turned them into one of the most popular comedy teams of the 20th century.

The '90s were tough on Cheech and Chong. The "Just Say No" generation wrote them off as comedic has-beens. Cheech Marin turned to serious roles in *Tin Cup* and *Nash Bridges*, while Tommy Chong picked up a recurring role on *That '70s Show* before being arrested and sent to federal prison in 2003 for selling bongs. (Not pot. Bongs.)

Now they're old men. Marin is 68. Chong is 77. And a funny thing is happening: they're popular again. On the casino circuit Cheech and Chong are cash money, a sure sellout.

Tommy Chong joined Marin and me backstage after a meet-and-greet with members of the Puyallup tribe. "Indian people, man, they love us," Chong said. "We're all brown people."

I asked them how they accounted for marijuana's comeback.

"It's funny," said Chong. "The other side always claimed there weren't enough studies. Never enough studies. But there were enormous experiments with marijuana." Woodstock was an experiment, he said. "Woodstock proved you could get 500,000 people together for four days and have a peaceful, loving concert." But straight America wanted scientific proof, Chong went on. And they finally got it. "Marijuana is a medicine. Listen to Sanjay Gupta. He went on CNN and said it. I believe marijuana can and has cured cancer. It cured mine."

"Cures halitosis too," said Cheech, always looking for the joke. "Doesn't take away the smell, just your senses, so you don't know. Or care."

Chong stayed serious. "For 70 years the government's been trying to prove there's something wrong with marijuana. And they couldn't."

"They were wrong and we were right," said Cheech. "So nah-nah-nah-nah-nah." Cheech looked kind of bored by the subject.

"Do you feel a sense of vindication?" I asked.

"The vindication that I want," said Chong, "is to be cleared of my felony record for selling paraphernalia." His nine-month stretch in federal prison—again, *for selling bongs*—was no joke.

Cheech will find one anyway. "That was a felony," he said, "so Tommy can't go in the strip bar with his gun anymore."

Chong's California MMJ card now allows him to legally grow his own. He's got a little rooftop garden that he harvests every few months. Even so, he's never been able to shake that old paranoia.

"There's always been a vicarious thrill associated with doing something illegal," he told me. "Smoking weed, there's always been that line there. No matter how legal it is, I still hide it. I go in the garage or up on the roof to smoke it by myself."

Chong's manager poked his head into the green room. "Five minutes, guys!"

The interview ended. Only then did I realize there was an element missing from the room. I stood backstage with Cheech and Chong, and there was no pot smoke in the air. Not a whiff, not a draw. As I left the green room and strolled to the front of the house, I spotted a guy sucking on a vape pen but saw nobody openly passing a joint. Then it hit me. We were on an Indian reservation. Federal law ruled here. State legality did not hold.

"Hey, Bruce! How were the guys?" Pete O'Neil asked me. He'd claimed a seat about 10 rows back. Sitting next to him was Steve, a pot grower from rural Mason County. Steve's grin made me suspect he'd inhaled a little of his own crop. ("Correct!" he said.)

Cheech and Chong took the stage.

"Who is it?"

"It's me, Dave. Open up, man, I got the stuff."

"Who?"

"It's Dave, man, open up, I think the cops saw me comin' here."

Pause.

"Dave's not here, man."

The room exploded with laughter.

10

THE MARIJUANA
MAGNATE ROLLS LARGE

I kept hearing about these marijuana millionaires. Ganjapreneurs. Cannabis capitalists. "Big Marijuana." Everywhere I went I saw small marijuana. Finally I made some inroads. Privateer founder Brendan Kennedy put me in touch with a Colorado businessman named Vincent K. "Tripp" Keber.

Keber embodied the latest incarnation of the American dream. In the space of four years, he'd turned himself into the Richard Branson of the legal-marijuana world. He was rich, smart, outspoken and brash. "In this business there are very few people out there building a mainstream brand and doing it in a smart, considered way," Kennedy told me. "Tripp is one guy who's doing it right."

Keber didn't just sell marijuana. He grew it. He packaged it. He sold it in cannabis-infused beverages, chocolates and breath mints. One of his companies provided security for medical marijuana dispensaries.

After a couple of phone conversations he invited me to spend a day with him. "I'll show you the industry," he said.

Three weeks later Keber pulled up to the Denver Ramada chewing an unlit cigar. It was a little past eight on a Wednesday morning in October 2013, two months before the scheduled opening of Colorado's first recreational pot stores.

"You ready to go, brother?" he said.

I nodded.

Keber smiled and invited me to ride shotgun. I climbed into his black Ford pickup, one of those roided-out King Ranch editions. "Got a lot to get to today," he said as we pulled into the rush hour on Colfax Avenue. "I need to get out there and check on things in my companies. You know what they say: inspect what you expect."

Solidly built and snappily dressed, Tripp Keber was a no-apologies empire-building capitalist. "I'm a serial entrepreneur," he told me. "I make companies to sell companies. Make me an offer and I'll ride off into the sunlight with saddlebags of gold."

Keber wasn't supposed to end up selling pot. As a young man he joined the Young Republicans and espoused the conservative religion of private enterprise. He sold bonds for a while, then dabbled in real estate. He developed luxury motor-home resorts in Gulf Shores, Ala., and then looked around and wondered if that was all that the good Lord intended for him to do on this Earth, because it all seemed kind of . . . boring. In 2009 he read a story about medical marijuana in Colorado. Farmers reported bumper crops. Dispensaries were mushrooming across the state. Inspiration struck in a word: edibles.

"I thought, What about all the people who need their medicine but prefer not to smoke?" he told me. "If we could find other ways of delivery, we might have something." Most people in his situation might think of brownies. Keber thought of an entire grocery store.

He found that cannabis extraction—the process of stripping out the essential oils from the plant—was a common practice. Cosmetic companies had been using high-pressure carbon dioxide to extract essential oils from lavender, rose and other plants for decades. Run a batch of marijuana through the same process, and voilà: cannabis oil, a thick amber fluid that resembles honey. "The mother's milk of our products," he said.

In 2009 Keber moved to Denver and founded Dixie Elixirs & Edibles. "I liked the way the name rolled off the tongue," he said. Dixie put out soda, candies, tinctures and baked goods infused with THC-rich cannabis oil. Dispensaries across Colorado couldn't get enough. By 2013 Dixie Elixirs had become one of the cannabis industry's best-known brands.

Keber made a truckload of money. Which presented its own problems. With pot still federally illegal, most banks wouldn't touch marijuana money for fear of losing their federal charters. So he farmed out his profits.

Keber snapped up properties like a Monopoly champion. By the time I caught up with him, he owned or held stakes in no fewer than 17 cannabis-related companies. The player owned half the board.

Victory was assured, he told me. "In Colorado, 100,000 patients drove a $300 million medical marijuana industry last year," he told me. "Now think about the coming adult-use market. Nearly every study shows that about 10 percent of the public has a relationship with cannabis. Ten percent of Colorado's 5 million residents—that's half a million people. We get 60 million visitors every year. Even if only 5 percent of those tourists make a purchase, that's 3 million people a year." He lets the numbers sink in. "We're talking massive, hockey-stick growth!

"Wall Street analysts believe there are going to be two or three billionaires minted in this industry in the next 10 years," he went on. "I'm not saying I'm going to be one of them"—humbly—"but this kind of opportunity comes around only once in a generation."

―――――

Keber took a call. "Jakester! How are ya, brother?" he said. "We're five minutes out."

As we pulled into a light-industrial district in south Denver, a fragrant note hung in the air. "Smell that?" Keber said. "Cannabis."

There are pockets like this dotting the city, places where a light breeze carries the unmistakable hoppy scent of state-legal, federally illegal grow operations hidden in unmarked warehouses. One of Keber's main grows is housed here in a nondescript 25,000-square-foot facility. Dozens of competing grows exist in similar warehouses within a three-mile radius south of Interstate 25.

Jake Salazar, the 30-something chief executive officer of MMJ America, Keber's dispensary company, met us at the heavily secured door. With his stout frame and rounded forearms, Salazar looked like a man who could handle himself in a bar fight. He ran nightclubs and a couple of Benihana franchises before starting his first indoor marijuana grow in 2007. "We were the second MMJ grow in Denver," he told me. "Those were sketchy days." He and Keber met in 2010 when Keber went looking for raw material for his edibles.

"When we first started up, I put a lot of faith in street growers," Keber told me. That didn't work out so well. "They weren't organized, they couldn't come in on time, and the quality was spotty. We had issues."

Salazar recalled the first time he took Keber to see his grow. "I made him wear a blindfold," Salazar said.

I followed Salazar into a gallery-white space the size of a small lecture hall. Hundreds of marijuana plants about four feet high sat in neat rows, each in its own 15-gallon pot. Reggae rhythms bounced off the walls. "This is our cloning area," Salazar explained.

Cloning involved snipping a stemmed leaf off a mother plant and nurturing it in an aeroponic chamber. "If you water it for two weeks you'll get a full rooting system—nice, white, healthy roots," Salazar explained. He held up a young clone with a beard of tendrils as pale and succulent as bean sprouts.

"It all starts here," Salazar said, sweeping his arm to take in more than 120 mature mother plants. Each represented a different strain of cannabis: Crazy Train, Cheesequake, Purple Agent Orange, Grape AK-47, Green Crack. "My personal favorite is Green Crack, the GC," said Salazar. "That's one that really needs to be renamed." Indeed. There seemed to be a disconnect between the people naming strains and the people promoting cannabis as a medicine. Try as I might, I couldn't imagine Pfizer branding its next miracle pill Yellow Meth.

Back in the grow room, Salazar walked me through the clone-to-flower process. Once the young clones sprouted roots, Salazar's farm crew transplanted them into individual soil pots and moved them upstairs into the veg room, an open loft dominated by dozens of 1,000-watt sodium halide lights. For every room there was a different soundtrack. Up in the veg room it was ZZ Top's "Sharp Dressed Man."

"You're looking at roughly 1,600 plants in their vegetative process right now," Salazar told me. "Looking" was a strong word. If I squinted hard I could see a crew of three strong men in their 20s moving plants in near darkness. "The lights are out because they're transplanting," Salazar said. "The rule is, if you're moving plants around, we want the lights off so they don't get stunted or burned. That's just corporate policy."

Before entering the next room Salazar requested that Keber and I put on headlamps with special green LEDs.

"This is the flowering chamber," Salazar said, "the last step prior to harvest."

Soundtrack: "Sugar Magnolia" by the Grateful Dead. What can I tell you? Sometimes clichés endure because they are true.

Our headlamps provided enough light to pick our way through the room without crashing into the plants. In previous rooms the plants were allowed to grow fat and bushy, but once they reach the flowering stage they're limbed up like an acacia tree, nothing but strong, thick stalks and broad canopies. That focuses all the plant's energy on the topmost stems where the buds emerge.

"Why the darkness?" I asked.

"The plants are in their sleeping period," Salazar said. Flipping on the lights in the middle of a 12-hour dark cycle might confuse the plant. Night turned day, day turned night, seas boiling, snowfall in July. "The plants think something's wrong," said Salazar. "The world is going haywire. They think they're about to die, so they seed themselves to carry on the line, to survive."

There are female and male marijuana plants. Only females produce the high-THC, high-value buds. This is another reason cloning, which results in a female every time, works so much better than growing from seed, which offers only 50-50 odds. If a female plant isn't pollinated by a male, it will pour all its energy into growing bigger, fatter, juicier buds.

Once the buds reach maximum fatness and stickiness, they're harvested and strung up in a drying chamber. "It looks dry, but if you touch it you'll feel that it's still very moist," Salazar said.

A member of the grow crew popped around a corner to consult with the boss. The grower wore latex gloves and a long butcher's apron. Salazar introduced us. I reached to shake the man's hand. Keber nabbed my arm before I could complete the gesture.

"Never shake a gloved man's hand in a grow facility," Keber said. Cannabis oils and resins can be absorbed through the skin, he explained. "You shake his hand, you could be in for a very long and mellow afternoon."

We moved on to the drying room, where dozens of cannabis bouquets hung upside down on wires bolted to the ceiling. Drying and curing are akin to the fermentation process in winemaking. Growers tend to be guarded about the details of these final steps, as they can mean the difference between low-grade joint weed and a top-shelf Cannabis Cup contender. "So if you do it wrong, you're spoiling wine into vinegar," I said.

"Not quite," said Salazar. "More like turning Château Lafite into jug wine."

In a natural outdoor setting, cannabis will usually produce harvest-ready buds at six or seven months. In the Denver warehouse, Salazar's production system cut that time in half. By manipulating light, soil, nutrients, temperature and airflow, his growers turned a six-inch clone into a five-foot flowering plant in only 12 weeks. Planting a new crop of clones every two weeks allowed Salazar to keep a crew of harvesters, trimmers, packagers and delivery specialists working five days a week.

"We've learned a few things over the years," Salazar told me. "We didn't invent the process, of course. We stand on the shoulders of giants." The science of indoor growing owes as much to law enforcement as it does to botany. In the '60s and early '70s, most American pot originated in the remote forests of Mexico, Jamaica, Hawaii and Northern California. In 1983, California began cracking down on outdoor cultivation by using helicopters to spot illegal grows. Over the next decade, state and federal agents destroyed hundreds of thousands of plants, arrested scores of growers and turned natural cultivation into a risky business. By 1990 the choked-off supply had driven the price of pot up from $2,500 a pound to more than $5,000 a pound. That inspired the next generation of pot farmers to grow indoors. After nearly a quarter century of innovation, indoor cultivation had far outstripped outdoor growing in efficiency, crop rotation, pest control, bud size and quality, employee safety, operational risk—almost everything except price. Sunshine was free. Electricity was not.

———————

Our next stop was a 100,000-square-foot light-industrial facility that Keber recently purchased for $1.2 million in cash. "It was a commercial bakery until about two weeks ago," he told me. As we pushed through the front door, you could smell the lingering odor of cakes and bread.

In a conference room sat a woman poring over documents and files. "Is Shellene here?" Keber asked her. She looked up. "I don't know," she said. "I'm the state auditor."

Keber apologized and left her to her work. Inspectors from the state Department of Revenue's Marijuana Enforcement Division regularly popped in for unannounced spot-audits to make sure every leaf and bud was accounted for.

Keber and I roamed through the largely empty building looking for Shellene Suemori, a molecular biologist whom Keber recently hired as his head of research. "I think this is her third day on the job," he said.

We passed a loading bay. "We've got space to load three 18-wheelers at a time here," Keber said. "We'll reach every retail outlet in Colorado from here."

In a small baking room near the shipping bay, four workers wearing hairnets and long white coats prepared Dixie Elixir Truffles, a chocolate treat dosed with a whopping 300 milligrams of THC. (Just 100 milligrams will put most people on the floor.)

Keber spotted movement behind a curtain across the concrete factory floor.

"Buckie!" he called. The curtain parted.

Clad in a mechanic's jumpsuit and a florid beard, Buckie Minor attended to dials and digits. "This is where we get the mother's milk," Minor said. "That's what Tripp calls the cannabis oil." Behind him hummed the Apeks 5000-5L Supercritical CO_2 Extractor. In one end Minor fed trimmed fan leaves and sugar leaves. Out the other dripped thick amber cannabis oil.

As Minor and I talked about the finer points of cannabis extraction, a large man joined us from across the room. At first he appeared to be human-size, but then I realized that was merely an illusion of perspective, because as he drew near the man doubled in size.

"Meet Big Wayne," said Keber. "He was my second employee. Big Wayne was there in the colorful days. I call him Henry Kissinger. The diplomat."

Big Wayne's size didn't just encourage diplomacy; it erased any notion of physical confrontation. His body was not something to be attacked but scaled. Big Wayne was in charge of product distribution and played an integral role on the company's security team. The man was a walking invoice.

Keber checked his watch. It was a little past noon. "Let's keep moving," he said.

―――――

As we pulled into the Denver Four Seasons, the valets came running. Keber was a known hitter at the hotel. He kept the twenties flowing.

"Hey Tripp!" said one of the young valets. "How you doing?"

Keber tossed him the keys. "Never better," he said. "Listen, I'll be back in an hour or so. Keep her close."

We strolled up 14th Street in the full warmth of the afternoon. Our destination was the Colorado Convention Center.

Keber pulled a trade show pass from his suit pocket. "Put this on; it'll get you in the door," he told me.

I slipped the lanyard around my neck.

I skimmed a convention guide as I followed at Keber's heels. The Champs Trade Show billed itself as "the premiere counterculture business-to-business expo." In plain English: it's a head-shop convention. As Keber strode the floor, old hippies and young heads glanced curiously at his pinstriped suit. We passed hundreds of products devoted to combustion, stealth and pleasure. It was like traveling to a foreign country and discovering a whole world of new brand names: Chrontainer, Hookahzz, Bethlehem Burners, Hydrostrike, VapeApe, Kindtray .com, PipePadz, Bud Vault, 420 Science, DabR USA, Captain Amsterdam. A number of exhibitors employed young women in hot pants and bikini tops as professional sirens. "Why do they still hire booth babes?" Keber said, shaking his head, and I felt myself a sadder person for now knowing the term *booth babe*.

"Does Dixie Elixirs have a booth here?" I asked.

Keber shook his head. "Not the forum in which we want to appear."

At the Apeks Fabrication booth, Keber introduced me to Andy Joseph, a former nuclear submarine engineer. "Andy's machines are changing the industry," Keber said.

Joseph made the machines that Buckie Minor used to extract cannabis oil. Keber had recently purchased a stake in Joseph's company. "This is what attracted my money," he told me, running his hand over the gleaming steel of the Apeks 5000 20-Liter Supercritical CO_2 System, a $120,000 piece of machinery that looked like a whiskey still built by a nuclear engineer.

I asked Joseph, a former military engineer, if he had any competitors at the show. He pointed to a balloon the size of a small bus hovering over a booth across the floor. It looked vaguely like a can of spray paint. The label said *Newport Butane*.

"That's our competition," Joseph said. "Butane extraction." He all but spat the words.

Cannabis oil extraction could be done in one of two ways. The clean and expensive way was to use one of Andy Joseph's supercritical CO_2 machines. The cheap and dirty way was to blast a solvent like butane through the plant material. You could do it for about $200. Shopping list: a dozen cans of butane ($25); a glass Butane Honey Oil (BHO) Extractor, which looks like an oversize test tube ($50); a vacuum pump ($150); a stainless-steel mesh filter ($20). And a few ounces of fan leaves and sugar leaves. After stripping out the oils with butane, you'd be left with a yellowish liquid. From that, the solvent needed to be slow-cooked away. Of course, the solvent was lighter fluid. So you can imagine. In 2013 a number of newspapers in medical marijuana states began to carry stories with headlines like "HASH OIL SETS APARTMENT ABLAZE."

Hash oil fires were not to Tripp Keber's liking. His vision of the future pointed toward OSHA safety regulations, state health department inspections and the controlled, responsible, sustainable use of marijuana. Butane cooks blowing up their apartments weren't good for the industry.

Neither were massively overpacked edibles. "Anyone can stuff 300 milligrams [of THC] into a chocolate truffle and call it 'Chasing the Dragon,'" Keber told me. With recreational sales just two months away, "those days are about to be over," he said. Colorado's recreational marijuana regulations limited each packaged edible to a maximum potency of 100 milligrams.

Like a lot of people in Colorado's pot industry, Keber prepared himself for the first adult-legal marijuana mishap. "Something's going to go wrong," he told me. "You don't know what it will be. Somebody might crash a truck into a bus. Or consume a 100-milligram bar and go out of their mind in a hotel room." It wasn't a matter of if, but when. And when it happened, folks in the marijuana industry needed to have clean operations and clear, concise answers.

It wasn't easy to raise these issues among the cognoscenti. Seventy-five years of marijuana prohibition had bred a culture with a bias against judging thy neighbor. Introducing the idea that maybe, perhaps, the promotion of home butane extraction might not be in the cannabis industry's best long-term interest went against the long-established code of not harshing a colleague's buzz. *No shame, no blame, brother. You run your business; I'll run mine.*

The result was a conspiracy of silence around the use of butane. Nobody in the industry had the cojones to step up and be the adult in the room.

As Keber and Joseph spoke privately, I strolled down the aisle and spotted Ross Kirsch selling Stink Sacks.

"Ross!" I called out. "Are you moving units?"

"Trying to," he said.

Kirsch was a Brooklyn boy who could have had a side career as a Neil Simon character. With thick black hair, chunky glasses and a borough rasp, he seemed to step out of the 1940s. Not for him the glamour of pot growing or bud tending. Kirsch was in packaging. I'd been introduced to him months earlier at a meeting of the ArcView Group, the leading organization of cannabis financiers. There he made a pitch for investment in his Stink Sacks, clear plastic baggies that trapped the tell-tale scent of fresh weed. "A must for your customers who desire a clean purchasing experience," he said.

The aroma of pot was so overpowering that Stink Sack's main competitor was a company that manufactured trash bags meant to block the smell of human shit. OdorNo, an Ohio company that marketed bags in step-up sizing (dog poop, baby diaper, Depends) under the trade-marked slogan "Why smell it?", had adapted its Odor-Barrier Technology for the cannabis market with a product known as the FunkSac. Stink Sack's logo featured a cartoon skunk. FunkSac countered with a cartoon weed dealer. Neither image inspired an overwhelming confidence in the product.

Truth be told, the Stink Sack wasn't setting the world on fire. Orders from medical marijuana dispensaries were arriving in trickles. The brand name wasn't helping matters. "Stink Sack" was pretty much the visual antonym of a clean purchasing experience.

"You gearing up for adult use in Colorado?" I asked.

"Yeah, as a matter of fact I got something going on there," Kirsch said. He drew me closer and lowered his voice.

"You know that the adult-use regulations in Colorado require childproof packaging, right?" he said. "Well, nobody's got any. Childproof packaging. Nobody even knows what it means. It hasn't even been invented."

"So you've got something?"

"I've got a design," he said. "It's not that hard. I just need some capital to make it happen. I get a little money, I'm on the next flight to my manufacturer in Dongguan."

Keber caught my eye and tapped his very expensive watch. We slipped out of the convention center and made our way to the Four Seasons valet station. Before we got there, though, Keber spotted a trio of men approaching him. "Uh-oh," he said. "Union organizers."

Three men wearing jackets embossed with the emblem of the United Food and Commercial Workers waved him down. "How's business, Tripp?" one of them said.

Keber made small talk and hustled away as quickly as he could. "They're nice guys, but they like to bust my balls," he told me. "They're trying to unionize the cannabis industry, and my company is a high-profile target."

After slipping the valet a twenty, he pulled onto 14th Street and dialed the office. "Christie, it's Tripp," he said. "I'm running behind. Let's move that marketing meeting to 4:30."

As we rolled through Denver, I thought about something I heard Ethan Nadelmann say a few days earlier. Nadelmann, head of the Drug Policy Alliance, warned a gathering of drug reform activists that there would be nothing fair about the economic rewards of the legalized market. "The forces at work in a prohibitionist market are violent and brutal," Nadelmann said, "but the capitalist forces at work in a legal market are even more brutal in some respects. We know that the people who may come to dominate this industry are not the people who are a part of this movement." He was right. And there was no tragedy in that. Activists are great at changing laws. They are usually lousy businesspeople. For marijuana reform to succeed, commerce would now have to take over. The activists probably would not have approved of Tripp Keber and his wheeling-dealing ways. But they needed him to succeed.

———

At 4:29 we returned to the old bakery building. In a conference room Lindsey Jacobsen, the company's 31-year-old marketing director, laid out four different versions of a new beverage bottle design. Colorado's new adult-use regulations required opaque packaging, so the company's clear glass bottles would be illegal on Jan. 1. "With the new laws, we're forced to change, but I think it's good," Keber said. "We want a more adult look."

"These are our four finalists," Jacobsen said.

The silver aluminum bottles reminded me of the Michelob shape.

"Anything jump out that you love or hate?" Keber asked.

Christie Lunsford, the company's administrative director, and Chuck Smith, chief operating officer, considered the designs.

"We're still playing with the color," said Jacobsen. "We're aiming for sophisticated but fun, without being too young."

Too young was code for the third rail of legal marijuana: underage use. When Colorado's recreational shops opened, the world would watch to see if pot use increased among teenagers. Edibles were especially vulnerable to charges of child marketing. Though he insisted on calling them *beverages*, Keber's infused sodas were clearly sodas. His infused candies were candies. His infused chocolate truffle, with its horse-stoning 300 milligrams of THC, was clearly a chocolate truffle. The products themselves were child-friendly. The packaging had to fairly scream *adult*.

The conversation turned to the font size of the THC content. "Do we want the '70 milligrams' larger?" Jacobsen asked.

Keber shook his head. "We want it to be clear, but we don't want it to dominate."

Dosage was expected to be an issue. Adults whose relationship with marijuana had lapsed after college would be sampling edibles. They were going to have to relearn their own levels of tolerance. Colorado and Washington weren't just rolling out a new post-prohibition marijuana system. They were opening one of the largest psychotropic dosing experiments ever conducted.

Keber held up one of the illustrated bottles. "Frickin' slick," he said. "Nothing on the shelves even comes close to this. I'm getting goosebumps."

The new design was approved. Now all Keber's team had to do was ramp up production to full speed for the next three months. The Jan. 1 deadline loomed. And the new factory echoed with the empty sound of beverages not being bottled.

"Come Jan. 1, the demand for edibles is going to be higher than anybody thinks," Keber told me. "If we can't meet all of the pent-up demand that's out there, our retailers will look elsewhere. There are other companies out there. We've got to be able to come through with the product."

His phone rang. He glanced at the caller ID and ignored it. As his staff dispersed, Keber stood on the cold concrete of his factory floor and rolled an unlit cigar around his mouth. Somewhere in his head, the ghost of the future moved.

11

AND THERE WILL BE

TREATS FOR EVERYONE

In early December I received an invitation to a Christmas cocktail party. It was from The Joint. This struck me as odd. In all my years of medical treatment I couldn't recall my local pharmacy throwing open the holiday lampshader to its patients.

> *Hello Bruce,*
> *Come to our 3rd Annual Patient Appreciation HOLIDAY PARTY!*
> *• Patient Raffle with TONS of prizes!*
> *• Dab Station!*
> *• Volcano!*
>   *And there will be Treats for EVERYONE!*
> *We hope you will come celebrate the holidays with us at the*
> *Royal Bar and Grill!*

This struck me as mildly unsettling. Here was a medical practice inviting its patients to an office party (a) at a bar, (b) with prizes and free drinks, where they would be encouraged to (c) indulge in extremely high doses of their medicine. Oh, The Joint.

I showed up fashionably late. As one does. (Of course I went! Please. Like you wouldn't.) Lucy had tickets to see NoFilter at the Neptune Theater that night, and about that I can't tell you much beyond my 15-year-old daughter's explanation that this was a group of transgressive female culture-forward comedians whom I and other fogeys would learn about in the Arts section of the *Times* six months hence.

"What time does the show get out?"

"Dunno. I'll text you!" And off she pranced into the early architecture of her influences.

The Royal Bar and Grill was about eight blocks and 20 years north of the NoFilter show.

"Are you a patient?" asked the bouncer.

"Indeed I am," I said, reaching for my wallet. I kept my MMJ card there at all times, like a young man's optimistic condom.

He banded my wrist. "Drinks in the front, dabs in the back."

I ordered a Pabst and made my way to the back room. It wasn't a room so much as an enclosed dirt-floor patio. Patients clustered on wooden picnic tables around the propane aureole of patio heaters. The party had drawn a mix of streetwise 20-somethings and hippie gray-hairs. Extremely loud dance music filled the room. I made eye contact with one scraggly old-timer. We nodded. It was the kind of acknowledgment men of a shared demographic exchange in a mixed room. My heart sank just a tick. *That* was my demographic? Old Prospector Jones? Yeesh. Maybe it was time to mix a little CrossFit into my morning.

I picked my way to the dab station. I wanted to know more about this. Dabbing was reputed to be the crack of marijuana, a highly concentrated, fast-rush form of pot smoking. Instead of smoking the leaf, dabbers inhaled a vaporized cloud of cannabis oil containing 75 to 90 percent THC. Dabbing emerged around 2009, and by 2013 concentrated oils, budders and waxes accounted for upward of 40 percent of sales at some dispensaries. "Before smoking with a newb dabber," *High Times* advised, "ask them if they smoke weed everyday. You want to make sure this is a pleasant experience for all parties involved, and you certainly don't want someone flipping out, passing out or vomiting all over the room." *High Times*, you really know how to charm a girl.

At a rudimentary bar, I watched a trim young man (the dabtender?) focus a crème brûlée torch on a small metal cup attached to an elaborate glass pipe known as a dabbing rig. The cup was about the size of a golf tee. It had been cast in titanium, which was reputedly the finest material for the job. That job was to turn red-hot in the tongue of flame. As the cup neared optimum glow, the dabtender signaled the, er, patient to be in readiness. The dabtender lowered a glass cowl over the cup and squeezed a drop of dabbing oil onto the end of a metal rod that looked vaguely dental in nature. He touched the oil to the cup. It vaporized instantly. The patient drew the white cloud into his lungs. I stood mesmerized by the timing and teamwork of the whole operation. An urge to try it welled within me, even as my conscience frantically flapped warning flags. The crack-iness of the scene was troubling. If a member of my generation knows anything, we know that when somebody breaks out a torch, it's time to leave the party.

I wasn't the only one a little creeped out by dabbing. Even some of the old heads at NORML were put off by the practice. "We've hosted national conferences for 40 years," Allen St. Pierre told me one afternoon at NORML headquarters in Washington, D.C. St. Pierre was the group's charming and witty executive director. I thought of him as the Neil deGrasse Tyson of cannabis. "We enjoyed the best marijuana in America. No problems. Then someone showed up around 2009 with the first concentrates and a blowtorch. This guy from Colorado stepped up and hit the rig. He turned, and it was like someone had cut the string from a puppet. He passed out and clipped the bar on his way down. Broke his jaw."

I stood and watched the dabbing continue. Nobody broke their jaw, but a couple of patrons wobbled to a nearby bench.

Patrons—or patients? Here was the problem with The Joint's holiday party. (One of many, to be sure.) Were they serving medicine to patients or hosting an all-you-can-dab open bar? The evidence of my lying eyes clearly pointed to the latter. Under the law, they were doing the former. With full adult legalization, marijuana moved into an ambiguous condition, existing as neither pure medicine nor naughty intoxicant but a third state of matter encompassing both.

I was reminded of something else Allen St. Pierre told me. We were talking about the future of legal pot, and whether liquor companies or cigarette companies were more likely to move in on the action. St. Pierre believed the beer companies would be the first to embrace marijuana. "Tobacco and cannabis are both smoked vegetable matter," he said, "but tobacco is not a psychotropic. The culture of pot is more in line with that of the alcohol industry. We're both Dionysians. We like pleasure; they like pleasure. And they are very experienced at working in an area I like to describe as 'problematic adult commerce.'"

What an excellent phrase. Criminologist Jerome Skolnick once defined *vice* as an activity involving both pleasure and wickedness, to which an ever-shifting moral ambivalence adheres. At the end of 2013 the moral ambivalence about marijuana shifted daily under our feet. No longer a dangerous and highly illegal drug, it was passing into St. Pierre's sphere of problematic adult commerce. Was it medicine? Yes. Was it vice? Yes. I realized the riddle wasn't going to be solved that night at the Royal Bar and Grill. Sometimes life is complicated. Substances, like people, can fit in more than one category at a time.

"Are you in line?"

The question came from an older woman in a sweatshirt. Apparently I stood between her and the dab bar.

"No, no," I said. "I'm just watching the man's technique." My daughter expected me to retrieve her, and I thought I'd pay her the courtesy of not vomiting all over the car when that moment arrived.

The old lady slipped closer to the bar. "What are you, a writer?" she said, eyeing my notepad.

"Yes," I said. "I'm working on a book."

"I'm writing a book too," she said.

I'll bet you are. Please. Tell me all about it.

"It's about our origins as humans," she said. She had to fairly shout to be heard over the *thumpa-thumpa*. "From space. About how we are all just the seed of an alien race who stopped by this planet and planted our DNA millions of years ago."

I was unsure whether this would be fiction or nonfiction. The plot sounded suspiciously like a Ridley Scott movie I'd seen a few weeks earlier.

"Have you seen *Prometheus*?" I asked.

"Which what?"

"*Prometheus*. The movie. Have you seen it?"

She frowned and shook her head. Probably for the best.

"How far along are you?" I asked.

"Oh, I haven't started *writing* it yet," she said. "But I will. It's all in my head."

She stepped to the dab bar and eyed the nail until it obtained an emberish glow. The dabtender set a glass dome over the hot nail and touched a glop of Dama Oil, a 79 percent THC concentrate, to the head. The oil vaporized instantly. The woman took the milky gas into her lungs and held it. She exhaled slowly, looked at me and smiled. Then she wandered off to find a place to sit and, I hoped, continue to work out the complex strands of her literary masterpiece. Because why not. We all want to reach for greatness. We all want to create a work of art that connects to unseen people out there in the void, that beats back the pain and expands kindness and kinship. Sometimes we're able to create those moments and those little works of art in our lives. And sometimes we fall short but still want to feel the warm, ecstatic vibe of that connection anyway. So we look for a way to feel it.

Two hours later, I picked up Lucy across the street from the Neptune. "Oh my God, I met Hannah Hart!" she told me. "She is *so nice*. We talked about her YouTube shows and how weird it is to finally meet people you've been sharing these jokes and shows and tweets with for so long." As we drove to the ferry, Lucy went on and on about connecting to her people and how the entire evening was thrilling beyond words. I drove through the rain and warmed myself in the glow of her happiness.

12

DAY ONE

IN COLORADO

"C'mon, junior, roll them bones!"

The stickman pushed the dice to the shooter, an older gentleman with flowing gray hair. A man in a tuxedo called out encouragement. "Throw 'em hard now!"

The dice bounced twice on their flight to the far wall.

"Nine!"

Tuxedo smiled. A young man to my left whispered to his companion. "He can afford it," he said, indicating Mr. Tux. "That's one of the heaviest growers in the state."

At 11:41 on the evening of Dec. 31, 2013, 19 minutes before the clock struck the end of marijuana prohibition in Colorado, a good portion of the cannabis industry gathered around the craps table at Casselman's Bar in Denver's NoDo district. Midnight approached, and with it the promise of a hugely prosperous new year. Marijuana was about to turn legal, and they were the people selling it.

The New Year's Eve party at Casselman's was billed as a

black-and-white "End of Prohibition" ball, and the organizers went to great lengths to create a Roaring '20s atmosphere. A jazz band filled the room with Artie Shaw standards; illicit pleasures were offered in dimly lit corners: top-shelf whiskey, a dab bar and a chocolate fountain flowing with THC-infused sweetness. Tickets went for a hundie per.

On the back porch, an attorney sloshed his Jack and Coke on my sleeve. "Sorry, man," he said. "Whew. That dab bar . . ." He told me he'd moved here from out of state. Set up a shingle in Denver last year. His specialty: cannabis law. "I've had work ever since," he said. I probed further, but he grew tired of my questions, or rather he wearied of the labor required to form vowels with his mouth. "Sorry, dude," he said. "That dab bar . . ." and his body drifted away.

Coupes of champagne appeared a few minutes before midnight. The band counted down to the new year.

"Ten . . . nine . . . eight . . ."

Cheers for midnight! Balloons falling, kisses offered, champagne toasting, "Auld Lang Syne" auld langing. The new arrived.

"Prohibition is over!" the bandleader shouted. "Cannabis . . . is . . . legal!"

Here and there, small joints appeared from breast pockets. Passing occurred. I pinched an offer between my thumb and forefinger. It felt so light. I flashed on the memory of a bird, cradled after a window strike, and the shock of its downy weight, the nothingness contained in flesh, blood and feather. I put it to my lips and drew.

A small stream of heat moved down my windpipe. I cooled it with a half breath of air and held the mix in my lungs.

The joint moved on. As did the party. By 1 a.m. the place felt like a wedding reception after the departure of the bride and groom. People had product to sell the next morning. Wait. *This* morning.

Happy new year, everybody. I gotta go.

7:45 a.m., New Year's Day 2014.

Snowflakes drifted like dust motes as I sprinted across Brighton Boulevard and up the steps to the 3D Cannabis Center. Across the city, hundreds of customers queued outside a dozen pot shops scheduled to open on Jan. 1. People drove in from all over the country. The first arrivals claimed their spot around 5 p.m. on New Year's Eve. From Georgia, Florida, Texas and Tennessee: they hunkered down in sleeping bags and tents. From Maine, South Dakota and Oregon: they smoked dope and laughed and sang songs and shared bottles of cheap champagne. When I asked why they had come, most people gave me a variation on the same answer: "I came to make history."

The bull at the door eyeballed my driver's license. "Nobody gettin' in without ID, boss," he said.

I stepped over the threshold into a writhing cockroachery of reporters. CNN, the BBC, Reuters, the *Los Angeles Times*, the *New York Times*, the Huffington Post, TIME, the AP, every local network affiliate plus Univision, Al Jazeera, Fox News and MSNBC. Radio reporters checked their sound levels and adjusted their goofy headphones. Prickly cameramen guarded their tripod of turf. Over the notoriously slow New Year's holiday, the world's media had dispatched their agents to Denver with a single mission: get the money shot. In this case there actually was money in the shot, with Colorado's first legal retail buyer handing over cash for cannabis. But there could be only one First Buyer and there were so, so, so many cameras.

At 7:50, Amendment 64 author Brian Vicente said a few words to the crowd. Betty Aldworth, spokesperson for the Amendment 64 campaign, declared that "today in Colorado we shift marijuana from the underground into a regulated market." Mason Tvert beamed. "We are going to set an example for the rest of the nation and the rest of the world," he said. "Regulating marijuana works."

Reporters stole glances at the time.

"Coming up on 8!" somebody shouted.

A murmuration of cameras pivoted to the buyer.

Sean Azzariti opened his eyes wide and smiled. The 32-year-old former Marine, the officially designated first customer, had been chosen for his symbolic value. Neither stoner nor hippie, Azzariti joined the Marines a few months before 9/11 and found himself on the tip of the spear during the 2003 invasion of Iraq. When he returned to civilian life in late 2006, Azzariti struggled with post-traumatic stress disorder. Veterans Affairs set him up on high doses of antidepressants, stimulants and sleeping pills. "Doctors just kept prescribing more and more pills," he recalled. Azzariti eventually weaned himself off the VA's drug regime by substituting cannabis. "It may not be for everyone, but it works for me," he told the pack of reporters.

Azzariti was the perfect new face of marijuana: a patriotic, self-sacrificing Marine. He also embodied the strange flaws that existed in the medical marijuana laws. Like most states, Colorado did not include PTSD among its qualifying conditions. So Azzariti was forced to lie to get his MMJ card.

The problem became moot, of course, at 8 a.m.

"What would you like, Sean?" asked Toni Savage, the owner of 3D.

"I'll have an eighth of Bubba Kush and one of those chocolate truffles," he said. Azzariti wore a sky-blue checked shirt and chinos.

Savage methodically sealed the bud and the Dixie Elixir edible in a childproof bag.

"Sean, your total is $59.74."

He handed her three twenties.

As this happened, more than 20 cameras whirred and clicked and flashed. The buying room, much smaller than the press conference area, felt like an elevator in a Marx Brothers sketch. "Hold it up!" one of the shooters hollered. "Sean, hold up the bag!"

He complied. A drop of sweat fell from his temple.

A blinding light clicked on. A TV reporter went live. "We understand that the first buyer, Iraq War veteran Sean Azzariti, has purchased a kind of marijuana called 'coosh' and a chocolate edible. . . ."

"Sean! Sean!"

A reporter pushed a microphone at him. "Sean, what do you think your mother would say if she saw you in here?"

"You can ask her yourself," he said. "She's right here next to me."

Azzariti turned his head this way and that.

"What does it do for you, Sean?" somebody asked.

He looked over the crowd. Cameras flashed. One reporter near the back fell into a glass case. Another texted a story into his iPhone. Azzariti smiled.

"It helps relax me," he said.

I had a list of open retail shops clipped from the *Denver Post*. The Grove, The Haven, The Shelter, DANK Colorado, LoDo Wellness, Evergreen Apothecary, The Green Solution. I drove over to Denver Kush Club on Welton Street, a seedy part of town. The line stretched down the block and around the corner. One circle of friends from New Mexico had been there for two hours. Another group of cargo-shorted bros road-tripped from Florida. "Did it in two days," one of them told me. "We drove in shifts."

At 10 a.m. customers continued to latch on to the end of the line. Around the corner, where the new arrivals stood, an old man shook a baggie of weed. He was rough and unkempt. He had good stuff right here, right now, he said. "No need to wait."

"How much you want?" I asked.

"Thirty for an eighth," he said.

Inside they were asking $40.

Here it was in the flesh, the great fear of the legalization theorists: the black market undercutting legal weed on price. I couldn't believe my luck. I joined the line to watch what would happen.

Minute by minute, others joined the line. Shake, shake, shake. "Thirty for an eighth. No waiting."

The old man found no takers. People wanted to make history. Besides, what he offered was old shake, stems and probably some seeds too. Buyers could purchase his brickweed on the cheap, or they could wait their turn at the Kush Club and select from among a dozen of the finest, freshest and purest strains of cannabis ever put under cultivation. There's a reason nobody buys beer in a bucket from a stranger on a street corner. It might be cheaper, but do you really want to drink it?

My hands grew cold. I turned and headed back to my car. At the end of the block, I glanced back. The old man stood in the freezing cold, still shaking his bag of weed.

Across town at Medicine Man, I found Andy Williams pumping hands like Bill Clinton working a rope line. "Thank you for coming out," he told a woman wrapped in a scarf. "We appreciate you waiting so patiently," he said to a group from Utah. "Good to see you, commander!" he said, clapping the dress-blue shoulder of Les Perry, head of the Denver P.D.'s Fifth Precinct.

For one day, the 45-year-old Williams may have been the happiest fellow in America. Hundreds of people lined up in merriness and peace outside his store. He had the supply to meet their demand. "We've been stockpiling for months now," he told me.

The Williams boys, Andy and his younger brother Pete, 43, served as the crown princes of Colorado's cannabis industry. Along with their older sister Sally Vander Veer, the Williams kids had bumped along through a rough childhood. They didn't have a lot of money growing up. Dinner was often noodles or Spam. As young adults, Andy and Sally got steady jobs with big companies. Pete, the free-spirited baby of the family, hustled cash by delivering pizzas and slinging weed. Then Pete discovered he possessed a kind of genius for growing mind-blowing bud. People came from all over the country to sample his crop. By the mid-2000s he was earning $100,000 a year growing for dispensaries around Denver. In 2009, when regulation came to Colorado's MMJ industry, Andy approached his brother. *You've got the green thumb*, Andy said. *I've got the business skills.* The new regs meant a grower could scale up with greater surety. "Let's go big with this," he said to Pete. "We could be the Costco of marijuana."

Andy invested the last of his savings, about $15,000, in a grow house and supplies. His wife was not pleased. "She cried when I told her," Andy recalled. At the time, Williams worked as a project manager for Jeppesen, an aviation company. The Great Recession was shaking the economy. In 2009, those who had jobs clung to them. His fears didn't revolve around money, though. "For those first few months I had nightmares about getting arrested, hauled away from my family," he told me. "It was awful."

As Andy and I spoke outside Medicine Man headquarters on Nome Street, we were approached by a tousled man smoking a cigarette. He looked like a 14-year-old boy trapped in a middle-aged body. "Meet my brother Pete," Andy said.

Pete took a tobacco hit and nodded toward the street. "Xcel is here," he told Andy.

"Finally," Andy said. He took off in the direction of the utility truck.

"We lost power earlier this morning," Pete told me. "We've been running on generators."

"What do you guys spend on power every month?" I asked.

Pete Williams smiled. "A lot," he said.

River Rock, a smaller dispensary and grow in Denver, spent about $20,000 a month on electricity. I figured the Williams brothers' power bill must be at least three times that amount.

Pete walked me through his grow rooms. We ended up in a small upstairs area where three women sat at a table trimming marijuana with nail scissors. Pete and Andy's mother, Michelle, a friendly woman in Midwestern eyeglasses, introduced herself. "I came in to help," she said. "I don't use it myself. Never even tried it." She laughed. "But we were the first investors."

No joke: Ma Williams owned 20 percent of Medicine Man. Andy and Pete split the rest between them. The company did $4.4 million in medical marijuana sales in 2013. With the opening of the recreational market, Andy reckoned they'd bring in $12 million in 2014.

"How much you figure you'll bring in today?" I asked.

"We might come close to 100,000," he said.

For the Williams family, the days of noodles and Spam were past. As we parted, Andy returned outside to thank the customers waiting in the three-hour queue. "Come back later tonight," he yelled at me. "I'll tell you how we did!"

By late morning, the lines outside Denver's pot shops showed no sign of shrinking. In fact, they appeared to be growing. Noon risers with New Year's hangovers were calling their friends and meeting up at the nearest marijuana store. The queues became impromptu block parties, with neighbors exchanging jokes, pot stories and shopping lists. There were old people and young people. Schools were on winter break, so a lot of college kids road-tripped to Denver that week. I met psych majors from Georgia, business students from Florida and engineering geeks from Iowa. A couple of middle-aged men pinned American flags to the backs of their jackets. Every now and then somebody—it was usually a fat guy with a beard—raised a victorious fist and cried, "Freedom!"

After mixing with the crowds, I drove over to an open house at O.penVape, a company that made the most popular vape pen on the market. O.penVape's headquarters were off Speer Avenue, near that Jonathan Borofsky sculpture of 70-foot dancing aliens. I arrived just as a group of pot tourists were exiting. Their guide, a smartly dressed woman in her 30s, pressed her business card on me. "I'm Jane West," she said. "I do cannabis events around town." I promised to follow up.

Inside I met Todd Mitchem, the company's chief revenue officer, who told me O.penVape had just closed out a phenomenal year. "We've grown 1,600 percent in the past 12 months," he said. Their success was the result of a superior product meeting a rising market. Vape pens had been around since 2009, but they weren't seen much until after the legalization votes in Colorado and Washington. Then the little licorice sticks became the hottest item in the dispensaries.

"We didn't invent the vape pen," Mitchem said. "What we did was give it a palatable coolness." I couldn't argue with him. Other vaporizers were chunky and ugly. The O.Pen was sleek. Its weight felt substantial. You could imagine Steve Jobs introducing it on an empty stage. "There's a smoothness to the high," Mitchem said. "It doesn't burn your lungs and it doesn't hit you like a bus."

I nodded. I was familiar with the O.Pen's silky draw. A few weeks earlier I'd purchased one at Fremont Gardens, a Seattle dispensary I'd begun to frequent when The Joint lost its ragged charm. The O. fit in any pocket and was indistinguishable from my black Uni-ball micro-point pens. I tested it while riding the ferry, walking down the street and in my own backyard. The O. was a lightweight's delight: a high as mild as a glass of wine, no smell, no pipe, no lighter, no roach. It offered everything traditional pot smoking lacked: discretion, convenience and cleanliness.

Mitchem was a handsome man with an athlete's build and a professional smile. In the cannabis industry this marked him as a fish out of water. A former management consultant, he'd been hired by O.penVape to develop its corporate culture. "My goal is to put cannabis in the daylight," he said. Mitchem received dozens of résumés every week. Passion and professionalism were more important than product knowledge. "We're building a new kind of cannabis company," he told me. "O.penVape is more like a high-tech start-up than a dispensary. We are the grown-ups in the space."

You may wonder, as I did: What exactly *is* vaping? I looked into it. Vaporizers heat marijuana or cannabis oil to a temperature of 180 to 200 degrees Fahrenheit, below the point of combustion. It's enough heat to release THC and other cannabinoids, but not enough to emit all the other toxic byproducts of full combustion. Beyond their convenience, vape pens overcame a concern often raised by the straight world but seldom addressed in cannabis culture: cancer.

Marijuana smoke contains many of the same toxic compounds found in tobacco smoke, including cancer-causing aromatic hydrocarbons. Tobacco smoking kills more than 480,000 Americans every year. But here's the weird thing: chronic pot smoking has never been shown to cause lung cancer. Numerous studies have been done on this. Pot smoking has been linked to an elevated risk of bronchitis and respiratory infection, which will come as no surprise to anyone who's suffered a harsh toke. But not lung cancer. Look, I may eat these words in 10 years. More research needs to be done. But so far, researchers who have looked into the question have come up empty. In a large case-controlled study at Johns Hopkins University, researchers found that their evidence "does not favor the idea that marijuana as commonly used in the community is a major causal factor for head, neck, or lung cancer in young adults." That's young adults. What about old adults? Scientists at UCLA looked into that. They found "no positive association" between marijuana smoking and cancer, even among pot users who had smoked the equivalent of a joint a day for 30 years. In fact, their data indicated that people who didn't smoke pot had *greater* odds of getting lung cancer than chronic pot smokers.

How can that be? One intriguing possibility is that the cannabinoids in pot smoke could be suppressing the carcinogenic effects of the other toxins released as a byproduct of combustion. The aromatic hydrocarbons in smoke are actually *pre*-carcinogens; they require the enzymatic activity of a protein to become fully carcinogenic. In tobacco cigarettes, nicotine activates and encourages that enzymatic activity. Researchers have found that THC does the opposite—it inhibits enzymatic activity. In other words, the THC in pot smoke could be protecting the lungs against those pre-carcinogenic toxins.

There are pot advocates who love to rave about the cancer-fighting properties of cannabis. I've tended to shut my ears when they hijack the microphone. I will give them this, though: the more time I spend in the medical stacks, the less delusional they sound.

While the U.S. government has gone to great lengths to suppress any marijuana research not devoted to showing its harm, scientists in Israel, Canada, the U.K. and other countries have been discovering the potential cancer-fighting properties of cannabinoids. British biotech firm GW Pharmaceuticals is known in marijuana culture as the producer of Sativex, a THC/CBD drug approved in 25 countries (but not the U.S.) to treat spasticity in multiple sclerosis. In the past few years GW Pharma has taken out U.S. patents on the use of pot-derived cannabinoids for the treatment of prostate cancer, breast cancer and glioblastoma, the brain cancer that nearly killed Jessamyn Way. That's not the delusional thinking of a stoned hippie. That's a $1.6 billion, NASDAQ-listed corporation investing millions of dollars in an area of cancer research that, according to the company, "is supported by an ever increasing body of available evidence."

There are a couple of theories about how this might work. Normal cells are created, live from five days to 15 years (depending on their function), then die on cue. This programmed death is known as apoptosis. Cancer cells ignore the usual signal to die; they just keep dividing and growing. Certain marijuana-derived cannabinoids may promote the re-emergence of apoptosis in cancer cells, which would cause them to heed the signal and die. Another possibility, also under investigation in GW Pharma's labs, focuses on blood vessels. Cancer cells send out signals to promote the growth of new vessels, which nourish the tumor. Cannabinoids may turn off those signals, cutting off the tumor's blood supply.

This brings us back to vaping. The Institute of Medicine's 1999 report on medical marijuana found cannabis to be effective for relief of chronic pain, epileptic seizures, glaucoma and nausea. The institute cautioned against the use of smoked cannabis, though, because of a generalized fear of lung cancer. Over the next 15 years, two things happened. Credible studies found zero connection between joint smoking and lung tumors. And the invention of the vaporizer removed toxins of combustion from the equation. The federal government responded to these developments by doing nothing.

At a certain point I began to wonder if science could ever overcome the marijuana phobia of America's ruling class. Among those heading federal agencies and holding public office, belief in the inherent malevolence of marijuana had become not just an article of faith but an assurance of virtue. It meant you stood for seriousness, order and sobriety. In the face of ever mounting evidence to the contrary, some public servants allowed their positions to evolve. In many, though, the old beliefs only hardened. As time passed and more research pointed to the medical promise of cannabinoids, the weedheads and the agency heads swapped positions. Twenty years ago, pot advocates who spoke of marijuana's cancer-fighting potential were written off as magical thinkers. Now it seemed that the authorities in D.C. were the ones increasingly clinging to long-debunked myths, superstition and sorcery.

I returned to Medicine Man that evening. The line outside the front door had winnowed to a stub. I joined it. I figured I'd buy a loose joint or two to mark history.

"Just want to let you all know," a security man told us, "by law we have to close at 7 p.m." State law allowed retail pot shops to remain open until midnight, but Denver's city council had decreed an earlier end to the cannabis day. "I'm not sure we'll be able to move everyone through."

That's OK, I thought. So did others. Nobody abandoned their place in line. Night fell. Time passed. Cold crept into my toes.

At 6:50, I made the front door.

My heart sank. Inside, the line snaked like an airport security queue. The shop had seven budtenders on duty behind a long glass case full of packaged pot.

"Ten minutes!" Andy Williams bellowed. "Folks, these registers are programmed to shut off precisely at 7 p.m."

Inspectors from the State Department of Revenue, Marijuana Division, had been by twice that day. No way were the Williams brothers going to screw up under that kind of scrutiny.

At 6:55 I passed by the clone kiosk. Tiny cannabis plants could be had for $15 apiece. I was tempted to buy one just to get the day-one receipt. But what would I do with a plant that was illegal to transport across state lines? I suppose I could eat it like a salad. Yecch.

My chances grew slimmer with every tick of the clock.

To my surprise, the crowd turned festive. Almost . . . giddy. "Four minutes!" people chanted. "Four minutes!"

"We can make this happen," said a budtender managing the line. "Please know what you want when you step to the counter!"

Easier said than done. When they reached the counter, many customers seized. Confronted with the widest array of marijuana products most had ever seen, they ordered one of this, and two of that, and oooh! what's that thing over there?, yeah, throw that in the bag too. . . .

"Three minutes!"

Shit. I was not going to make it. I took out my phone and snapped a couple selfies.

"Come on!" cried a woman behind me. "We can do it!"

"Cash is quicker!" a budtender shouted.

Andy Williams grinned and checked his watch. "Go! Go!" he told a customer, pointing to a waiting budtender.

"Two minutes!"

There was a chance. Two people stood in front of me. They were a couple. They cleared together.

A budtender waved at me from across the way. I locked eyes and sprinted to him.

"I just need a couple of joints," I said.

"Seven dollars each," he said.

"Yes. Done."

His cash register hadn't worked for the past hour, he told me. I would have to pay over at the medicinal side of the store. I crossed open ground. I stood behind a couple finishing their selections. And . . . finishing. And . . . finishing.

"One minute!"

Holy Christ would you buy your fucking weed already, I did not say.

"Two sixty-seven forty-two," the budtender told them. The couple paused. The woman fumbled in her purse for . . . *dear God, no!* . . . a debit card.

The budtender slid the card through the reader. And waited.

"Fifteen seconds!"

My eyes bugged out of my skull. *Just two goddamn joints!* I waved a $20 bill above my head.

"Can I pay for this?"

"Sorry," the budtender said. "The register only takes one sale at a time. It's part of the tracking system."

"Ten . . . nine . . . eight . . ."

I stared at the opaque package that held my two joints. So near.

". . . three . . . two . . . one!"

"We're done!" yelled Andy Williams.

The $267.42 sale went through. My $14 joint purchase did not.

I slunk out of the store empty-handed.

Outside it was dark and snowing. Peaceful.

I drove away slowly. Before reaching my hotel I stopped at a Walgreens to pick up some batteries for my tape recorder.

As I stood at the kiosk debating with myself—Duracell or Energizer? Energizer or Duracell?—a woman in her 30s burst through the front door. A faint whiff of skunk attended her.

She charged the register clerk.

"DO YOU HAVE NILLA WAFERS?" she said. Not angry. Desperate.

The clerk and I shared a glance. "I think . . ." he said—

"NILLA. WAFERS. THEM COOKIES," she said.

"Try aisle seven," he said.

I waited, wanting to see the end of her show.

I suddenly became aware of the Muzak playing around us. "No Rain," the old Blind Melon hit. *And I don't understand why I sleep all day . . . .*

She reappeared clutching two boxes of toasted-brown cookies.

"Yeah!" she said, pleased with her triumph.

The woman paid for her cookies and trundled off into the night.

The next day I stopped by Sean Azzariti's condo in south Denver. I wanted to talk with him away from the crush of reporters.

"Come on in," he said. "I just got off work."

Azzariti lived in a typical bachelor's condo. A couch, an extremely large television, last night's pizza box on the kitchen counter. A dabbing rig sat on his coffee table. It looked like a tiny hookah. Next to it was a copy of that morning's *USA Today*. A photo of Azzariti holding the nation's first bag of legal weed played across page one, top of the fold.

He lit a small torch. The sound was unnerving, yet I found myself drawn to its miniature roar, something so dangerous and tiny, like a bonsai rocket flame.

"Do you partake?" Azzariti asked.

"Not today," I said. "Still got some work to do."

Azzariti painted the flame across the metal dabbing nail until it glowed orange. He squeezed a dollop of concentrated cannabis oil on the end of a metal dabbing rod, then touched oil to nail. The oil vaporized instantly. Azzariti inhaled, held the vapor, then let it go. A moment passed.

I asked if he'd recovered from the events of the previous day. He laughed.

"Quite the shit show, wasn't it?" he said. "I think my favorite picture is this one where the photographer's got his camera resting on my mom's head."

His smartphone squirted out one of those R2-D2 duck farts. He ignored it. "Just a text," he said. "Another request."

"Interview requests? Friend requests?" I asked.

"Both," he said. "I got 60-some today. Got more than 100 yesterday." He held open his hands and looked at me like, *What can you do?*

I wanted to know how he got here. How a 32-year-old former Marine living in a Denver condo became, for one 24-hour media cycle, the most desired "get" in the news business. Azzariti grew up in the Northeast and joined the Corps a few weeks after high school graduation. It was the summer of 2001. Then came 9/11. His unit didn't see action in Afghanistan, but in 2003 Azzariti shipped out to Iraq. He was a supply specialist and sergeant of the guard.

"What led you to re-up?" I asked. I'm not a military guy, so re-enlisting for combat seemed insane to me.

Azzariti nodded, as if to say, *There's an explanation.* "I had a friend," he said. "We met in boot camp and became roommates, then best friends. I got to know his family. We looked out for each other during that first deployment. His contract was a little longer than mine, and he got called to deploy again just about the time my contract was up. I couldn't let him go back a second time by himself. I felt it was my duty to go with him. I re-enlisted for another two years and we redeployed together."

And survived together, I added in my mind. Full respect.

Azzariti mustered out in October 2006. "What were your plans?" I asked.

"Right after I got out, I got a job developing software for an online college, but I was miserable," he said. "Staring at computers would activate my PTSD."

I asked him to describe what exactly that meant. "For most people who haven't had military experience, it can seem like such a vague catchall term," I said. "What does it actually feel like when it kicks in?"

"With me, it came on gradually over time," he said. "When I first got out, I'd feel a little anxiety or maybe a little extra stressed. Then it would progressively get worse and worse. There'd be a snowballing effect where some days I couldn't leave my house or be social."

"Was it set off by anything in particular?"

"Stress," he said. "I don't have a trigger like loud noises or something.

If I get into a quick, high, fast, stressful mode, that can set it off because it puts me back into that Marine Corps mentality. And then unexpected things, like staring at computers for a long time. I had a job developing software for an online college. I was really successful, doing well, but I was miserable. Staring at the computer would make me ruminate on things. My mind would start racing about how unhappy I was, and it wouldn't stop. I'd wonder whether I should have ever gone into the military, and eventually I'd be questioning every step I'd ever taken in my life. It was crippling. When I'd have a bad episode I'd pull the blinds, shut off the phone, just not talk to anybody for a day or two. I know it's hard to understand if you've never experienced it. It's kind of like describing blue to someone who's blind. But it's real. Even sitting here talking with you about it, my hands are getting a little sweaty."

It got so bad he had to quit his job and enter therapy five days a week. VA doctors put him on heavy meds. "At one point I was taking six milligrams of Xanax, four milligrams of Klonopin, 30 to 50 milligrams of Adderall to keep me awake, and Trazodone at night to help me sleep," he said. He looked at all the pills and knew he had to change. "I was going to become a zombie or die of an overdose," he told me. "So I started experimenting with cannabis."

"On your own?"

"I went through the black market at first. Before I got my medical card. And I noticed that it helped."

"How, exactly?" I replied. This was a point on which I still wasn't convinced. I wondered if medical marijuana users were just smothering their symptoms with a pillow of pot intoxication.

"It took away my anxiety," he said. "I got my card and started learning about what I was putting into my body. It took a while to figure out the right strain and dose. It wasn't an overnight thing. Everyone's different. I use only indica-dominant strains, which are more relaxing, calming. If I smoke sativas it can actually make my symptoms flare up. If I smoke a sativa concentrate it'll throw me into a full-blown PTSD episode. But eventually I figured out my body's chemistry and how it interacts with this substance. And it let me be the normal person that I am now. I'm an outgoing person.

I like to interact with people." Using a certain dose of cannabis, he said, relieved the tension in his head. It stopped his mind from racing. "It's not the cannabis alone," he told me. "I did a lot of therapy as well."

His own experience led Azzariti to a job counseling other patients at a dispensary near Denver's upscale Cherry Creek neighborhood. Kind Love had a reputation as one of the city's cleanest, brightest dispensaries. It shared a shopping center with PetSmart, Starbucks, Walgreens, 24 Hour Fitness, Payless ShoeSource, Wendy's, Wells Fargo bank and an Extended Stay America hotel.

"The place I work is . . ." Azzariti said, pausing. "Well, their mission statement is, they want to be the kind of place you could bring your mother and your grandmother. That's a big thing for them. So you try to put people at ease, talk with them, ask what brought them in today, joke with them a little, let them know you're not in any kind of rush; you're just here to help. I've been to a lot of places that aren't like that. It's more like you're bothering them. I had one older lady come in; she must have been in her 60s, and she'd just walked out of another dispensary. She'd been asking the kinds of questions any newcomer would have, and the guy behind the counter actually told her he'd help her if she did a little dance for him. Literally, that's what he said to her!" Azzariti shook his head. "In this business, we've got to be nurturing with everybody. We're going to have to accept the idea that it's going to take some people more time to get comfortable with legal cannabis. And that's OK. It's only the second day."

———————

Later that evening I laid down 20 bucks at Denver Kush Club—I happened to be in the neighborhood—and pocketed two joints. It was not an especially pleasant experience. The Kush Club had embraced a hard-core urban aesthetic. Graffiti decorated the walls. The budtenders were . . . well, they were not Sean Azzariti.

In 2014, hundreds of thousands of tourists would stop in at retail pot shops to make exactly the same purchase. A little souvenir bud or joint. Just for fun.

Then came the challenge: where to smoke it.

Smoking cannabis in public is illegal in Colorado. It's also against the law to smoke anything—tobacco or pot—in an indoor public space. That rules out bars and hotel rooms. At the front desk of the Denver Quality Inn the manager posted a sign warning of all the ways he would kick the ass—up, down, sideways and out the door—of anyone caught smoking weed in his family-friendly establishment.

So where are you supposed to partake?

There was an abandoned Denny's next to the Quality Inn. After dark, I shuffled over to the side of the building. I put flame to joint. I inhaled.

Check left. Check right. Nobody near me, I puffed and puffed. I held the smoke deep in my lungs for as long as I could. I'd taken a hit on that passed joint on New Year's Eve, but it did nothing for me. It was an auntie-peck kiss of pot smoking.

On one long draw the smoke seemed to crack my windpipe. Or the top of my lungs. I wasn't sure. *Ow. Ow ow ow.* Throat and chest burning. I hacked a horrible cough. Mucus flowed into my mouth. My breathing system wanted to expel the poison. How glad I was not to be in the company of experienced pot smokers. *Hack, hack, hack.* Sandpaper to the lungs. Cool air calmed the attack. I took shorter tokes on the joint. Still the hurt stayed in my lungs like a burning web. Fuck! I didn't know whether the problem was my smoking technique or the poor quality of the weed. Either way, Kush Club had seen the last of my business.

As the doobie smoldered down to a nub, I wandered back to the Quality Inn.

Head check. Anything? Nothing. Damn.

I waited for the elevator. The lobby, jammed with all-night ravers on New Year's Eve, now sat empty.

Something must have happened on the way up.

The elevator stopped. The doors opened. A recorded voice said, "Fifth! Floor."

Oh. My. God.

That was the most beautiful thing I'd heard in, in, I don't know how long. "Fifth! Floor." The way she sang it. The tone. Gorgeous.

I had to hear it again. I rode the elevator down to the lobby. Pushed

1 through 5. The other numbers were nice. But none as sublime as five. "Fifth! Floor." Yes! Woman, make me weep.

I made my way to my room. It took a while. Time slowed. *I am walking and enjoying the walking down the carpeted hallway. Pleasant, the walking. Yes, me and the walking and all.* This is what looped in my head.

Keycard, open door, straight to the bed.

I wrote down the time: 10:14 p.m.

My hands felt strangely heavy, like they'd been weighted down as part of some sort of interval training. The burning sensation in the chest continued. I wondered if I'd done some permanent damage there.

My mind began to embark on a kind of pot-induced walkabout. I opened my Mac and began to type whatever thoughts came into my head. This is what came out:

> What would be the most beautiful type font?
> Sounds of a train off in the distance. Made me think of Kerouac and Neal Cassady riding the rails, and how Denver becomes a minor character in *On the Road*, something compelling about its position as the First Western City. I looked out the window. Lights of the city. How they twinkled.
> Ugh! The ugly double curtain of Room 509.
> No, wait, the curtains arc okay. They're beautiful in their own way. The lacy under one and the rough thick outer one. Nice. Now I've sexualized the Quality Inn curtains. Ugly! Pretty!
> Ugly and Pretty are quarreling. Stop fighting, Ugly and Pretty! I hate it when you fight.
> I really dislike microwave oven clocks.
> Must keep the cell phone turned off. I don't want to talk. And I would be incredibly annoying. (In the original, I wrote that as "incredibly ennoying." That's enraging and annoying.)
> 10:37 p.m. Lung burn is subsiding.

Turn on the TV. They're broadcasting an old AC/DC concert. The boys are slamming through a song as Phil Rudd, the drummer, smokes an entire cigarette, flailing his way through the crashes and rolls. This strikes me as an amazing feat of willpower and technique. Not once does he pause to remove the fag. Just keeps on smoking. It sticks there on his lip like a mustache. Phil Rudd you are amaaaazing.

10:40 now though it feels like a long time has passed. Like an hour.

This is far past high. This is *stoned*. And it is quite pleasurable.

Who's got something to eat around here? Mmm, pretzel crisps.

A wrinkled brown paper bag would make an awesome Jeff Koons sculpture.

What time is it? 10:48. You're shitting me! Gad it felt like . . . well not like *hours* but many more minutes than eight have passed.

Pretzel crisps. They're thin and bladey. Like they could cut you.

Y'know, some pretzel crisps look kind of like a mask. A scary mask. I will *eat you*, scary mask. Now who's scared, eh? That brown paper bag: Now I'm seeing it more as a Frank Gehry museum than a Koons sculpture. A museum of . . . product packaging! I would go to that museum. See packaging through the ages. Sheep's bladders. Burlap sacks. A tin can from World War One.

11:16. Stoned for an hour! Getting sleepy. I've got to—

The next morning I woke up with my laptop open and all my clothes on, including my shoes.

THIS IS YOUR
BRAIN ON POT

What the hell was that?

Seriously. What just happened to my brain?

Yes, I know, I got stoned. Fine. Let's move ahead. Let's talk about the scientific processes involved in my experience between 10:14 and 11:16 on the night of Jan. 2.

The past 20 years have seen tremendous growth in neuroscience, the study of the brain and nervous system. We now have the technical tools that allow us to peer into the electrical and chemical workings of the mind, the body and the systems that regulate, propel, excite, depress, harm and heal us. Some of that knowledge has to do with marijuana's effect on the body and brain.

Here's what we know. The brain's pleasure circuitry is profoundly complex, but one of the main control boxes exists in the ventral tegmental area (VTA), a pea-size cluster of neurons near the spot where the spinal cord connects with the brain. The VTA plays a vital role in cognition, motivation, pleasure, orgasm, feelings of love, and drug addiction.

When activated, the VTA sends electrical impulses out into the brain along fibers known as axons. Axon terminals are storehouses of neurotransmitters, amino acid molecules that control everything from muscle contraction to appetite, mood and pain. So far, more than 60 different types of neurotransmitters have been identified, and researchers continue to look for more.

Dopamine is the primary neurotransmitter responsible for feelings of pleasure. VTA-sent impulses trigger the release of dopamine molecules, which spill out into the gap between the axon terminal and the end of a receiving neuron. It's like this: Imagine hundreds of swimmers diving into a river from the northern shore. Some of the swimmers make it to the southern shore, resulting in a jolt of pleasure. Not all of the swimmers make it, though. Many return to the northern shore, where they're re-absorbed into the axon terminal.

Psychoactive drugs alter this process. Cocaine, for example, blocks the reuptake of dopamine by the axon terminal. In *Bright Lights, Big City*, Jay McInerney famously called cocaine "Bolivian marching powder," and in this case it's like the Bolivian army standing at the northern shore with long pikes, forcing all the swimmers over to the other side. The result: a stronger and longer jolt of pleasure. Antidepressants like Prozac, Zoloft and my preferred brand, Celexa, act by similarly inhibiting the reuptake of the neurotransmitter serotonin, which is involved in mood regulation. Heroin is a central-nervous-system depressant. It mimics neurotransmitters known as endorphins, which block pain and enhance pleasure throughout the body. Unfortunately, heroin can relax the central nervous system too much. Most heroin deaths are caused when the user nods out, brain function slows and the body forgets to keep breathing.

Cannabis is complicated. The plant's main psychoactive ingredient—delta-9-tetrahydrocannabinol, or THC—wasn't known to science until 1964, when an Israeli biochemist named Raphael Mechoulam isolated and identified it in his lab. Mechoulam went on to identify the plant's other major constituents, which he named cannabinoids. Of those cannabinoids, only THC caused the psychoactive response marijuana is famous for. But Mechoulam noted early on that another constituent, cannabidiol (CBD), produced a variety of medically promising effects. In 1988 American scientists discovered that the human body contains specific neurotransmitter receptors to which cannabinoids like THC and CBD bind. Those receptors exist because the body produces its own natural cannabinoids, known as endocannabinoids, that serve to modulate emotions, pain, memory, appetite and other systems. The more researchers looked into it, the more complex and profound the endocannabinoid system's regulatory effect on the body seemed to be.

Is it crazy that of all the plants in the vegetable kingdom, only this particular species produces cannabinoids that so precisely mimic the human body's own? Yes, but only in the same amazing way that certain species of poppies produce opiates that mimic human endorphins. Johns Hopkins University neuroscientist David Linden has observed that endocannabinoids "are the brain's own cannabis in the same sense that the endorphins are the brain's own morphine."

This is where it gets tricky. Remember VTA, the neuron cluster that sends the dopamine-release signals? Well, the body has checks and balances to regulate the VTA. One of them is gamma-aminobutyric acid, an amino acid known by its acronym GABA. GABA is an inhibitory neurotransmitter, which means it has a calming effect on the VTA. GABA cautions the VTA to moderate its release of dopamine impulses.

The endocannabinoid system, in turn, regulates the release of GABA. When THC molecules enter the body, they bind to endocannabinoid receptors. Those receptors believe they're being told to slow the flow of GABA. With less GABA around to moderate the VTA, the VTA goes a little overboard with the dopamine signals. More dopamine, ergo more pleasure.

Because it isn't a central-nervous-system depressant like heroin, marijuana contains no risk of death by overdose. There are no recorded deaths from marijuana overdose. None. Zero. That doesn't mean users can't overserve themselves and trigger a psychotic episode, which is the medical term for a bad trip. It just means the drug itself won't set off a deadly system shutdown.

That explains the pleasure of the trip. What about the other distortions? Time dilation, for example. Charles Richet, a 19th-century French doctor, was one of many early cannabis users to note the perceptible slowing of the clock. "With hashish the notion of time is completely overthrown," he wrote. "The moments are years, and the minutes are centuries; but I feel the insufficiency of language to express this illusion, and I believe that one can only understand it by feeling it for himself." This expansion of time, the feeling that each second opens and stretches and invites some looking around, was a major part of the drug's appeal to jazz musicians in the 1930s and 1940s. Time, measures, beats— these were the rooms in which they swung, and marijuana pushed the walls back and gave the players more space to move, dance and explore. One of the best descriptions of the phenomenon was captured, ironically, by James Munch, a pharmacology consultant for the narcotics bureau. Munch told Larry Sloman, author of the cannabis history *Reefer Madness*, that marijuana "lengthens the sense of time, and therefore [jazz musicians] could get more grace beats into their music . . . In other words, if you are a musician you're going to play the thing the way it is printed on a sheet. But if you're using marijuana, you're going to work in about twice as much music in between the first note and the second note. That's what made jazz musicians." Research has established that cannabis alters the cognitive functioning of memory, but scientists haven't yet done the research to find the neurological causes behind the phenomenon of time dilation.

About those pretzel crisps. It's long been known that marijuana suppresses nausea and stimulates the appetite. That's why chemo patients use it and why Jack in the Box runs late-night ads featuring heavy-lidded dudes ordering 30 tacos. Researchers are only now starting to uncover the scientific reasons behind the munchies. Recently an Italian neuroscientist found that THC stimulated receptors in the olfactory bulbs of mice, increasing their ability to smell food and their eagerness to eat it. Other researchers have found that THC, interacting with cannabinoid receptors in the hypothalamus, spurred the production of the hunger-stimulating hormone ghrelin. UC Irvine pharmacology professor Daniele Piomelli recently discovered that endocannabinoid receptors in the intestine also affect feelings of hunger and satiety. Researchers have long suspected that breaking the code behind the munchies could lead to a spectacular weight-loss drug. One such drug, Acomplia, briefly came to market in Europe. Marketed as an obesity fighter, Acomplia reduced feelings of hunger by blocking cannabinoid receptors in the brain and body. The drug was never approved by the U.S. Food and Drug Administration, though, and its manufacturer ultimately pulled it from the shelves in Europe due to concern over increased anxiety and depression in some users.

———————

The mechanism of marijuana's psychotropic effects also carries implications for its addiction risk. In his book *The Compass of Pleasure*, neuroscientist David Linden puts it this way. "Those psychoactive drugs that strongly activate the dopamine-using medial forebrain pleasure circuit (like heroin, cocaine, and amphetamines) are the very ones that carry a substantial risk of addiction," he writes, "while the drugs that weakly activate the pleasure circuit (like alcohol and cannabis) carry a smaller risk of addiction."

Here are the generally accepted addiction rates for some of America's best-known drugs. Of all the people who try injected heroin, approximately 23 percent go on to become addicted. For cocaine, the rate is 17 percent. For alcohol, it's 15 percent. For marijuana, it's between 7 and 9 percent, although those rates increase the younger a person starts smoking pot. None of these is the most addictive drug in America, though. The unrivaled champion is tobacco. One in three people who try cigarettes becomes addicted.

The comparative death rates are astonishing in their imbalance. According to the Centers for Disease Control and Prevention, cigarettes cause 440,000 deaths every year. Forty-six thousand Americans die from alcohol-related causes. About 3,000 die from heroin overdoses. Nearly 17,000 die from overdoses of prescription opioids like OxyContin. Zero die from marijuana overdose.

Within the drug reform movement and recovery culture, there's a heated debate about whether marijuana is addictive. Most of the people I've encountered in the cannabis industry scoff at the notion. Professionals in the recovery industry think that attitude is a self-serving delusion.

The existence, nonexistence and definition of marijuana addiction matter. Legalization's continued rollout, or its halt, will turn in part on the public's perception of how legality affects marijuana addiction rates. An addiction spike in Colorado and Washington could derail the entire movement.

That's unlikely to happen. In fact, marijuana addiction rates might actually fall in legalized states.

Here's why. Marijuana addiction rates are often calculated using the number of people in drug rehab for pot. Right now those numbers are skewed. Fifty-eight percent of all people in marijuana rehab are there to serve out a drug-court deferral. In other words, they were arrested for possession. Given a choice between jail and rehab, they chose the latter. Most of these people aren't addicted to marijuana. They're just among the unlucky 650,000 Americans still popped for simple possession every year. Another 15 percent are in pot rehab because their parents sent them there. Many of those kids probably aren't addicted to marijuana. Their parents caught them smoking, freaked out and packed the kid off to residential rehab.

In Colorado and Washington nearly all of those court-ordered rehab deferrals have disappeared because nobody is getting arrested for possession. No adults, I mean. Underage rates may rise for related reasons—not necessarily because kids have greater access to pot but because the police can ignore the adults and focus their enforcement efforts on illegal underage use.

But let's get back to the meat of the matter. Is marijuana addictive? Ryan Vandrey, a Johns Hopkins University behavioral psychologist, and Margaret Haney, a clinical neurobiologist at Columbia University, collaborated in 2010 on a systematic look at the evidence. Their conclusion: marijuana addiction exists. It's not as deadly and all-consuming as heroin addiction, and it's not as innocuous as caffeine addiction. Vandrey and Haney concluded that "it appears clear that a subset of marijuana users meet the criteria for a diagnosis of drug dependence (addiction) as described in the *Diagnostic and Statistical Manual of Mental Disorders*," the standard reference for the diagnosis of psychiatric conditions.

I once heard J. Michael Bostwick, a clinical psychiatrist at the Mayo Clinic, offer a succinct definition of addiction. "When I see a patient," he said, "I don't weigh their personality type and brain chemistry. I ask, 'Is your life screwed up? How are your relationships doing? How are you doing in school? How are you doing at work?'" If a drug is negatively affecting those circumstances, he said, then his patient has a substance abuse problem.

A pot grower from Texas once told me something along similar lines. "If you're using cannabis to engage with the world, that's good," he said. "If you're using it to disengage from the world, that's not so good."

According to Vandrey and Haney, the criteria that cut to the heart of the matter centered on the question posed by Bostwick. Between 3 and 8 percent of current users "report that their marijuana use has caused problems at school, work, or home, strained interpersonal relationships, or caused a reduction in social, occupational, or recreational activities."

That corresponded with the findings of Roger Roffman, one of the nation's most experienced marijuana dependency researchers. Roffman, a professor of social work at the University of Washington, studied marijuana dependency for more than 25 years. His conclusion: "Most people who use pot occasionally do not become dependent," he wrote. "But that doesn't mean it's impossible to become dependent on pot."

I met Roffman for lunch one day in Seattle's University District and put the question to him directly: Is there such a thing as marijuana addiction?

He nodded. "I'm aware of the power that the word *addiction* holds in the context of politics and the current legalization debate," he told me. "And I say *addiction* very clearly when it comes to marijuana." If we're going to legalize, he said, we've got to face up to all the consequences, negative and positive. Over his career he saw plenty of addicted pot smokers. They typically tried pot at 15, used daily at 19, got high for six hours a day, and tried and failed to quit an average of six times before succeeding. When pot interferes with your job or alienates your spouse and you still can't quit it, that's addiction.

Roffman, by the way, was one of the sponsors of Washington's legalization initiative. "There are many excellent reasons to legalize marijuana," he told me. "But it is not a harmless drug."

I'm hesitant to say that habitual pot smoking is a problem only if it's causing trouble in one's day-to-day functioning. Most adults of a certain age have known functioning alcoholics in their lives, and their functionality is often buoyed by a deep and unnoticed sea of emotional harm suffered by those around them. It might be the same with cannabis. Years ago my wife's old college friend, Alex, told her that his father had just dropped a bomb on his family. His dad revealed that for 20 years he'd smoked marijuana on the sly at work and at home. For most of Alex's childhood, his father, who ran one of the biggest advertising agencies in Chicago, had been high. He did it, he told his son, because he felt marketing wasn't a worthwhile use of his life. The revelation floored Alex. A profound sense of disappointment and betrayal ran through him. Alex is a producer at *This American Life*, and years later he wrote about it for the radio show. "My dad was a good dad," he said. "He read to us every night, took us on long hikes in search of snakes and salamanders to keep as pets. But his drug use did leave at least one lasting effect on me. I can't hear any story about a seemingly functional pothead with anything but a skeptical ear." Alex couldn't help but suspect that people who are functionally high are running from something. "And there's always at least one person wondering," he said, "is that something me?"

14

THESE ARE REASONS
TO KEEP IT ILLEGAL

Colorado's rollout caused no ruckus. There were no fights, no robberies, no underage arrests, no dabbing tourists vomiting all over their hotel rooms. This did not come as a shock to most people. Still, a certain segment of the population found it incredible that Denver hadn't erupted in a citywide crime riot. A few days after returning home, I heard that Mason Tvert was going to be on Nancy Grace's show on the HLN network. I tuned in to catch the fireworks.

"Also with us, Mason TUH-vert, communications director of the Marijuana Policy Project," said the helmet-coiffed host. The control room split the screen into three panels: Tvert on the right, Nancy Grace in the middle, and some anti-marijuana fellow on the left.

"Mason. Let's first ask you: What is the 'Marijuana Policy Project,'" she said, exercising finger quotations, "and do you get *paid* by them?"

Tvert was an old hand at this game. "Well, yeah, that's my job," he said. "Our goal is to end marijuana prohibition and replace it with a system where marijuana is regulated and taxed and treated similarly to alcohol. It's a system that a majority of Americans now think would be a much preferable system to the one that we have."

"Well, OK, yeah, and again, in a nutshell if you could, you think that marijuana should be legalized because, why?" Grace asked. "I mean, you do know it's addictive. *Highly* addictive. Right?"

"Well, marijuana's addictive properties have been found to be pretty mild compared to not only alcohol and tobacco but even caffeine, so . . ."

Grace broke in. "Sir, are you admitting that it *is* addictive?"

"Yeah; so is sex; so are video games," said Tvert. "I think what's apparent is that you do not like the people who use marijuana."

Grace began to shout. "I completely disagree with you!"

"The fact is, you don't like people who use marijuana and you want to see them punished," Tvert said. "But they're normal people just like you. They enjoy using marijuana for the same reasons people like having a drink after work, and they shouldn't be made criminals for it."

At this point Nancy Grace trained her Stare of Contempt Unto Death upon Mason Tvert. The guy in the third panel watched the proceedings like he was ringside at WrestleMania.

"Actually," Grace said, "the reason I'm against pot is that I've seen too many *felonies*, and I don't mean pot sales . . . I mean people on pot that shoot each other, strangle each other, kill families, *wipe out a whole family!*"

Tvert slowly shook his head. "You sound like someone from the 1930s," he said.

———

It was time for me to talk to the other side. I'd spent so much time coming up to speed on the new marijuana world that I hadn't done my due diligence. I wanted to talk, seriously, with the leading voice against marijuana legalization. So I got hold of Kevin Sabet.

In the early months of 2014, Sabet seemed to be everywhere. His confident baritone purred out of NPR news shows. His op-eds appeared in dozens of newspapers. His round, jaunty face filled the half-screen of countless he-said-she-said TV yakkers. He toured like a pop singer. This was his schedule for the first three months of the year:

Jan. 7–8 Washington State • Jan. 13–16 Oregon • Jan. 21–22 New York City • Jan. 23–24 Missouri • Jan. 30 New Hampshire • Feb. 3–6 Washington, D.C. • Feb. 7 Salt Lake City • Feb. 10 Hartford • Feb. 12–13 Minnesota • Feb. 14–22 Hawaii • Feb. 24–25 Tampa • Feb. 25 Miami • Feb. 26 Gainesville • Feb. 27–28 Orlando • March 1–3 Atlanta • March 7 Atlantic City • March 11–21 Vienna

He spoke to Rotary clubs. He spoke to civic forums. He spoke to addiction groups. He spoke to just about any gathering of human beings willing to set a lectern in front of him. In a nation where more and more people saw marijuana legalization as fine and inevitable, Kevin Sabet said, *Hold on. It is not fine. And it is in no way inevitable.*

At 34, Sabet had spent most of his adult life fighting drug abuse. At the age of 21 he had been invited by Gen. Barry McCaffrey, Bill Clinton's drug czar, to work at the White House Office of National Drug Control Policy (ONDCP). After earning a master's degree in public policy at Oxford, he returned to ONDCP under the George W. Bush administration. Sabet took a break in the mid-2000s to earn a Ph.D., then returned to the drug czar's office when Barack Obama took over the White House in 2009. In 2011 he left that post, not over a policy disagreement but because a freak medical event forced him to reconsider how he was spending his days.

Then Nov. 6, 2012, happened. Washington and Colorado went legal. And Sabet realized that almost nobody was pushing back against the forces of legalized marijuana.

He reached out to an old Capitol Hill acquaintance, Patrick Kennedy. Kennedy, son of Sen. Ted Kennedy, championed mental health issues while serving eight terms as a congressman from Rhode Island. Kennedy knew Sabet from his ONDCP days. And he saw legalization as a force working against mental health. Sabet and Kennedy formed Project SAM: Smart Approaches to Marijuana and offered themselves as public speakers and talking heads. When legal pot appeared as an issue, they were ready and eager to argue against it. Salon.com called Sabet the quarterback of the new anti-drug movement. *Rolling Stone* called him the No. 1 enemy of legalization.

I got in touch with Sabet, and we agreed to meet in Portland, Ore., where he was scheduled to speak to a gathering of narcotics officers.

The gathering of narcs was a curiosity in itself. It took place at a hotel in Vancouver, Wash., across the Columbia River from Portland. I arrived expecting Det. Jimmy McNulty and the squad-room dicks from *The Wire*. What I found were a bunch of deckhands from *Deadliest Catch*. The hotel conference room filled with about 75 men wearing black T-shirts, hoodies, jeans, beards, ponytails, sunglasses, tattoos and ball-caps. In other words, men who looked like they might be in the market to score.

"I'm excited to be here in the belly of the beast!" Sabet told the cops. He was 34 but played younger, with a moonish face, caterpillar brows and a boyish layer of plumpness around the midsection. There was nothing of the finger-wagging scold about him.

"What you're doing in Washington and what's going on in Colorado, a lot of people call it a 'grand experiment,' " he said. "I don't like that phrase. An experiment is carefully planned; you adapt as you go along. That's not happening here. This is a reckless policy pushed through by powerful political and financial interests."

The narcs were attentive but unmoved.

Sabet launched into his stump speech, a 90-minute presentation on "Seven Great Myths About Marijuana."

Myth No. 1: Marijuana is harmless and non-addictive. "What we know is that one in six teens who tries marijuana becomes addicted," Sabet said. "That's compared to a one-in-10 rate among adults who try it. Teens have a greater chance of addiction because their brains are under construction; they're just being primed."

Addiction rates were bound to increase, he said, because of the increased potency of today's marijuana. "When we test your seizures of marijuana," Sabet said, giving a nod to the men in the room, "we find an average of 12 to 14 percent THC." I found that . . . low, actually. Weed in Seattle dispensaries typically ranged from 18 to 22 percent.

"Recently I spoke at a high school and used the term 'roach clip,' " Sabet said. "Nobody knew what I was talking about. Now it's all dabbing, waxes and hash oil. That's one of the major disconnects among voters. Adults and policymakers have a memory of marijuana that's not current. The marijuana of today is not the Woodstock weed most adults smoked."

This was old news to the narcs. But they listened patiently.

Sabet hit the mental health angle. "We know the connection between marijuana use and mental illness is very strong," he said. "When you look at the recent mass shootings, the theater shooting in Colorado, the Boston Marathon bombing, it's interesting to look at the marijuana connection."

This seemed a stretch, and Sabet knew it. "I'm not making any claims here, but it's a connection worth exploring."

Next came a short fugue on the theme of national competitiveness. "This is the worst time since the Great Depression to be on the job market," Sabet said. "And this is what we're saying to the younger generation: we don't have a job for you, but we're going to make sure you have plenty of marijuana available to smoke." He paused. "Kids in China, India and Brazil are not smoking marijuana at the rate our kids are smoking."

Myth No. 2: Smoked or eaten marijuana is medicine.

I must confess that when this PowerPoint slide went up, I glanced at my watch and thought, *Oh my God, we're only on Myth Two.*

"We don't smoke opium as medicine," Sabet said. "If it's a medicine, we should dispense it at a pharmacy. Ninety-eight percent of medical marijuana patients smoke it. We don't smoke any other 'medicine.' If it's a drug, let's treat it like any other drug."

He mentioned Sativex and Marinol. "These make a lot more sense to me." Sativex, GW Pharma's THC/CBD inhalant, was still unavailable in America. Marinol, a synthetic THC pill given to cancer patients to control nausea, had been available in the U.S. since 1985. Its main drawback was its form. Vomiting chemo patients often found it easier to smoke pot than to swallow and keep down a pearl-size Marinol pill.

Myth No. 3: Countless people are behind bars for smoking marijuana.

"This is the biggest myth of all," Sabet told the cops. "Why are people in Seattle, the most educated city in the country, voting to legalize marijuana? Because they truly believe that 70 percent of your time is spent going after a guy with a joint in his pocket."

That raised a little chuckle among the narcs.

"By the way: it is almost impossible to find a person now serving in state prison who is there for only smoking a joint."

I frowned as I took down that quote on my legal pad. That simply wasn't true.

———————

Later that night, Sabet and I met at Little Bird, a bistro in downtown Portland. I wanted to find out more about his background, what led him to embrace his role as legalization's number one enemy. He was happy to chat.

"I grew up in Anaheim Hills, just outside of Anaheim in Orange County," he told me. His parents immigrated from Iran in the late '60s. "They're of the Baha'i faith, and they don't drink. We never had alcohol in the house."

A server stopped by to take our order. I had a glass of $10 Cabernet. Sabet had a club soda with a sprig of fresh mint. "I don't drink, so I've become kind of an expert in the mocktail," he said.

I told him I enjoyed his presentation to the narcotics officers. A few things bothered me, though. I told Sabet I'd been researching marijuana laws and prison sentences. "When you talk about it being nearly impossible to find anyone in prison for pot, that's not been my experience," I said. "I've found those people. They exist. There are a lot of people in prison for pot. That aspect of the drug war is ruining lives. It's a problem."

He turned serious.

"It is a problem," he said. "And I'm not diminishing it. What I'm saying is, Why would we think legalization would solve that problem? There are more people in prison for alcohol than for all drugs combined."

"But people aren't getting arrested for possessing alcohol," I said.

That didn't slow Sabet down. "They're getting arrested for violating regulations around alcohol," he said, "which happens when you legalize alcohol and you provide availability and accessibility. In other words, the effect of allowing people to use a substance is that more people are going to get into trouble with that substance and need enforcement action."

People aren't serving 10 years in prison for drinking a bottle of Corona on the beach. That's nonsense. I think what Sabet was referring to is the clear relationship between alcohol and crime. Research by the U.S. Department of Justice has determined that booze is a factor in one quarter to one third of all violent crime. The worse the crime, the more likely the bottle. Alcohol figures in 25 percent of assaults, 37 percent of rapes and 40 percent of murders. People tend to do stupid, angry, regretful things when they're drunk.

"When you have more marijuana users, you're going to have more impaired drivers than you do now," Sabet continued. "You're going to have more people using in public, and you're going to have more people selling to minors."

Wait, what? He seemed to be hopping from one paradigm to the other.

Let's go back to the connection between marijuana and crime for a minute, because I think it's worth exploring.

The causal link between drugs and crime has long been a main driver of our drug laws. And with some drugs it makes sense. Heroin addiction not only ravages the lives of its users, it often drives them to steal in order to support their habit. In the 1930s marijuana was outlawed on the claim that the drug turned inhibitions inside out, made fiends of men and slatterns of women. The La Guardia report debunked that theory in 1944, and research since then has only confirmed the fallacy of the pot-driven criminal.

The problem isn't pot. It's alcohol. In 1994 psychologist Klaus Miczek and his colleagues at Tufts University published an overview of the known research on drugs and crime as part of a National Research Council report on understanding and preventing violent behavior. Miczek and his team found a "persistently overwhelming alcohol-violence link," with alcohol as a causal factor. That is, the booze triggered aggression-specific brain mechanisms. With marijuana they found no such link. All major studies of cannabis and human aggression dating back to the 1970s, they wrote, "conclude that cannabis has no effect on, or actually decreases, various indices of aggression."

Subsequent studies have done nothing to disprove Miczek's conclusions. In 2009 a study in *Addiction Research Report* found that crime statistics initially suggested that pot smoking might be causing criminal activity. But when the researchers looked more closely at the data, they found that the criminal activity mostly consisted of pot smoking. "The association seems to rest on the fact that use, possession and distribution of drugs such as cannabis is illegal," they concluded.

―――――――

Our food arrived. I had the pork shoulder. Sabet tucked into a pair of pork chops.

"Let's talk about the racial disparities in marijuana arrests," I said. "That's one of the main reasons I voted in favor of legalization."

"Sure, let's talk about them," Sabet said. "Why do we think legalization is the way to solve that issue? Can't we fix our current laws to make sure that disproportionality doesn't happen?"

"How do you do that?"

"You make sure your policing practices aren't skewed," he said. "You make sure your arrest practices aren't resulting in low-level offenders serving time or getting a black mark on their record. These are relatively easy fixes you can do without jumping off the cliff and legalizing marijuana."

I killed off the last of the Cabernet.

"I agree to a certain extent," I said. "But it's not easy to change those policing practices. For the past two years the Seattle Police Department has been under federal supervision because of their excessive use of force." We couldn't stop the cops from escalating a simple street stop into a shooting, I said. The culture was too entrenched. The mayor tried to change it, the city council tried to change it, and it didn't change. So the feds had to step in.

Sabet nodded sympathetically.

"I understand," he said, "but why can't we change those ordinances around marijuana possession? Let's not call it a criminal offense. Let's say it gets expunged after a year if you don't have any more offenses. Done! You can do these things. It's a lot easier than passing legalization. If your headlight is broken, fix your headlight. Don't total the car."

My pork shoulder was growing cold.

"Well, the trick is that those sorts of actions have to take place at the level of the state legislature," I said. "That's where you have politicians voting on the record. And they're well aware that their opponents in the next election will run ads broadcasting their support for drug dealers. They'll be branded 'soft on crime' and lose their seats."

Sabet shook his head.

"I think the 'soft on crime' thing is so '80s and '90s," he said. "People who want to reduce criminal justice involvement around marijuana are actually more popular than those who don't. I think the mood has changed. The desire for legalization isn't based on people liking pot. It's based on people not liking how the criminal justice system is working right now. What you're saying was true in the '80s and '90s. But it's different now."

I shook my head. It wasn't so different now. Voters were ahead of politicians on marijuana, but few members of Congress were willing to bet their seat on a vote to ratchet down marijuana penalties. They weren't even interested in voting to allow banks to handle state-legal pot money. Sabet's claims simply didn't correspond with the facts on the ground, no matter how much he wanted them to be true.

15

THE SCHIZOPHRENIA
QUESTION

At a friend's birthday party not long ago I fell into a conversation with an acquaintance I hadn't seen for a few years. Doug was a friend of a friend. His son Josh used to babysit my kids when they were little. (I've changed their names to protect Doug's and Josh's privacy.) Josh was in high school then. Great kid. Polite, thoughtful and a little gawky in that way that makes old people fall a tiny bit in love with the coltishness of teenage boys. He must be, what now, 20?

"Twenty-three," said Doug.

"How's he doing?" I said, expecting to hear about college, girlfriends, a first job.

"Not well, honestly," Doug said. "At the moment he's homeless."

Like . . . couch-surfing homeless? Or *homeless* homeless?

The latter, Doug said.

Oh.

Hell of a thing, Doug told me. Josh went away to college and was doing great. Then he started having these psychotic episodes. Periods when he'd lose touch with reality.

"They started about the time he began to smoke a lot of pot," Doug said. The marijuana seemed to trigger some sort of malfunction in his brain. Josh's mental health deteriorated. He went to see a psychiatrist at the college health center. The doctor advised him to immediately stop smoking dope. Josh promised he would, but he didn't. Things went downhill. He obsessed about tiny slights and perceived humiliations. He got into fights with strangers at bookstores and coffee shops. Imagined girlfriends—women who barely knew his name—had to take out restraining orders. To calm his mind, he smoked more pot. The college eventually asked him to leave. They feared for the safety of other students.

Josh returned home and lived with his parents for a while. Then he went out on his own. He was 19.

"He's his own adult," said Doug. "Legally, we can't do much for him if he doesn't want to get help."

Doug had bailed Josh out of jail more times than he cared to remember. Little stuff: Misdemeanors. Fighting. Shoplifting. Sometimes Josh broke the law in order to go to jail and rest. "When he's in jail he doesn't have to think about what to eat, where to go, how he's going to find a bed to sleep in that night," Doug said.

Doug told me all of this in a calm and accepting voice. It was as if he were telling the story of calamity that had befallen a distant cousin. Clearly he had been through years of work and worry. To raise a kind and beautiful son for 18 years and then watch as he fledges into the open jaws of madness seemed obscenely cruel, like being forced to watch your own child drown.

I asked if Josh had shown any indications prior to college. Doug shook his head. "It's there in our family," he said. "We saw it once we knew what to look for. My grandmother would have episodes of what was then called hysteria. And I've got an uncle who struggles with episodes of mental illness. So there was a genetic disposition. But who thinks to look closely at that when your kid is graduating from high school with honors? That's the kind of stuff families sweep under the rug. Nobody likes to talk about it."

"What about the marijuana?" I said.

"The stuff is like kryptonite to him," Doug said.

At 23, Josh had been diagnosed as bipolar, and it sounded like he was edging toward schizophrenia. He did his best to stay clean. He knew pot was no good for his mind. "But once in a while he'll go out with friends and they'll pass around some pot and he'll partake, you know, to be social and all," said Doug. "It hits him like a train. For a week or two after, I can tell he's smoked. We all can—his mother, his sister. He's . . . off-kilter. Altered."

The experience Doug shared forced me to confront one of my worst fears about marijuana. In 2013 and 2014 there were vague news reports about a possible connection between pot and schizophrenia in young people. With Doug and Josh's experience as a starting point, I began looking into the schizophrenia question. What exactly was the connection between pot smoking and mental illness? Was this just another piece of chicanery from Harry Anslinger's bag of tricks? Or was there more to it? My father's generation had Art Linkletter's daughter seared in their minds. Now I was the father, and I had schizophrenia on the brain. If I was going to pass along the cautionary tale to my own children, I had to know if it was true. More to the point: I had to know *why* it was true.

———

Darold Treffert is one of the world's leading experts on autistic savants. When the producers of *Rain Man* wanted the movie vetted for accuracy, they asked Treffert to give them notes on the script. Before his long career in autism, though, Treffert was known for his expertise in another area. During the 1970s he was one of the world's leading researchers on schizophrenia and psychoactive drugs.

He came to it by accident. As a young psychiatrist in the 1960s, Treffert directed Winnebago State Hospital, the largest mental health institution in Wisconsin. From the mid-'60s to the early '70s, Treffert watched Winnebago's teenage patient population triple in size, reflecting a larger nationwide trend. By early 1972, half of his hospital's 550 patients were under the age of 21.

Many of those young patients struggled with schizophrenia. Fortunately, the anti-psychotic drug Thorazine had come into common use in the mid-'50s. Before then, schizophrenic patients were treated by locking them in asylums and sedating them with tranquilizers or electroshock. Antipsychotics like Thorazine knocked down the worst symptoms and allowed many patients to resume their normal lives.

In the early '70s Treffert began to notice a disturbing pattern among some of his young adult patients. Schizophrenic men and women who had brought their symptoms under control with Thorazine were suffering abrupt relapses. One day they'd be calm; the next day they'd find themselves slipping back into the funhouse of hallucinations, delusions, agitation and paranoia. The trigger seemed to be marijuana.

One case illustrated the pattern. Mr. D, as Treffert called him in a later article, was a bright 24-year-old graduate student at the University of Wisconsin–Madison. During the summer of 1973, D suffered through the worst stages of schizophrenia. In the rare moments when his thoughts weren't jumbled, they coalesced around sexual obsessions and delusional scenarios. By the time he checked himself into the Winnebago Mental Health Institute, D was sobbing uncontrollably.

Treffert discovered his patient was a frequent flyer: D estimated he'd tripped at least 100 times on LSD or mescaline. He mixed in a steady supply of marijuana and amphetamines.

Under Treffert's direction, D went off the recreational stuff and got himself onto a carefully dosed regimen of antipsychotic medications. By and by, he recovered. The hospital discharged him, and he resumed daily life. A little more than a year later, D had been weaned off the antipsychotics and returned to his graduate studies.

That's when he started back up with the pot.

D's marijuana use quickly escalated to three or four times a week. He became increasingly agitated and developed a delusional scenario involving United Nations Secretary-General Kurt Waldheim. D possessed enough mental cohesion to purchase a plane ticket and board a flight to Newark, where he planned to meet with Waldheim.

He never made it to New Jersey. His agitation and delusional cycling erupted in a midflight psychotic outburst. The pilot diverted the plane and had D arrested. After his transfer back to Winnebago, D returned to the care of Dr. Treffert.

The doctor asked if he'd gone back to the psychedelics.

Only marijuana, D said.

Nothing else? No alcohol?

No, D told him. Just pot.

After looking over his case files and inquiring with other doctors at Winnebago, Treffert spotted a pattern. A number of patients with controlled and clearly documented schizophrenia had suffered relapses after smoking marijuana. After culling cases with multiple variables (patients who had also used alcohol or other drugs), he found four patients in whom marijuana touched off a recurrence of psychotic episodes. One patient described marijuana as "ungluing" him.

Treffert's research, published in the *American Journal of Psychiatry*, alerted the medical world to the dangers of marijuana in patients dealing with schizophrenia. "Perhaps some persons can safely use marijuana," he wrote, "but schizophrenics cannot."

———

I tracked down Darold Treffert in Fond du Lac, Wis. He's now in his 80s, and he continues to see patients. He was pleased to discuss his early work. "Nowadays people exclaim, *My God—look what we've discovered!* about the hazards of marijuana and schizophrenia," he told me on the phone. "But we knew it back then."

Mental health professionals in the '60s saw plenty of bad trips. Psychiatrists exchanged shop talk about marijuana as a psychotic trigger. But there were no studies to back up the anecdotal accounts.

Once a patient was aware of marijuana's specific toxicity, I asked, why did he keep smoking it?

"They wanted to feel good," Treffert said. "There's always that allure with marijuana." Depression is a common symptom of schizophrenia. Sometimes a person just wants to take a two-hour vacation from his own head. "Patients will rationalize it. They figure it's the safest thing to take compared to psychedelics or heroin."

Treffert's research established that marijuana could trigger a psychotic relapse in people already diagnosed with schizophrenia. But could pot smoking actually *cause* schizophrenia?

He couldn't tell me. "I specifically avoided that question," Treffert said. "I didn't have enough clear data. Many of our patients had their first psychosis after using a variety of controlled substances. LSD was more popular at that time. So I didn't have enough 'pure culture' cases to make a judgment."

Could you make a judgment now? I asked.

"You mean of those kids that came into Winnebago, how many would never have been psychotic if they'd never used marijuana?" he said. "I can't answer that in a scientific way. But I'm convinced there were some."

————————

Here's what we know about the developing brain. During infancy and childhood, brain growth is all about volume. Above the neck, the body has one job: make more. More gray matter, more white matter, more neurons, synapses and dendrites. A newborn's brain is about one third the size of an adult's. It takes years to grow into full three-pound maturity.

With the onset of adolescence, development shifts from raw growth to the refinement of neural pathways. If the brain were a house, the childhood years would be spent pouring the foundation and framing up the walls. Adolescence is when the wiring and plumbing get finished. During this period the volume of gray matter in the brain actually declines because those network connections are refined and strengthened through pruning. At the end of childhood the brain finds itself overstocked with synapses, axons and dendrites, the mechanisms that transmit and receive electrical signals. So a thinning occurs. The brain takes inventory. The strong are selected and preserved. The weak are culled. The process, according to Columbia University psychiatrist Gregory Tau, enhances the "efficiency and fidelity of signal transmission." In other words: less noise, more signal.

This synaptic thinning doesn't occur in one great purge. It plays out in fits and starts. It's constrained by our genes and shaped by our lived experience. Nobody knows exactly when certain types of thinning occur. Brain researchers use the term "sensitive period" to describe these discrete moments during which certain mental capacities or capabilities are fixed. Within those sensitive periods there are "critical periods" that result in irreversible changes in brain functioning. The Nobel-winning animal behavioralist Konrad Lorenz invented the "critical period" concept to describe the brief stage, 13 to 16 hours after hatching, when geese imprint on the first moving stimulus they see. (The mother goose, or a dog, or Lorenz's boots.) Stanford neuroscientist Eric Knudsen and others have applied Lorenz's "critical period" concept to brain development. Once the critical period ends, Knudsen writes, the particular brain function "does not change with subsequent experience."

The best we know about schizophrenia is that it's caused by some sort of breakdown or wrongly flipped switch that occurs during one or more of these sensitive periods during adolescence. Just as the brain is finishing its final wiring, in other words, some wires get crossed.

Why? It's partly nature, partly nurture. Genes play a role. Some researchers believe a genetic predisposition accounts for as much as 85 percent of schizophrenia. Scientists have yet to identify a single genetic marker, though, in part because it's believed that inherited susceptibility to schizophrenia is caused by disruptive mutations across many different genes. But we've known for nearly a century that your chances of suffering from schizophrenia increase greatly if a relative has a known history of the illness. Schizophrenia occurs in 1 percent of the population but in 46 percent of people with a biological mother and father who both suffered from the disease.

Heredity isn't destiny, though. Environmental stressors come into play. Schizophrenia is more likely to occur among young adults of lower socioeconomic status, who suffer from poor nutrition, live in big cities, and are socially isolated or endure the psychological harm of endemic racism. (Yes. Racism can literally drive you crazy.) Young men and women who have experienced the death of a parent are at increased risk of developing schizophrenia, as are adolescents who regularly smoke marijuana.

The research on that last point is pretty unequivocal. Soon after publishing his Winnebago observations, Darold Treffert diverted his attention to the study of autistic savants. But a few others picked up the scent.

In the mid-1980s a group of researchers at Sweden's Karolinska Institute got their hands on two rich data sets. The first came from the Swedish military. In 1969, more than 50,000 conscripts (about 85 percent of the country's 18-year-old population) entered compulsory military service. The army had each soldier fill out a detailed questionnaire about their upbringing, schooling, home life and drug use. The drug questions were unusually specific: which drugs, when they started, how much they used, for how long, etc. Fifteen years later, scientists at the Karolinska Institute compared that data with Sweden's national register of psychiatric care, which contained all inpatient admissions in the country's nationalized health care system.

What they found was striking. Of the 41,280 conscripts who had never smoked marijuana, 197, or 0.5 percent, had been diagnosed with schizophrenia. Among the 752 who self-identified as heavy users (smoked pot more than 50 times before age 19), 21 had become schizophrenic. That was nearly 3 percent, a sixfold increase in risk. The risk seemed to increase with consumption rates. Those who used pot rarely (fewer than 10 times) had only a slightly elevated risk. Those who used at least occasionally (11 to 50 times) were diagnosed with schizophrenia at three times the rate of their non-using peers.

Further research confirmed the correlation. By 2010, nearly a dozen independent studies had established cannabis use as an important risk factor. The problem was, none of those studies could prove causation. One of the first maxims that every student of science and statistics learns is: correlation does not imply causation. In 1970 young men with long hair were more likely to smoke marijuana than men with short hair. That didn't mean marijuana caused long hair.

The authors of the Swedish conscript study wrote, in fact, that cannabis consumption might cause schizophrenia to emerge—but it was also possible that cannabis consumption might be caused by an emerging schizophrenia.

When I read that, I couldn't help but recall the "self-medicating schizophrenics" who delivered their pot plants to Jeff Gilmore, the old pot farmer. If diagnosed schizophrenics turned to marijuana to escape their depression and feel better—even at the risk of throwing gasoline onto their smoldering condition—perhaps those predisposed to the illness were also drawn to the drug.

I put the question to Michael Compton, chairman of psychiatry at Lenox Hill Hospital on Manhattan's Upper East Side. He's one of the nation's leading researchers on substance abuse and the earliest phases of schizophrenia.

"It's possible," he said, though his voice registered as skeptical. "Maybe young people destined to have early onset psychosis have a genetic makeup that somehow drives them toward greater use of marijuana at a young age."

"However," he continued, "since there's research to suggest that there really is something biological about the tendency for marijuana to be associated with psychosis, when we put all the evidence together I have some reason to believe the association might well be causal."

———————

Around the time I was looking into marijuana and brain development, I paid a visit to Dr. Erickson, my physician. I'd survived a bout of pneumonia some months previous, and I wanted to make sure my lungs had recovered. As he listened to me breathe, we got to talking about my marijuana project. I still hadn't confessed my procurement of an MMJ card. But I wanted to know how the medical research on marijuana and the adolescent brain filtered down to doctors who treated dozens of patients a day.

"I'm kind of having an ongoing conversation with our kids about it," I said. "In the same way we're talking with them about alcohol."

Dr. Erickson seemed taken aback.

"Ah, but it's not like alcohol," he said.

"How?"

"Teenagers are going to experiment with various aspects of their lives," he said. "They're trying to figure out who they are; they're curious about things like alcohol, drugs and sex. When I talk to them, I want to be realistic. I want to be their ally. But I'm not their best buddy. I'm the person who's supposed to keep them alive and safe. The main things I tell them are to do everything in moderation and don't make big decisions under the influence of any drug. About marijuana, I say, lay off until you're 25 or 26."

"That late? Really?"

"Yes! That late," he said. "Because your frontal cortex keeps developing until that late in life."

He plucked the stethoscope from his ears.

"In a funny way," he said, "alcohol is a more dangerous drug later in life, as we approach our senior years, because of the way it affects memory loss. And marijuana is such a more dangerous drug early in life because of the developing brain. Everything I read—about IQ loss, and the sensitivities of the brain—leads me to caution young people to stay away from it."

He added that there were plenty of problems with underage drinking, of course. As a doctor he encountered many of them firsthand.

I asked him what he made of the possible connection between marijuana and schizophrenia. "That's a tough one," he said. "I liken it more to people who have seizures. It may be that they're able to go without seizures for a long time, and then they hit some kind of imbalance or threshold where the seizures kick in. With some people, they may have a tendency toward schizophrenia just below a certain threshold, and then using marijuana can kick them up above that threshold."

"So," he said, signaling the end of our appointment, "I say don't use it at all. And if you're going to try it, wait until you're 25 or 26."

———

Waiting. It seemed to be an emerging theme.

Dr. Erickson's advice jibed with an earlier conversation I'd had with Lenox Hill Hospital's Compton. Over the past few years, he's conducted a number of studies looking into adolescent marijuana use and what's known as "early onset psychosis," or the appearance of schizophrenia-like symptoms before age 18.

The main question he wants to answer isn't whether underage pot smoking causes schizophrenia. It's whether underage pot smoking can trigger the emergence of schizophrenia earlier than it might otherwise appear. It's a subtle difference, but an important one.

"The earlier a person's age at the onset of psychosis," Compton told me, the worse a schizophrenic patient's outcome tends to be. "Delaying the emergence of psychosis by even one month can make a difference."

I expressed surprise. Four weeks?

"It matters," Compton said. "More social and psychological development goes on from ages 15 to 25 than in any other 10-year period in our lives. You're getting to know how the world works. How to drive. Study. Get a job. Relate to other people. And you're learning about how you work. What your desires, wishes, needs and strengths are. Who you are."

Recovering from a psychotic episode at age 25 is a lot easier than at age 15, Compton said. At 25 your world is fairly well set and centered. You know who you are, who your friends are, what your work is and what your day-to-day schedule is. The normal world of a 15-year-old is already kind of schizophrenic even without psychotic episodes. Your friends are transient and changing; your life's path is unsettled; your sense of who you are changes week to week.

"So if you're able to delay the onset of psychosis by even one month, that may be the month in which you pass an important test, or get your driver's license, or graduate high school," said Compton. "Which gives you that much more grounding" and ability to recover from and manage the onset of schizophrenia.

Compton's research reinforced the wisdom of waiting. His first study, published in 2011, looked at the lifetime marijuana use of 509 people hospitalized for the first time for a psychotic disorder. He found that the onset of psychosis happened an average of three years earlier for pot smokers than for patients who had never used cannabis. The more quickly an adolescent moved from initiating marijuana use to smoking pot daily, the earlier their first psychotic episode tended to emerge.

To further test the theory, Compton ran a second study with 247 subjects. "We're finishing up our data analysis right now," he told me. "And it's looking much the same. Marijuana use is associated with earlier onset by at least a couple of years."

———————

Risk factors mean little without context. The chances of a young person becoming schizophrenic, with or without a pot habit, are fairly small. Without taking genetic disposition into account, the general public has a one in 200 chance of developing schizophrenia. Adding a chronic teenage marijuana habit raises that chance to six in 200. Again, that's small—but it's not insignificant. Consider that MC1R, the recessive gene that gives people red hair, is carried by four in every 200 people. Six of every 200 people are afflicted with psoriasis.

When you factor in the other risks that young people face, those odds appear more concerning. Among all Americans, young men ages 16 to 19 face one of the highest risks of dying in a car crash. Car accidents are the leading cause of death in that age group, in fact. Their risk of death by smashup: two in 10,000.

Perhaps the best way to think about underage pot smoking and schizophrenia is to consider it next to cigarette smoking and lung cancer. The lung cancer rate for nonsmokers is about 15 to 17 per 100,000 adults. The rate for those who currently smoke is 149 to 363 (studies differ) per 100,000. That's a 10- to 30-fold increase in risk.

We can say a few true things about those numbers. The majority of cigarette smokers don't contract lung cancer. Not every lung cancer patient is a smoker. Among smokers with lung cancer, other factors may have contributed to their disease. But a half century of research and hard experience have led us to conclude that smokers have a frightfully higher chance of developing lung cancer than nonsmokers. The connection is so clear that we speak of smokers "giving themselves" cancer.

We don't have all the data we need to draw airtight conclusions about schizophrenia and pot smoking. At this point, though, the research is trending in a cigarettes-and-lung-cancer direction. The overwhelming majority of young pot smokers don't develop schizophrenia. Not all schizophrenics smoke pot. There are many other contributing factors involved. Still, heavy marijuana users develop the illness at six times the rate of non-users. We can't yet say that chronic teen pot smokers are giving themselves schizophrenia. But one day we might.

16

FATTER, DUMBER
AND SLEEPIER

At 6:27 on the morning of Jan. 3, less than 48 hours after the first retail pot sale in Colorado, former *New Yorker* editor Tina Brown tweeted out this little gem:

. . . legal weed contributes to us being a fatter, dumber, sleepier nation even less able to compete with the Chinese

Brown's 19-word essay was embraced by many as the smart take on legal pot. Fans of the movie *Animal House* will recognize in its cadence an echo of Dean Wormer's advice to "Flounder" Dorfman: "Fat, drunk and stupid is no way to go through life, son."

Brilliant in its provocative arrogance, Brown's tweet managed to pack elements of classism, stereotype, wrong information, xenophobia and competitive anxiety into the strict confines of the 140-character space. As a thumbnail of the fears of America's striving class, you could do worse.

In the media business, January is the "New Year, New You!" month. Everybody's exhausted from the five-week bacchanal we run from Thanksgiving to New Year's Day. January is for life assessing, goal setting, body trimming and bill paying. The rent has come due. That January it felt like half the adults in America were "doing a cleanse." The other half were rummaging through the fridge to cobble dinner together out of something other than quinoa and kale.

Given that mind-set, what Tina Brown offered was a national stock taking. By hitching *-ers* to her freight cars, Brown made it clear that Americans were *already* fat, stupid, sleepy and powerless to stop China's economic ground game. Marijuana would only make us more so. Perhaps what America needed was an on-trend cannabis cleanse.

———————

Brown's tweet struck such a nerve in part because it glanced at so many things we think we know about marijuana. But as it turns out, what we think we know isn't quite true.

Take the bit about marijuana turning us fat. This is hitting us where we live. Cannabis stimulates appetite. So is our national cannabis intake contributing to our obesity epidemic?

In a word, no.

The French looked into it. Yann Le Strat and Bernard Le Foll, researchers at the Louis Mourier hospital in Colombes, France, wanted to know if there was an association between marijuana use and weight in America. They ran the numbers on more than 50,000 Americans, comparing body mass index with marijuana use and stripping out factors like alcohol and other drugs.

What they found was this: "The prevalence of obesity was significantly lower in cannabis users than in nonusers." Sixteen percent of pot smokers were obese; 22 percent of non-users were obese. "The proportion of obese participants decreased with the frequency of cannabis use," reported Le Strat and Le Foll. The more often people smoked pot, the less likely they were to be obese. A twice-yearly pot smoker was 25 percent less likely to be obese than a non-user. A heavy three-days-a-week stoner was nearly 50 percent less likely to be obese.

Remember: correlation doesn't imply causation. Don't fire up a bowl of Blueberry Kush as a slimming strategy. But it's worth noting that over the past decade, one state has consistently ranked at the top of polls and studies ranking the fittest states in the nation. That state is Colorado.

––––––––––

Cannabis isn't going to make Americans fatter. But surely it's going to make us dumber, right? We've all heard about the study that found that pot smoking shaves six IQ points from your brain. The evidence of our own eyes doesn't lie. Stoners and valedictorians form a Venn diagram with negligible overlap.

Tina Brown's tweet was driven in part by a famous study published in late 2012 in the *Proceedings of the National Academy of Sciences (PNAS)*. It came from a group of Duke University scientists led by Madeline Meier, a postdoctoral researcher in psychology and neuroscience, and it got a lot of media play because it came out just weeks before Colorado and Washington voted to legalize. "EARLY MARIJUANA USE LINKED TO I.Q. LOSS," read the *New York Times* headline. The takeaway in news accounts was dramatic and simple: between high school and middle age, heavy pot users smoked away six to eight IQ points.

The study itself told a more complicated story. The Duke team had gone data mining in the Dunedin Study, a famous research project that's been tracking a cohort of 1,037 New Zealanders since birth. It's a scientific version of Michael Apted's classic *Up* film series. The Dunedin subjects, born in 1972 and 1973, have been revisited and retested as they've aged. They were questioned about marijuana use, among many other things, at ages 18, 21, 26, 32 and 38.

IQ tests established baseline scores for the Dunedin subjects at age 13. Most kids scored in the 100–102 range. (Average intelligence is generally regarded as 90 to 109.) A follow-up test was given at age 38. During the intervening years, the subjects had a variety of relationships with cannabis.

What happened between 13 and 38? Separation. At 38, the IQs of marijuana abstainers and marijuana dabblers remained more or less unchanged. Those who smoked pot regularly during one stretch of their lives lost an average of three IQ points. Those who smoked heavily through three or more stretches lost six. At middle age, abstainers scored 101, dabblers 101, once-stoners 98 and heavy users 94.

The results were especially grim for those who had embraced marijuana as youngsters. Of the 38 Dunedin Study subjects who turned out to be heavy adult cannabis users, 23 started smoking pot before they turned 18. By middle age, those 23 had lost an average of eight IQ points.

Meier, the Duke researcher, hammered her data prior to publication. She looked for confounding factors like socioeconomic status, schizophrenia, alcohol or other substance abuse. In the end, after controlling for all those factors, she couldn't deny what the data revealed. "The younger the cannabis user and the more years of use," she wrote, "the worse the cognitive outcome."

Meier's study caught nobody in the field by surprise. Earlier research had turned up similar results. A 2002 Harvard study examined 122 middle-aged heavy cannabis users. "Heavy" meant they had smoked pot at least 5,000 times. That's a joint a day for 13½ years. The researchers split them according to age of onset: those who started using before age 17, and those who were 17 or older when they first lit up. Their verbal IQ scores were compared with a control group of dabblers. (Not *dabbers*. Important distinction.) The dabblers had smoked pot at least once but no more than 50 times in their lives.

Heavy lifetime users who were 17 or older at age of onset scored nearly as well as the light dabblers. The former averaged a verbal IQ score of 116, the latter 118. Heavy users who started at an early age, though, fell far below the other two groups. They scored 104. Here was the same conclusion I'd taken away from studies of pot and mental health: age of onset matters.

The Harvard researchers cautioned that other factors might explain the verbal IQ gap. Cannabis might be harming the developing brain, certainly. But the gap could also reflect innate differences in verbal IQ, which might lead to a greater propensity to reject academic study and rebel against mainstream conceptions of intelligence and success—and smoke pot. Cannabis as cause, or cannabis as symptom: it's a chicken-and-egg problem that runs through a lot of research on pot smoking and the brain. A 2011 study out of the Scripps Research Institute noted that "acute cannabis use promotes more impulsive behavior and less inhibition of maladaptive responses." It could just as easily be argued, though, that the natural impulse toward risky, exploratory or "maladaptive" behavior promotes cannabis use.

—————

"You know what I told Tessa?"

I'd been talking with my friend Chris about talking about marijuana with our kids. Chris works on databases for Microsoft. We met during our junior year at the University of Washington. He and his wife had raised two kids a little older than our own. His older daughter, Tessa, had gone back east to college a few days earlier.

"No, what?"

"I got out my UW transcript," he said.

I nodded and thought, *You have your transcript?*

"I showed her the 3.8 grade point I had before I started smoking pot," he said. "Then I showed her the 3.2 I got the quarter I smoked a lot of pot. I told her, 'Pot makes you dumb.'"

"That's it, huh?"

"That's the information. What she does with it is up to her."

The grade fall made him change his ways. He stopped hitting the pipe. His GPA rebounded. He graduated, got hired at Microsoft, got married, had kids and built a life that pleased him. He and his wife Diana are those pioneer parents the rest of us watch for clues about how to raise bright, creative, healthy and happy children.

I kept asking around for advice. Other parents told me they used variations on the alcohol talk. Some didn't touch marijuana, verbally, at all.

The best advice came from my Colorado friend Dan.

Dan and I met in middle age. We were both freelance writers. Dan had a successful career writing books and national-magazine pieces. I was a few steps behind him. He raised two kids on his own in Boulder. By the time Colorado turned legal in 2014, both his kids had graduated and gone to college. I flopped in his guest room now and then. Dan wasn't a stoner. He was an adult experienced with marijuana. He'd grown up in Berkeley in the '70s. He lived in Boulder. Now and then, when I was in town, I'd stop by and we'd enjoy a glass of wine and a couple moderate puffs of cannabis. It was a nice, safe setting in which to figure out what sort of dosage my body and brain could handle.

One night we got to talking about kids and pot. Dan said he'd struggled with it at first. His kids went to high school in Boulder; they were going to be exposed to the stuff. He talked with them about his own history, about alcohol and various drugs, and age and setting and the various legalities involved. He knew they'd try the stuff in college. But he wanted them to stay off it in high school.

"The main thing I told them," he said, "was something I kinda ripped off of Nancy Reagan."

I leaned forward. He handed me the pipe.

"I don't expect you to just say no. Think about saying 'not yet.'"

When other parents ask me about pot, I give them a variation on Dan's answer. Smoking an occasional joint is not going to lower a person's intelligence. I think that if you adopt it as an adult habit, marijuana will shift your brain into a lower gear for a good portion of your day. For some people that means they're not operating at full brain capacity—but there may be individuals who need that downshift, to deal with stress or PTSD or some other factor in their life.

The chipping away of a couple of IQ points in adulthood isn't the primary issue. Kids, young adults and the developing brain—that's the real problem. Beyond increasing the risk of early-onset schizophrenia, teen habitual pot smokers are gambling with their brains. Every time they smoke, they're flooding their brains with cannabinoids. That flood may happen during a dormant moment in neurocognitive development. Or it may occur during a critical period when the brain counts on precise doses of cannabinoids to calibrate the fine wiring of the mind. One day the roulette ball lands on black. Another day it lands on red. The only way to make certain that marijuana doesn't screw up the developing brain is to smoke on neither day.

Early on I thought my research would lead up to One Big Talk with my kids about the real and scientifically true risks of marijuana use. I imagined myself dazzling them with dead-sexy data and piercing analogies, all Robin Williams in *Dead Poets Society*, as they curled beside the fire on pillows and leather chairs. A rap session, as it were. You will be shocked to hear that this did not occur.

What happened instead were a series of short conversations, usually in the car on the way to school, rehearsal, practice or to pick up somebody from the ferry.

"What's on your schedule today?"

"The usual," Lucy or Willie would say. "School. Theater tech until 5. What do you have going on?"

I am not making that up. They actually ask me this once in a while. It helps that because of my job I can reply, "I'm driving to Canada to interview the world's leading camouflage expert" or "I'm talking to the guys who created the frickin' sharks with frickin' laser beams for that Austin Powers movie." Sometimes I bring a little value-add to the situation.

Lately I can answer, "I'm talking to a researcher who studies how long-term pot use affects IQ" and take off from there.

Recently, though, an opportunity arose to expound at more length. I brought home a tiny marijuana clone, a baby plant about eight inches tall, in order to write about it and take a few photos before tossing it in the garbage. (You can't smoke a clone. Or eat it. Or rather, you can, but it's not going to do you much good, tripwise.) Claire got angry at me for bringing it home, and Willie grew noticeably uncomfortable in its presence. Lucy rolled her eyes and chuckled. We called a family meeting.

I set the clone next to a bottle of Jim Beam on the coffee table. Put the cards on the table. Give us a visual.

After acknowledging my wife's legitimate feelings about the presence of marijuana in our home (about which—read her book), I directed everyone's attention to the clone.

"This," I said, "is a plant. It's a marijuana plant. But it's just a plant.

When it's this small, you can't smoke it; you can't get high from it; it's not going to make you become a heroin addict. For the past 70 years we've been treating it like it's nuclear waste. But it's just a plant. Go ahead. Touch it. Smell it."

The kids leaned forward and had a whiff. Lucy patted the delicate leaves.

"It doesn't become a useable drug until it gets about four feet tall and produces a flower," I said. "Then it's got to be harvested, dried, trimmed and cured. It's not as complex a process as making this whiskey," I said, indicating the Beam bottle, "but it takes some doing."

We talked about the fact that they would run into both pot and alcohol in the next few years, or even the next few days. "It's going to be at a party, or at somebody's house," I said. "I can't tell you 'just say no,' because they tried that on us and it didn't work." I told them the best advice I'd heard came from Dan: "Just say not yet." I gave them my spiel about cannabis and the developing brain, how the wiring up there is finishing itself off and how chronic pot use can mess with the final connections. "This isn't a bunch of BS I'm making up to scare you," I said. "I am literally writing the book on this stuff. Take the information. Make your own decisions."

"Don't make your own decisions!" said Claire. "Just wait till you're 25!"

"The other part of this is pragmatic," I said. "You're doing all you can to keep up with your homework and get A's." I looked at Lucy. "Imagine trying to do that while drunk."

When I have a drink, I explained, or when I've tried pot, "my workday stops. It's over. My brain's no good for writing until the next day."

That's about it. The parents talked. The kids listened. We tossed in a few jokes. Then I threw away the pot plant and we all watched an episode of *New Girl* in which Jess falls for a cute new math teacher. Lucy finished her homework. Claire answered some email. I paid some bills. Willie cleaned out the cat's litter box. Life carried on.

GOING

INTERNATIONAL

The United States isn't the only country relaxing its marijuana laws. Other nations are taking tentative steps toward legalization. Spain has allowed private cannabis clubs to operate in a legal gray area, much like medical dispensaries in the U.S. Uruguay has gone further. In 2013, President José Mujica legalized cannabis by setting it up for sale through licensed pharmacies. Other countries are considering their options. Throughout 2013 and 2014, I-502 author Alison Holcomb found herself in great demand as a legalization consultant. Every week seemed to find her jetting off to Mexico City, Warsaw, Amsterdam and other capital cities.

Canada was also getting in on the action. In the late '90s, Health Canada established a medical marijuana program. The national health service contracted with a single biotech firm in Saskatchewan to grow marijuana for all of Canada's 40,000 registered patients. In 2014 the rules changed to allow private growers to sell medicinal cannabis to patients. That sparked a medical marijuana rush.

In British Columbia, where black-market "B.C. Bud" had been grown for decades, a number of small growers scrambled to ramp up and join the new system. Well-financed outsiders jumped in as well. Tweed, a start-up backed by hedge-fund money, bought an old Hershey's chocolate factory in Ontario and turned it into a medical marijuana grow. On the West Coast, a company called Tilray planted its flag in Nanaimo, a small port town on Vancouver Island. Tilray, it turned out, was owned by none other than Privateer Holdings.

Brendan Kennedy, Michael Blue and Christian Groh were going international.

I got Kennedy on the phone.

"Yes! We're expanding into Canada," he said. "Health Canada used to have a single cannabis supplier. Now they're allowing a number of private licensed producers."

Smelling opportunity, Kennedy and his partners formed a Canadian holding company, Lafitte Ventures. (It was unclear how long the Privateer partners planned to milk the whole pirate theme, but apparently they hadn't wearied of its raffish pleasures.) Privateer marketing director Tonia Winchester met with Scott Lowry at Heckler Associates and set him on a task. "We need a brand for Canada," she told him.

"What's the company going to do?" Lowry asked.

"Grow and distribute medical cannabis," said Winchester.

They would finally touch the leaf. Privateer had never promised investors that the firm wouldn't directly deal in cannabis. The commitment was to never engage in illegal activities. Because Health Canada operated that country's medical marijuana system, the whole thing was legal under Canadian federal law.

At Heckler Associates, Lowry came up with a name: Tilray. It rolled off the tongue. It contained notes of transparency, honest toil and warm summer days. Till the soil under rays of sunshine.

"You should come up and see our facility in Nanaimo," Kennedy told me. "We bought the property for 3½ million, and we're putting 10 million into the build-out. It's going to have 36 grow rooms in 70,000 square feet. When we get it running it'll produce 20,000 pounds of cannabis."

I caught a ferry north the next day.

———————

I met Kennedy outside an unmarked warehouse on the outskirts of Nanaimo. He looked underslept. "It's a hectic time," he said. In late 2013 his firm closed a $7 million funding round. By the middle of 2014 he expected to close a $50 million round. Investors were crashing the door. Leafly was booming. Arbormain, a subsidiary set up to lease grow spaces to licensed marijuana farmers, had already purchased land in Eastern Washington. Tilray was poised to go nationwide in Canada. "And we can't go public with this yet," Kennedy told me, "but we're negotiating with the Bob Marley family about a deal to create the world's first global cannabis brand."

Nanaimo is an hour's drive north of Victoria on Vancouver Island. Nanaimo is known for three things: Its major industry is timber. Its most spectacular yearly event is a bathtub race. And it is the town that Diana Krall fled in order to become a world-famous jazz singer. It's unknown whether these are causally related.

Tilray's main office was a tangle of phone lines and makeshift desks. Winchester gave me a wave from across the room. She wore a yellow construction helmet and held a phone to her ear. Pointing to the receiver, she mouthed, "Health Canada." Kennedy signaled, *How's it looking?* She scrunched her face and gave him a 50–50 hand tilt.

"We looked all over Canada," Kennedy said. "Toronto. Winnipeg. Calgary. Vancouver." Finally, they heard that Nanaimo had adopted some of the most pot-friendly zoning ordinances in Canada. "When we saw this building, we knew it would work," he said. The former nursery warehouse was about the size of a Home Depot. Surrounding it were nothing but light-industrial manufacturers and fir trees. "The neighbors are thrilled we're here. The building is clean, well-lit, and we've got security here 24 hours a day."

Something was missing, though. "Where are the plants?" I asked.

Kennedy smiled. "It's complicated."

Tilray couldn't legally bring marijuana plants into its grow facility until Health Canada signed off on its license. "We're still waiting on their final inspection," Kennedy said. "That's why Tonia's on the phone with them." At the same time, he explained, the new law required licensed growers to acquire their cannabis strains by May 1, which was 11 days away.

Kennedy cast a despondent look at the empty rooms.

"What can you do about it?" I asked.

"Christian, Patrick and Jeff are out in the field right now securing our inventory."

"What do you mean by 'securing'?"

"It's hard to describe what they do without seeing them in action," he said. "You should go for a ride-along with them."

———

Tilray's three-man scouting team roamed the British Columbia countryside seeking quality weed. I joined them on a drizzly and cold Tuesday evening. Christian Groh, Patrick Moen, Jeff Guillot and I wedged into a rented Hyundai in the basement parking garage of Nanaimo's Coast Bastion hotel.

"Where we heading now?" said Guillot.

"Chemainus," said Groh. A small timber town.

As we drove south, Moen and Guillot introduced themselves. Moen was a former U.S. Drug Enforcement Administration official. Until recently he'd run the DEA's field office in Portland, Ore. Guillot was a gregarious Texan. He'd been in the steel industry for a number of years. After reading an article I'd written about Privateer, Guillot had quit his job and moved to Seattle. He knocked on Brendan Kennedy's door and talked himself into a job.

Moen wheeled the Hyundai into the parking lot of a Tim Hortons. Outside it was growing dark. The drizzle had turned to heavy rain. He checked the dashboard clock: 6:55. We were a few minutes early.

"Who we meeting with here?" Moen asked.

"His name's Ben," said Guillot. "I have no idea what we're in for."

We sat and listened to the sound of the wipers clacking. "We could be pleasantly surprised," said Groh. "Who knows."

Inside, our man sat in a corner of the doughnut shop. Ben was a tall guy, early 30s, a clean-cut bring-home-to-Mama character. He looked like a business major at a state college.

"Sorry, man, we usually don't roll four deep," Groh told him. He spun his eyes at Guillot, Moen and me. "Got a crew tonight."

"Not a problem," said Ben.

Groh gave him a five-minute version of his pitch deck. *Here's our operation. We're looking for strains and suppliers.*

Ben started talking. He opened his mouth. By the time he closed it, we'd all grown beards.

"You ask anyone on the island, I'm the guy to talk to about pricing," he said. "I've got my own grow, but I've been brokering for 20 years. There are a number of levels of quality: dubs, trips and quads. Your dub is the lowest-cost product, less than ideal, wasn't dried and cured well, it's maybe a little old, and that's anywhere from 900 to 1,150."

Nine hundred to 1,150 Canadian dollars per pound, he meant. At the time, Canadian and American dollars were trading one-for-one.

"Then there's trips. That's excellent quality, a known strain, your Pink Kush, Purple Kush. Twelve hundred to 1,500. And then there's quads and exotics, which go for as much as 1,900 to 2,000."

At about this time, Ben's partner Steff joined us. Steff was a rangy kid in his 20s, sloppily dressed, in a hoodie and a Stussy cap. He worked his way through a bag of cinnamon-sugar doughnuts. I wondered if he'd been hanging out at the counter this whole time, waiting to lend some muscle if Ben got into trouble. He didn't introduce himself. Just smiled and chewed his fried dough.

Ben continued. "You ask anybody, they know I know quality. I've got a number of ways to tell. There's the smell test." He pantomimed the act of a man inserting his nose in a plastic baggie.

"And the burn-and-smear test. You light a little of the bud and smear the carbon on a table. If it leaves a smear, it's good stuff. Oily."

The six of us gazed at the imaginary smear.

"The squish test is what I like to use with fresh bud." He worked an invisible spring between his thumb and forefinger. "Is . . . it . . . sticky?"

I shot a glance at Groh. He was listening patiently. It was as if he were practicing a kind of zen exercise known by a phrase meaning *Letting the fool chatter on*. At a certain point he closed his Moleskine and let Ben's stream of consciousness flow like water into an overfilled tub, each word more useless than the last.

Eventually Ben ran out of string. We agreed to follow him to his production facility.

In the Hyundai, I asked, "What the hell was that all about?"

"Dubs and trips?" Guillot said. "Just the usual bullshit. Voodoo testing. Guy trying to find a way to justify his price. It's no different than guys back in the '80s taking a dab of coke and putting it on their tongue and saying, 'That's really good shit.' It's nonsense."

I wondered if they encountered that a lot.

"He's by no means the worst we've seen," said Moen. His tone carried the weariness of a man who'd spent too many hours with Canadian blowhards in squalid circumstances. "This is the tricky part," he told me. "We're trying to bridge the gap between the guys that have been doing this for so long, and the next generation. We're trying to bring them into a legitimate system."

———————

We followed Ben's truck down a country road to a muddy driveway cut through a shaggy field choked with Scotch broom. We came to a locked gate. Ben opened it and waved us through.

"Six months ago I would've been scouting this place to figure out how I was going to take it down," Moen said, recalling his DEA days.

Guillot looked up from his phone. "Now you're thinking about how to get a truck up this driveway to haul away the product. HAW-haw-haw-haw-haw!"

The driveway continued up to a compound in a clearing at the top of a hill. At one point this was somebody's proud little farm. Skeletal apple trees stood near a single-story house from the 1940s. On the porch an old bicycle leaned against some rusting chairs. A scope-sighted .22 rested on a wooden bench next to the front door. The property looked out over the Cowichan Valley. Below us, houselights twinkled here and there like stars in a hazy night.

Ben led us to a pale-blue three-story outbuilding. It resembled a cheaply built house, with vinyl windows that still bore the remnants of its manufacturer's labels. It struck me as the kind of place the farmer's lazy son might call "my crib."

Lo and behold! We stepped through the door into a Seth Rogen Playhouse. The open and airy main floor held a dirty vanilla-colored couch, two stained recliners, three folding camp chairs, old potato chip bags, half-empty cans of Coke and Mr. Pibb, a workbench littered with bits of cannabis trim, and a 72-inch flat-screen television. Onscreen a hockey game was playing. Stereo speakers were propped here and there. A full-size refrigerator stood against the north wall, and a Red Bull mini-fridge, like the kind you'd find in a convenience store, sat next to one of the recliners. Old joints dotted the poured concrete floor. Two Molson beer mirrors hung above a foosball table. A lone hockey stick leaned against the back wall.

"Boys got yourself quite a place here," Guillot said with his Texas smile.

"We had it purpose-built," Ben said. He nodded and took it all in as if weighing the measure of his estate.

Upstairs, we—

—but wait.

Allow me to say something that needs to be said about the marijuana grow houses of North America. Farmers, it's time to upgrade those staircases. As a weary veteran of the grow house tour, I have come to recoil at the sight of naked plywood. Among ganja growers, the frayed edges of a crude unvarnished staircase may bespeak a commitment to the cannabis. No time for sanding and painting! Yes, I know, your duty is to bud quality and yield alone. But listen. Visuals matter. Take an afternoon. Splash a little Sherwin-Williams on those steps. You'll be amazed at how an updated growing space will brighten the price of your crop as well.

As we were: up the naked plywood stairs to Ben's grow rooms. "We've got Hindu Kush going in the main room here," said Ben.

There were 224 four-foot-tall marijuana plants bunched in pods of

16, each plant in its own five-gallon grow pot, bathed under the glow of more than 20 1,000-watt sodium halide lights hanging from the ceiling. A cabinet-size air conditioner pumped a cooling breeze into the room.

Groh pulled a flower up to his nose.

"When you figure on harvesting?" he said.

"This room's about ready to go," said Ben. "We've got a crew of trimmers scheduled next weekend."

Guillot disappeared into a second room with Steff. He emerged nodding. "Got some nice Pink Kush in there," he told Groh.

When it came time to negotiate, we repaired to the main house. The six of us bantered around a retro '50s kitchen table with tubular steel legs. A half-empty bottle of Jameson sat next to a couple of unwashed coffee mugs.

Guillot and Ben talked price and weight. The Tilray team liked Ben's product. They considered it trips, not quads. Didn't want to pay more than $1,500 a pound.

Ben nodded. He could live with that.

The more Ben and Steff talked, the more it became apparent that the sticking point wasn't price. It was timing. Tilray couldn't legally take delivery of Ben's cannabis until Health Canada approved Tilray's grow space. That might not happen until after Ben's scheduled harvest-and-trim date.

"I suppose we could hold off on harvesting for you guys," said Ben. "But we've got the trimmers coming."

I was confused. Couldn't he just cancel the trimmers? It seemed like that would actually save him money.

"Who are these trimmers?" said Guillot. "They some local guys?"

"Oh no," said Ben. "There's a team of girls from Hornby Island. They work as a crew, up and down the coast. They're in pretty high demand. You gotta book 'em weeks ahead."

"Yeah," said Steff. "They stay over here in the house for two or three days. It's a party."

Ah. Ben and Steff weren't using the Hornby Island crew as a negotiating tool. The two growers—single men stuck in the boondocks tending a garden of weeds—eyed the upcoming trimmers' visit like sailors dreaming of shore leave. They loved the idea of selling their entire stock to the Tilray team. But not if it came at the price of a visit from the Hornby Island girls.

Guillot stepped in with a solution.

"What if we took . . ." he said, tapping his finger to his lips, ". . . a *portion* of your harvest? That way you wouldn't have to cancel the trimmers."

Deal.

The next morning I met up with the three amigos after breakfast. "Where we headed today?" I asked.

Guillot rolled his eyes. "Back to Chemainus."

Their first appointment was with a grower in a light-industrial park off Highway 1. This was Mike's joint. Mike was a trim, compact man who wore his jeans pressed and his silver hair combed neat. Mike's grow contained the most enchanting strain of marijuana I'd ever encountered. A few steps through the door of his inner grow room, I rubbed a bit of flower on my thumb. I held it to my nose. Fragrance exploded in my brain. The plant smelled of lemon, but so much more. Lemon crossed with gardenias, lavender and musk. Mike had cultivated the Chanel No. 5 of cannabis.

I shot a look at Jeff Guillot. He was smelling it too. Whatever it was, I wanted more of it. I had to suppress the urge to rub it all over my body. "What . . . what is this?" I asked.

"This one's our special strain," said Mike. "We call it Harmony. Nice, eh?"

"Really nice," I said. I shut my mouth as a courtesy to Guillot. I didn't want to undermine his negotiating position.

When it came time to talk price, Mike and his lead grower chewed over terms with Groh, Moen and Guillot.

Guillot inquired about Harmony. "We're open to selling that as a finished product," Mike said, "but not clones."

Guillot shrugged off the loss. "What about that Kush you got growing?" he said. "What are you thinking about a price?"

Before Mike could speak, his grower blurted, "Thirteen hundred."

Mike shot him a cold look.

"We could do that," said Patrick—$1,300 a pound was a steal.

Mike tried to salvage what he could. "We'll have to think about it," he said. We shook hands and departed.

An hour later, the Tilray team met up with their second appointment of the day. This grower was located, I am not joking, three doors down from Mike's operation.

"You think they know about each other?" asked Guillot.

"Anybody's guess," said Groh.

The gentlemen three doors down were ready to cut a deal. The Tilray team took a quick spin in their grow house, then settled in at a conference table in a nearby office.

Doug and Jim were longtime B.C. bud growers in their 60s. Doug had a fleshy face and a heavy nose. He looked like he played a lot of hockey back when the game was 60 percent brawling. His partner, Jim, was a strange-looking dude: tilted face, small eyes, short spiked hair.

Moen opened his laptop. "I've got a standard contract that we've been working from," he said. "Well, actually there is no standard. This is a contract that's never been created before. We start with a two-year contract with a two-year option. So after two years, if you're happy and we're happy, we renew."

Jim countered. "Three years," he said. "We want a three-year with an option for two after that."

Time for a little of Jeff Guillot's Texas tea. "For us it's all about quality and consistent production," he said. "There's a minimum we want to make sure you produce. So we'll have it on hand to market."

Jim nodded. "So we should build in some contingencies for a catastrophic event."

"We'll put in some minimums and maximums, in case you start producing more than we can handle," said Moen. "We just want to make sure you and we agree about 35 pounds a month."

"Forty is about what we've been producing," said Jim.

"If you're producing 40, we'll contract for 35 to give you some room."

Doug wanted some assurance on the high side. "If you're not obligated to take more than 50 pounds, we should have the ability to market that overage to somebody," he said.

"We'd want a right of first refusal on that," said Guillot. "If you can produce 50 and we're not ready for that much, you can sell that extra, yes. But you should let us know. Most people are seeing this as a supply-driven market."

Doug brought the conversation back around to the option. "So, ah . . . three and a three?" A three-year contract with an option for an additional three years.

"Three and a two," said Moen. "Others have taken a two and two."

"I'm OK with three and a two," said Guillot.

Jim was an old man. He didn't want to spend his time chasing new buyers and better prices. He wanted to lock in stability. "If you're gonna want to renew for two, you're gonna want to renew for three," he said.

Doug shifted to price. "What about contingencies for price fluctuation?" he said. "It would be great to buy from us at 15 a pound when you're getting 32. But not so good when you're paying 15 and selling at 16."

Guillot handled it. "I come from the steel business, where there's a published spot price. Every day we can look in the paper and say, 'OK, that's the price of steel now.' We could link our contracts to the price index. That doesn't exist yet with cannabis. It will someday."

"We're creating it now," said Doug.

Doug floated the idea of a moving spread. What if, he said, we structured a deal such that the wholesale price is always 50 percent of the retail price? "That way our prices change as your prices change, and the spread stays the same."

Jim nixed the idea. "We gotta be careful of that," he said to Doug. "If their prices bottom out, our costs still stay the same. We could get into a position where we're trying to supply these guys at a loss." He circled back to his desire for security. "I'd rather lock in a minimum wholesale price," he said. "Then if there's upside to be had," he motioned to Moen, "that's *your* gig."

"Yeah . . ." Guillot said, meaning no. "That could leave us in a bad position, where we're selling at a loss and your price is inflated relative to the market. I'd rather have something where you get a little upside, we get a little upside."

Moen continued to type on his laptop as the contract evolved. He wrote in a clause about "a substantial change" in the market price, which would trigger a resetting of the wholesale price. "It's got to be a really big change," he said. "We don't want to be haggling over this every month, right?"

"So maybe we put a percentage point to that," said Jim. He shot a glance at Doug.

Guillot suggested 25 percent as "a good number to watch."

"But which retail price?" said Moen. "Ours? A market average?"

It was fascinating to watch the market take shape before my own eyes. The old Canadian growers, Doug and Jim, spun numbers and scenarios in their head. The Tilray team did the same. Everybody was making it up as they went along. Everybody was trying not to get screwed.

There was a silence.

"I would suggest," Guillot said, drawling his drawl, "that we tie the price change to our retail price. The reason is that it's going to be to your advantage."

Doug understood. "Because you're going to get as much as you can get."

"Right," said Guillot. "We're not branding ourselves as the low-cost supplier. We're all about quality."

Jim put his finger to his lips. "I think we're fine with that." He waited a couple of seconds before coming back to the strike point. "So back to the price, then," he said. "We were thinking 1,500."

The room hushed.

Moen stopped typing. Guillot ran the numbers in his head—*$1,500 per pound, 453 grams per pound; that's about $3.35 a gram wholesale, $7–8 a gram retail; yeah, that works*—but he kept his mouth shut. As the firm's founding partner, Groh outranked his colleagues. It would have to be his call. For his part, he thought $1,500 a pound was a fine wholesale price. Agreeing too quickly, though, might infect Doug and Jim with a case of buyer's remorse. *Had they offered too low? Would he have gone to $1,700?* So Groh waited.

"Fifteen hundred . . ." he said, running the figure over in his mind. Finally he nodded. "I'd be OK with that."

Done and done. The men leaned in to sign one of the first legal marijuana commodities contracts ever written. The new world: this was how it was created. Price by clause by contingency.

LOUISIANA
RAIN

As Tilray's flying squad continued its quest to secure quality Canadian weed, I returned home via the ferry *M.V. Coho*. The *Coho* was an old steel warhorse that sailed a daily route between Victoria, B.C., and Port Angeles, Wash. The bow cut through the chop with a rhythmic rise and fall. I sank into a vinyl seat and let my mind wander.

I liked Brendan Kennedy. I liked his Privateer Holdings team. If the marijuana industry was going to find legitimacy and knit itself into the fabric of the North American economy, it would be due to the work of people like him.

And yet. I didn't vote for Initiative 502 in order to expand the corporate portfolio of wealthy white guys like Brendan Kennedy. My vote turned on social justice. I agreed to legalize marijuana to stop the madness of the War on Drugs. I voted for 502 to end the incarceration of a generation of men exactly *not* like Kennedy.

It was time to look into that. By the time the *Coho* docked in Port Angeles, I had booked a flight to New Orleans.

———

The United States has the highest incarceration rate in the world. No other country comes close. In 2014, America held 2.3 million men and women behind bars. That's the population of Pittsburgh. It works out to a rate of 707 for every 100,000 adults and children. The next nearest nation, Russia, had a rate of 471 per 100,000. Most developed countries are in the 100s. It's one of the signs that a country is, in fact, developed. Spain and the U.K.: 147. Canada: 118. Germany: 79. The U.S. has 5 percent of the world's population and 25 percent of the world's prisoners.

It didn't used to be like this. From the 1940s through the 1970s, the prison population in the U.S. held steady at around 200,000. In the early 1980s a rising tide of drug arrests swelled the population to 300,000. Over the next 30 years, incarceration rates continued to rise, driven almost exclusively by drug convictions. American prisons and jails held 41,000 drug offenders in 1980. By 2011 that number had grown more than tenfold, to 501,500. During that same time, the federal prison population grew by 790 percent. A graph of the U.S. state and federal prison population from 1925 through 2014 looks like the Himalayas rising from the plains of India.

Those convictions weren't spread equally among drug users. White people and black people use marijuana at roughly equal rates. When the War on Drugs gained steam under the Reagan administration, however, the prison population gained a decidedly darker hue. To put it bluntly: dark-skinned people got imprisoned and light-skinned people did not. That's not a rule, of course. Plenty of white people are serving long sentences for drug crimes. But in 2010, the rate of incarceration among black men was 4,347 per 100,000. The rate among white men was 678. By November 2012, the U.S. held a higher percentage of its black population under lock and key than South Africa did during apartheid.

The hard truth is that most white Americans don't care. For white people, the American prison complex remains largely invisible. The penal system is something other people get caught up in, people not like themselves. One in 23 white men is likely to serve time at some point in his life. For black men, the chances are one in three. There's a widely held assumption among white people that those behind bars deserve their punishment. It's circular reasoning: they're prisoners; therefore they should be in prison. For the past 35 years it has been nearly impossible for an American politician to lose an election for being too tough on crime.

It wasn't until 2010, two years into Obama's first term, that things began to change. Very quietly, the president signed legislation reducing federal sentencing disparities between crack and powder cocaine. For more than 20 years, crack users received far longer sentences than powder users. It wasn't a coincidence that crack tended to have more black users, and powder more white users.

That same year, Michelle Alexander published a remarkable book called *The New Jim Crow*. Alexander, a civil rights litigator and law professor at Ohio State University, put forth a startling thesis. The War on Drugs, she argued, had become a stealthily instituted system of racial oppression. Her title said it all: under the guise of law enforcement, American had enacted a new form of Jim Crow, the system of racial segregation outlawed by the Civil Rights Act of 1964.

It was an idea that Alexander herself found almost laughably radical when she heard it first proposed. But the more she investigated, the more she found the evidence leading her to that disturbing conclusion:

> In this era of colorblindness, it is no longer socially permissible to use race, explicitly, as a justification for discrimination, exclusion, and social contempt. So we don't. Rather than rely on race, we use our criminal justice system to label people of color 'criminals' and then engage in all the practices we supposedly left behind. Today it is perfectly legal to discriminate against criminals in nearly all the ways that it was once legal to discriminate against African Americans. Once you're labeled a felon, the old forms of discrimination— employment discrimination, housing discrimination,

denial of the right to vote, denial of educational opportunity, denial of food stamps and other public benefits,
and exclusion from jury service—are suddenly legal. As
a criminal, you have scarcely more rights, and arguably
less respect, than a black man living in Alabama at the
height of Jim Crow. We have not ended racial caste in
America; we have merely redesigned it.

I wanted to know what role marijuana played in that disparity. Pot
laws have been gradually loosened in Washington, Colorado and other
states over the past decade. That's not the case in many other parts of
the country. I went looking for the other extreme. Where was the anti-
Colorado, the bizarro Washington state?

The answer wasn't hard to find. People told me: look to Louisiana.

That surprised me. I'd been to New Orleans. I'd spent the better
part of a month crisscrossing the state during the Deepwater Horizon
oil spill. I loved Louisianans—their friendliness, their food, their rich
culture and joie de vivre. When Americans look for the worst in something, we traditionally turn to our national barrel bottom, Mississippi.
But Mississippi's marijuana laws were positively progressive compared
with Louisiana's. Texas? Ha! Louisiana's draconian pot sentences made
Texas smell like Berkeley on 4/20.

I got tipped to a case.

Bernard Noble. A 47-year-old truck driver. Born and raised in New
Orleans. Father of seven. Two of the kids have significant medical problems. As a young man he'd gotten into a few scrapes with the law. Got
caught with cocaine on the wrong corner at the wrong time. He did
his time and got his act together. Landed a job, raised a family. When
Katrina hit New Orleans, Noble's job disappeared, along with his house,
his car and all his possessions. He spent two hellish days and nights in
the Superdome before catching a bus to Kansas City. There he started

over. Got a job as a truck driver. Caught on with a towing service. Saved enough to buy his own truck. Things were looking up.

In 2010 he returned to New Orleans for a couple of days to see his father, who worked as a sound system installer at a shop on Washington Avenue. On the afternoon of Oct. 10, Noble left his car with his father to have a new radio installed. He borrowed a bicycle leaning against the shop wall. A few minutes later, as he pedaled down Miro Street, a New Orleans Police Department patrol car appeared. Noble turned to get out of the car's way. The officers read this as an evasive maneuver. Or they found a 47-year-old African-American man on a bicycle to be suspicious. (Did I mention that Bernard Noble is black? I haven't yet, but this is the point in the story where it becomes relevant. The cops were white. Noble is not.) Or they just needed to meet their stop-and-frisk quota. For whatever reason, they stopped him.

Noble was holding.

Just a couple of joints, nothing serious. Less than three grams of marijuana wrapped in rolling papers and stashed in a brown bag in Noble's pocket.

Here was the point of decision. The cops could have let it go. They could have tossed the joints in the gutter and told Noble to go about his day. They did not.

Bernard Noble went to jail. He was tried and found guilty. Felony possession of marijuana. In Louisiana, a first conviction for marijuana merits a few months in jail. But this wasn't Noble's first conviction. Because he had served time years earlier, the Orleans Parish District Attorney triple-billed him. In his sentencing brief, the D.A. asked for $13\frac{1}{3}$ years at hard labor.

Triple-billing: in Louisiana it's a term of art. Many states adopted tough three-strikes laws during the 1990s as a way to keep violent recidivists off the streets. In Louisiana, lawmakers adopted a grotesquely punitive three-strikes law meant for the worst of the worst, to be used rarely and with discretion. But prosecutors do not use this power, which came to be known as triple-billing, rarely or with discretion. They use it just about every time they can. Once an offender is convicted of a third felony, no matter how insignificant, Louisiana prosecutors will commonly triple-bill the offender, which means pressing for a three-strikes sentence that can keep him in prison for the rest of his natural life.

The trial judge, looking over Noble's impressive work history and child support, refused to give him 13$\frac{1}{3}$ years. Instead he sentenced him to five years without parole. Noble, the judge said, "is one of the few truly deserving" a lesser sentence. He called the mandated range "constitutionally excessive."

That did not please Orleans Parish District Attorney Leon Cannizzaro. Cannizzaro didn't win elections by being soft on crime. He appealed Noble's sentence.

The appeals court judge found himself handcuffed by state law. In an extraordinary opinion, he wrote: "This Court believes with all of its heart and all of its soul that this is injustice." Then he declared that Noble's sentence had been increased to 13 years and four months. The law allowed no possibility of parole.

––––––––––

How does something like that happen?

The whole thing seemed to illustrate the divide between the two nations of America. Bernard Noble and I were the same age. When I desired two grams of marijuana, I strolled into The Joint, paid 20 bucks, and exited with my purchase in a brown paper bag. When Noble hankered for the same, he bought from (I assume) a local pot dealer and stuffed a similar paper bag in his pocket. Had I spilled my weed in front of a Seattle police officer, the cop might have bent over to help me sweep it into the bag. Noble got caught with the same weight and lost 13 years and four months of his life. He lost the childhood of his children. The children lost their father.

One of the lawyers I spoke with, a longtime New Orleans defense attorney named Gary Wainwright, took Noble's tale in stride. "You might think this is a horror story," he told me, "but not in Louisiana. We've had people receive sentences of life without parole for marijuana here. Twenty-five years in prison? In Louisiana that's a *deal*."

For most of its history, Louisiana, like other states, locked up about one fifth of 1 percent of its population. In 1980 the state housed 8,900 prisoners. During the Reagan-era drug war, those numbers began climbing. By 1990 the state had doubled its incarcerated population. By 2000 the state's prisons strained to contain 35,000 offenders. The inmates kept piling up. By 2012, Louisiana had become the prison capital of the world: 39,709 prisoners. Together they would constitute Louisiana's 10th largest city. If you included inmates awaiting trial, the incarceration rate was 1,619 for every 100,000 people in the state. That was five times the incarceration rate of Iran.

On the ride in from the airport, a Gulf Coast thunderstorm hammered New Orleans. In the back of a taxi I paged through the *Times-Picayune* and the *Gambit*, the city's alternative weekly. The French Quarter Festival had wrapped the night before. The Saints were looking for a cornerback in the draft. A local parish council voted to outlaw saggy pants. In Baton Rouge, state legislators argued over the state's "crimes against nature" statute, which still outlawed blow jobs, and a bill to designate the Bible as the official state book. The arguing wasn't about church-state separation but rather over which edition of the Good Book should be so enshrined. Some championed the traditional King James Version. Others championed the Catholic St. Joseph Edition. One senator held out for an ancient Latin Vulgate edition published in the early 1500s. I wondered if the Vulgate version contained one of those archaic lost chapters, like the Book of Enoch, that laid down proscriptions against oral sex and the wearing of breeches that doth saggeth and offend The Lord Our God.

As long as we're talking racial disparity, allow me to own my own white privilege. While in New Orleans I fully enjoyed the advantages of my social class and skin tone. Friends of friends had kindly offered Claire and me the use of their Garden District mansion for the week. The house was magnificent. Twelve-foot bay windows, Jacquard silk curtains, a front-porch gas lamp, vases that cost more than my car. Located a few blocks from Magazine Street, the house fronted a magnolia-lined boulevard that led to Trent Reznor's plantation-style crib. The Manning brothers, Peyton and Eli, grew up a few blocks away. When the storm subsided, I poured myself a bourbon and listened to the birds chirp in the live oaks. The emerging sun glinted off Mardi Gras beads looped on a wrought iron fence. A breeze wandered across the veranda. The white upper-class New Orleans lifestyle: not so bad.

Prosecutors in most states have the upper hand against defendants, but Louisiana prosecutors had upper hands, legs and feet. The state didn't require a unanimous jury for a criminal conviction; a defendant could go down on a 10–2 vote. That gave prosecutors an inordinate amount of power. Faced with a tilted jury box and the probability of a long prison stretch, defendants often accepted even the harshest plea deals. In some parishes, prosecutors play with such a stacked deck that an entire year may pass without a single defendant going to trial.

Gary Wainwright, the defense attorney, was a bow-tied New Orleans dandy with a reputation as an outspoken champion of the poor and dispossessed. At the time we spoke, he'd been suspended from practice for 18 months for a minor financial infraction. The setback seemed to faze Wainwright not a bit; he relished the role of the courthouse rascal. It didn't surprise me, then, when he rolled out an incredible explanation for the prison state in which he practiced. "You can't run a prison without inmates," he told me. "We have an entire industry with a vested interest in maintaining full jails. And the easiest way to keep the jails full is to arrest black men for pot possession."

Oh, come on, I thought. I'd been to enough left-wing hootenannies to know hyperbole when I heard it.

With each passing day, however, I found Wainwright's claim accruing more and more plausibility.

I stopped in to talk to Bill Rittenberg, a veteran New Orleans civil rights lawyer. Rittenberg practiced out of an 1830s firehouse on Girod Street. "Back in the late '60s, I'd get calls from Tulane parents when their kids got busted for pot," he told me. "The laws on first-time offenses were really bad back then. Cops would go through your pockets and arrest you for 'gleanings,' what you and I would call crumbs. People did five years for that. No probation."

Louisiana has always enjoyed a notoriety for its brutal prisons and chain gangs. What set it on the path to becoming a prison state, though, was the practice of triple-billing. Prosecutors seemed to bring three-strikes charges against anybody and everybody who was black or poor. What began as a law to lock up violent criminals became a tool to lock up minorities and the poor, no matter how minor the crime.

Drug offenders and triple-billed longtimers swelled Louisiana's prisons to the point where a federal court ordered the state to reduce overcrowding. Louisiana could either draw down its incarceration rate or build more prisons. The state didn't have much money. So legislators found a third way.

Instead of constructing more state prisons, the state began paying local sheriffs to house state offenders. It cost $63 a day to bunk a prisoner at Angola, Louisiana's notorious maximum-security state prison. Local parishes (Louisiana's counties) could do the job for $24.39. So parishes invested in new jailhouses, anticipating a steady inflow of customers from the state. They issued bonds to construct parish jails that held more beds than state prisons. Prisoners became an income stream. By the late '90s, imprisoning its citizens had become a substantial profit-making industry in the state of Louisiana.

In 2012 the staff of the *Times-Picayune* published an eight-part series detailing how Louisiana became the world's top jailer. Its conclusion: money drove the machine.

> Today, wardens make daily rounds of calls to other sheriffs' prisons in search of convicts to fill their beds. Urban areas such as New Orleans and Baton Rouge have an

excess of sentenced criminals, while prisons in remote parishes must import inmates to survive. The more empty beds, the more an operation sinks into the red.

—*Times-Picayune*, May 13, 2012

Fred Schoonover, deputy warden of the Tensas Parish jail in northeast Louisiana, spent his days scaring up new bodies for his beds. "We struggle," Schoonover told the *Times-Picayune*. "I stay on the phone a lot, calling all over the state, trying to hustle a few."

A handful of private prison corporations run many of the operations for smaller parishes. The companies get the per diem; the parishes get a payout. The *Times-Picayune* reported that Emerald Prison Enterprises paid an annual fee of $200,000 for the lease of a parish jail from the village of Epps, La., population 854. In parishes that run their own prisons, the sheriff is often the region's biggest employer. He spreads the patronage, and voters respond with their ballots. "A drop in the incarceration rate could spell doom for both LaSalle Corrections and the sheriffs," the *Times-Picayune* reported. As you might expect, prison corporations and the Louisiana Sheriffs' Association operate some of the most powerful lobbying groups in the state.

———

Bernard Noble was ensnared in this madness. Because he already had a few nonviolent, low-level convictions, the New Orleans District Attorney automatically triple-billed him. Didn't matter that the previous crime had occurred eight years earlier. Or that he'd proved to be an exemplary, hardworking middle-aged father. In Louisiana, Noble was just another African American caught in the gears of the mill.

It wasn't easy to reach him. I think many of us, by which I mean me, have a fanciful notion about inmate visitation. We think prison visiting hours are like hospital visiting hours. You show up, request some time with an inmate and, after a short wait, are ushered into a room containing cubicles, stools, thick glass, and telephone receivers. Like on *The Sopranos*.

It wasn't like that in Louisiana.

First you had to find your inmate. The state's 39,709 prisoners were scattered among dozens of state prisons and parish warehouses. Like most people convicted of a crime in New Orleans, Noble was shipped out to a rural parish jail. I discovered that he was being held at the Concordia Parish Correctional Facility in Ferriday. A northern Louisiana town of 3,700, Ferriday was the birthplace of Jerry Lee Lewis and his two cousins, country star Mickey Gilley and evangelist Jimmy Swaggart. Nowadays what Ferriday produces are prisons and prison guards. The state's River Correctional Facility (602 beds) stands alongside the Concordia Parish Correctional Facility (510 beds) on the outskirts of town. When people in Ferriday go to work, they drive to prison.

If 1,112 beds seems excessive for a parish of 20,365 residents, that's because it is. King County, Washington, which contains Seattle and about 2 million residents, maintains a county jail with 3,039 beds. That's one bed for every 658 residents. Concordia Parish maintains a bed for every 18 residents. Except they're clearly not for parish residents. They're to warehouse the convicts from down South. "The economic benefits to the parish are enormous," the Concordia Parish Sheriff's Office boasted in its 2012 annual report: a payroll of $8.5 million, a $2 million surplus, nearly 300 employees and ultra-cheap rent-a-convict labor. "Inmate crews work year-around on beautification crews in the parish and municipalities, at great cost-savings to governmental agencies," wrote the office.

When Bernard Noble filled a bed at the Concordia Parish jail, he pumped $24.39 per day into the local economy.

I called the prison. The officer on the other end of the line seemed extremely busy. Or else just perturbed that I was interrupting her day.

Was it possible to call Mr. Noble?

No.

Could he call me collect?

"If you're on his list and you have an account."

"How would I get on his list?"

"He would have to put you there."

"Could I visit in person?"

"Offenders are allowed visiting privileges once every two weeks, and only with those persons on their list, attorneys, or clergy. Are you one of them?"

"No."

She sighed. "I suggest you write a letter."

————————

I wrote a letter and waited. In the meantime, I set about tracking down Bernard Noble's court records. As with all things judicial in Louisiana, this took some doing.

The Orleans Parish Criminal Courts Building is a standing seminar in the architecture of state power and intimidation. Built in 1930 at the height of Jim Crow, it's fronted by massive ionic columns and a long skirt of steps, like the U.S. Supreme Court building. It's grand and imposing and intended to be. From its portico I surveyed the breadth of Tulane Avenue, from bail bond row to the old Dixie Beer brewery down east. Past the front door, a phalanx of mustaches and metal detectors blocked my passage. "No electronics allowed in courthouse," a sign declared. "No computers, no cell phones, no recorders, no laptops."

The sign caught me short. What kind of courthouse banned cell phones and computers in 2014? Answer: a Louisiana courthouse. Fortunately, Claire had accompanied me. I handed her my cell phone, Marantz recorder, handheld scanner and MacBook. We agreed to meet in a nearby diner in an hour or so. I walked through security with only a legal pad and a pen. The deputies cast a sour look at the pen.

Navigating the courthouse was like wandering back to the days of Huey Long. My footfalls echoed off the white marble walls. Each courtroom was set off by imperial 12-foot doorways with signs spelling out the rules peculiar to the judge who reigned within. "NO FOOD • NO DRINK • NO EXCEPTIONS • PENALTY 24 HRS O.P.P.," decreed Judge Julian A. Parker. (That's 24 hours in the Orleans Parish Prison for those who dared to smuggle a Twizzler past the door.) Lawyers, defendants and their families huddled outside courtrooms. All the lawyers were white. All the defendants were black.

Courthouses across America have by and large accepted that computers may be more than a passing fad. Louisiana is a late adopter. Orleans Parish clerks had access to ancient machines running what I could only imagine was that ghastly software from the '80s, Atex. I requested a copy of Bernard Noble's court records. After a sufficient wait, I was informed that his papers had been sent to an off-site archive. Somewhere east of Tallahassee, I assumed. I would have to come back another day.

I sighed.

This is how oppressive state power works. It grinds away at you. It strips you of all the tools of modern civilization—mobile phones, computers, video and voice recorders, which is to say *access to information*—and allows you into the halls of justice with nothing but a pen, paper and pants. Those electronics aren't just beeping, buzzing annoyances. They're the essential tools of a working democracy. They provide immediate evidence to rebut a prosecutor's charge or a judge's outlandish claim. They etch a record of injustice or malfeasance. They allow an attorney or a defendant to communicate with the outside world, to check a fact, to reschedule an arraignment, to let a boss know they'll be arriving late to work. They are a necessary check on the overwhelming power of the state. In Louisiana they are not allowed.

———

Later that afternoon I stopped by the public defender's office not far from the courthouse. It was just as shabby as you might imagine. As a young lawyer photocopied Noble's file, I sat near the elevator and listened to the comings and goings of court-appointed attorneys. All seemed to be young, short on time and overworked. At one point a harried young man in a cheap tie sought out his supervisor.

"The defendant is somewhat mentally challenged," he said. "The prosecutor wants to triple-bill him."

The supervisor, a woman in her 40s, pursed her lips. "What's your offer?"

"We take 10 years, they pull the bill."

"What do they want?"

"To pull the bill they want 20."

The supervisor's body deflated.

"What do we do?" the defender pressed. "They need an answer." He glanced at his watch.

"Try again for the 10 and no bill."

––––––––

Claire had claimed a booth at Avery's on Tulane, a po'boy sandwich shop with a two-pedal Adler organ by the door and a wicked dish of fried green tomatoes. "Iko Iko" played on the jukebox. You'd think people in New Orleans would be sick to death of that song, but maybe it's like hearing "Smells Like Teen Spirit" in Seattle. Reminds you of home.

I read through Noble's file, looking for something, anything, that might justify his sentence. A past rape conviction. An assault charge later dropped. A scuffle with weapons.

Here's what I found. Between 1989 and 2003, Noble was convicted four times for using small quantities of marijuana or cocaine. That's it. He had no prior conviction for a crime of violence, or any offense committed against a person or property. In 2010—eight years after his last arrest—he was picked up for holding two joints in New Orleans. Bernard Noble wasn't a violent criminal. He wasn't a drug dealer. He was a truck driver and a supportive father who'd come down from Kansas City to see his dad.

I reached the Orleans Parish District Attorney's office later by email. I asked why they were so adamant about giving Noble 13 years for two joints. "The D.A.'s office took into account his lengthy criminal record that included multiple felony convictions," a spokesperson wrote. The D.A. appealed Noble's original five-year sentence "because the sentence imposed by the court was illegal," the spokesperson wrote. "Neither the D.A.'s office nor the court makes the law. The legislature—the elected representatives of the citizens of Louisiana—makes such decisions. The

D.A.'s office and the courts possess a legal obligation to enforce the laws that exist."

This is nonsense. The D.A.'s office makes judgment calls every day about which arrests to prosecute, which defendants to triple-bill and which court decisions to appeal. They work within the bounds of the law; they're not helpless before it. That "lengthy criminal record" with multiple felonies? A few convictions for personal drug use over a 14-year period.

After Orleans Parish D.A. Cannizzaro succeeded in sticking Noble with the full triple bill, Noble appealed the sentence to the Louisiana State Supreme Court. The court declared that a judge could waver from triple-bill mandatory minimums only in exceptional cases. And in Louisiana, Bernard Noble was entirely unexceptional. His appeal was denied.

My phone rang. The caller ID said "CONCORDIA PARISH CORR."

Bernard Noble was grateful that someone had taken an interest in his case.

"I don't know what I'm doing here, Bruce," he said. "I'm in here with a bunch of murderers and rapists. People ask what I'm in for and I'm afraid to tell 'em marijuana. Because they just laugh at that."

I asked how he filled his days.

"I try to keep away from the crazy ones, the guys in here with aggravated charges," he said. State prisons, because they're built for long-haul sentences, often have programs for inmates. Work programs. Study programs. Therapy. Parish jails, which are set up as temporary warehouses, often lack these amenities.

"I'm in this room with 45 other people," he told me. "The smoking is driving me crazy. Every couple of blue moons they'll let us go outside. But it's so small a yard that we end up just staring at one another."

I asked if there was a prison library.

"They don't give us books to read," he said. "It's hard to get any information at all in here. I understand this is jail. But really it's more like a human warehouse."

I asked if it was possible for me to visit him while I was in Louisiana. "I think my visiting day is this Saturday," he said.

I checked with the prison. No, they said, it was the following Saturday.

I sent a note to Cassey Byrnes, the prison's warden and chief of security. I called and left a message. He called back a couple of days later.

"Mr. Barcott," he said. "This is Chief Byrnes at Concordia. Yeah, we're gonna have to decline your request for a visitation with offender Noble. As it is not his regularly scheduled visitation day."

———

That night Claire and I attended a birthday party in New Orleans's Warehouse District. The fete was thrown for a friend of a friend's sister. We were crashers, essentially. But the people there welcomed us like old friends. They offered us cake and soda and five kinds of beer iced in a big metal tub. We drank and swayed to the sounds of a drum-and-bass combo. There were white people, black people, Cajuns, Hispanics and an older couple of Asian heritage. One man danced in nothing but overalls and skin. Young men wore white singlets and porkpie hats and smoked tobacco as if their lungs were made of leather. Twinkly lights hung from nails inside the old shack, which was little more than framing studs and facing planks. It was a party you dream of falling into during a visit to New Orleans.

As I stood there swaying to the music, cold beer in hand, I tried to reconcile Louisiana's rich cultural depth, its diversity and the warmth of its people with the utter nightmare of its legal system. The people around me were in a state of bliss. It was as if their enjoyment of life's pleasures was heightened by the fact that they lived on the edge of a cliff and could tumble off at any moment.

———

"This is crazy," I said to Bill Rittenberg, the civil rights lawyer. "How does it continue?"

We were back to discussing Louisiana's marijuana laws.

He smiled and nodded, as if to say, *Yes. It is crazy. And I have been living with the crazy for all of my natural life.*

"You have to understand," he said. "Marijuana laws are enforced against black people. They aren't enforced against middle-class and upper-class white people."

At a certain point Louisiana's marijuana law had become simply a pretext to trap African-American men in the state's prison system. Think back to the reason for Bernard Noble's stop: bicycling while black. The cops fished through his pockets and found two joints. Arrest, jail, conviction. It's as if NOPD officers were patrolling with dip nets, fishing for black men to fill their jails.

Marjorie Esman told me I wasn't far from the truth. Esman directed the Louisiana chapter of the American Civil Liberties Union. Where I come from, the ACLU's annual Bill of Rights dinner is one of the highlights of the city's social calendar. The mayor shows up. Movie stars like Kathleen Turner keynote the event. That sort of thing doesn't happen in Louisiana. The ACLU does not publish its address in New Orleans. The locked office door is marked only by a sign that says "PRIVATE." I rang a jerry-rigged doorbell. Esman answered. "It's a security measure," she told me. The ACLU: not overly popular around these parts.

I stopped in to see Esman because the ACLU had recently published a nationwide study on the racial disparity in marijuana arrests. Between 2001 and 2010, there were more than 8 million arrests for marijuana in the U.S. Eighty-eight percent of those were for possession. Despite the passage of medical marijuana laws in nearly half of all states, marijuana arrests had increased during the century's first decade. By 2010, marijuana accounted for more than half of all drug arrests in the U.S.

That rise in arrests resulted from the widespread adoption of data-driven policing, which rewarded officers and precinct captains for recording high arrest numbers. New York City's notorious "stop and frisk" policy, which targeted black and brown people for indiscriminate sidewalk interrogations, was the most infamous example. But it happened all over the country.

The ACLU report, co-authored by Ezekiel Edwards, focused on the racial component of those arrests. On average, a black person was four times as likely as a white person to be arrested for marijuana possession, even though blacks and whites used marijuana at similar rates. In Louisiana, the state's 30 percent black population made up 60 percent of the marijuana arrests. In St. Landry Parish, the Creole/Cajun region east of Baton Rouge, the black-white disparity in marijuana arrests was more than 10 to one.

During the week I stopped in, Esman was busy fighting the expansion of "saggy pants" laws across the state.

A chuckle escaped me when she mentioned this. Outlawing saggy pants. Ha! What next—10 years for untied shoes?

Esman did not share my amusement. "Who wears saggy pants?" she demanded.

Was this rhetorical? "Um . . . young black men?" I said.

"This is the thing," she said. "These ordinances are intended to create an entry point into the criminal justice system for young black men."

The worst of these ordinances put young black men in jail for low-hanging pants. The lesser laws resulted in a citation. "But that citation becomes a pretext," she said. "The officer says, 'Pull your pants up, here's a ticket, oh, and by the way, do you mind if I check your pockets?'"

"A stop-and-frisk."

"Right. And very few people know they have the right to refuse. Or the courage to refuse a police officer."

———

Was there hope for Louisiana?

Perhaps. It was small. A glimmer. But it was something. A New Orleans–based think tank called the Pelican Institute had stirred up some new ideas in Baton Rouge. The institute, run by a forward-thinking conservative named Kevin Kane, moved fresh thinking about school choice, free-market environmentalism and crime policy into a state where new ideas are not generally received with rose bouquets.

Kane and the ACLU's Esman had found common cause on the issue of crime reform. Esman saw Louisiana's medieval sentences and prison system as an affront to social justice and human dignity. Kane saw it as taxpayer money wasted on a failing government program.

"I heard about this new approach a few years ago at a policy conference," Kane told me over iced coffee on a sultry New Orleans afternoon. "A group from Texas calling themselves 'Right on Crime' approached legal reform from a fiscal-conservative point of view." Around 2007, Texas realized it was running out of prison space. With a rising population and tougher drug laws, the state needed to spend hundreds of millions of dollars on new prisons. "Or they could explore other options," said Kane. That meant finding alternatives to prison, incarcerating fewer people and spending less taxpayer money.

Texas passed the first of its "Right on Crime" reforms in 2007. The state saved millions of dollars, imprisoned fewer people and saw recidivism rates drop. That was the amazing thing. Putting fewer people in prison and reducing sentences resulted in fewer convicts re-offending.

Georgia adopted similar reforms in 2012. Mississippi followed in early 2014. Louisiana would be a tougher nut to crack. Kane and the Pelican Institute championed nine bills dealing with issues like sentencing, parole and alternatives to incarceration. One bill downgraded marijuana possession to a simple misdemeanor for every offense. "Ten years in jail for a joint offends many people's sense of justice," Kane told me, "including my own."

Passing those bills, he said, "isn't realistic this year." It would probably take another year to move more votes to his side of the ledger. A number of parish district attorneys had warmed to the "Right on Crime" way of thinking. The sheriffs had not. They probably never would. "Half of our state prisoners are held in parish jails, and local sheriffs depend on that revenue," Kane told me. "They're not eager to see it go away."

It had become a simple issue of finance. Parish officials had bond payments to make on those new prisons. They needed the income stream. And for that they needed prisoners.

———

Bernard Noble appealed his case one last time to the Louisiana State Supreme Court. He waited all year to hear whether the court would accept his appeal. Through the middle of 2014, he called me on my cell phone every couple of weeks. I'd accept the charges and we'd talk. Mostly he'd ask whether I'd heard anything new about his case. Every time I had to tell him no.

By and by, his calls became less frequent. I couldn't blame him. I had little to give beyond my outrage and sympathy.

At a certain point Noble's calls stopped altogether. I sent him a letter. It came back marked "Return to Sender." A note on the envelope said Offender No. 798891 was no longer incarcerated in the Concordia Parish Correctional Center. Another parish prison had put in a bid for him. There was an empty bed that needed to be filled.

19

SMALL CATASTROPHES
IN COLORADO

The bad thing happened in Colorado.

The unforeseen event that Tripp Keber and others in the cannabis industry expected, feared and prepared for played out in a Denver hotel on the night of March 11.

Levy Thamba was a 19-year-old college student from the Republic of Congo. The Kinshasa native earned a scholarship to Northwest College, a small two-year college in the town of Powell, Wyo. In early March he and three friends road-tripped to Denver. They all went in on a room at a Holiday Inn. The desk clerk put them on the fourth floor. The group went downtown, where 23-year-old Bessie Gondwe bought some infused edibles at Native Roots Apothecary on Denver's 16th Street Mall. Gondwe was the only one over 21. She picked out four Sweet Grass Kitchen lemon poppy seed cookies. They sold for $10 apiece. Each contained 65 milligrams of THC. A Native Roots budtender told Gondwe that each cookie contained six servings and she should go easy on them. Cut them up and eat one serving at a time. Edibles take some time to kick in, so wait a while before eating more.

Back at the Holiday Inn, Gondwe handed out the cookies and made sure everyone broke theirs into pieces. Each of the friends ate a piece. After a while, Thamba grew impatient. He said he didn't feel anything. So he ate the rest of his cookie.

Later that night Thamba awoke in a panic. He was shivering and speaking incoherently in French. Gondwe and the others calmed him down. But he couldn't sleep. One time he started talking to a lamp. "This is a sign from God that this has happened, that I can't control myself," he told his friend Anna Jakaovljeveic. She urged him to close his eyes and sleep. Not long after, Thamba began smashing furniture and pulling pictures off the walls. He ran out of the room, down the hallway, then tumbled over a railing overlooking the lobby. The fall killed him.

———————

One month later, a worse thing happened.

On the evening of April 14, Richard Kirk, a 47-year-old father of three, stopped in at Nutritional Elements, a marijuana store in southeast Denver. He bought a single joint and a 100-milligram candy edible called Karma Kandy Orange Ginger.

Richard had been having money troubles and marriage troubles. He and his wife Kristine had racked up $40,000 in credit card debt. The couple had been fighting about it. In March, Richard asked a friend if he could stay with him for a few days. He and Kris were having problems, he said.

About an hour after he bought the pot products, Richard arrived home and ate the candy. It's not clear whether he smoked the joint as well.

Around 9:00 that night, he began hallucinating and acting irrationally. He started talking about the end of the world. He asked his wife to shoot him.

At 9:30, Kris called 911. "We've been married 15 years; my kids and I have never seen him acting like this," she told the operator. Richard was acting drunk and paranoid, but he didn't seem violent. "Please hurry," she said.

In the background of the call, Richard Kirk could be heard telling his wife that she was "smarter and stronger" than him.

Kris Kirk stayed on the line with the 911 operator. Twelve minutes into the call, the police still hadn't arrived. "Don't go in there!" she yelled at her husband. "Stay away from the gun." Kris told the operator, "He's getting into the gun safe."

The operator stayed on the line. Kris didn't know where to go. Richard reappeared with the gun. Kris took off running and screaming. A shot was fired. The screaming stopped.

The operator stayed on the line. Seven minutes later, nearly 20 minutes after Kris Kirk placed the 911 call, police officers could be heard knocking at the door.

Kris Kirk was found dead from a single gunshot wound to the head. Richard Kirk was arrested for murder.

AT THE
CANNABIS CUP

Five days after the murder of Kristine Kirk, I flew to Colorado to attend the High Times Cannabis Cup. It was being held on April 19 and April 20, the traditional stoner's holiday. I had been poking around marijuana and the cannabis industry for more than a year. It was time to enter the belly of the beast. In pot culture, the core doesn't come any harder than Cannabis Cup.

In 1987, *High Times* editor Steven Hager got the idea for a cannabis harvest festival during a visit to the Netherlands. Part competition, part tribal gathering, the Cannabis Cup grew to become an international pot convention, with thousands of cannabis connoisseurs descending on Amsterdam during late November.

When Colorado and Washington went legal, the Cup finally came to America. In April 2013, *High Times* put on a Cannabis Cup in Denver. When the doors opened, 17,000 people poured in.

In 2014 the Cup opened at the Denver Mart, a downscale meeting barn. Sold out—37,000 people each day. Lines wrapped around

the building. Two hours just to get in the door. I did a rough calcula-
tion. Thirty-seven thousand people at $75 a day, for two days: let's say
$5 million, give or take. Vendors: 600 at about $2,500 per booth. That's
another $2 million. Let's say you've got $2 million in costs: hall rental,
deposit, security, administration. You do the math.

"This is crazy, my friend! All people going here. Is blocked. No good,
Bruce. No good."

Ali, my cab driver, was not happy.

At a few minutes past noon on a Saturday in April, Ali and I found
ourselves gridlocked on Interstate 25 about half a mile south of the trade
mart, a B-list convention center on the northern edge of Denver. I stuck
my head out the window. Looked north. Looked south. Nobody was
moving. People were Woodstocking their cars on the shoulder.

A Toyota 4Runner packed with six gentlemen in their early 20s inched
alongside us. Elbows jutted out windows.

"Hey!" One of them gestured to Ali. "You going to Cannabis Cup?"

Ali shook his indignant head. "No I am not!" he said.

The bro blew a lungful of smoke out the window.

"Y'should, man. Lot of money to be made."

The SUV six-pack cracked up. That was definitely the funniest thing
they'd heard in at least 10 seconds.

"Bruce, where is this place we are going?" Ali asked. He shot me eyes
in the rearview mirror.

"It's a . . . it's a marijuana convention, Ali."

His look of confusion turned to a sly smile.

"Ah. You like the marijuana, Bruce?"

"No, Ali, I'm more of a whiskey man."

That made him laugh.

"Oh, yes. A whiskey man. You are going to a marijuana convention
but you do not like the marijuana. I see. For you, whiskey."

He said this as if I had just explained to him that I retained my *Playboy* subscription for the magazine's excellent selection of fiction.

Ten minutes later we had registered zero forward progress. I passed two twenties to Ali, exited the vehicle and walked off the freeway. There was no need for a map or directions—37,000 people were racing to the Denver Mart like schoolchildren tardy for the bell.

———————

"Is this your first Cannabis Cup?" Melanie Holland shouted at me.

I nodded. House music *thumpa*'d my skull.

"Great," she said. "You're gonna love it. You might get a contact high. I'm just warning you."

I followed Holland, *High Times*'s media manager, to the magazine's booth at the edge of the outdoor smoking area. She wrapped a red MEDIA band around my wrist and bid me follow. "Let's introduce you to Michael," she said.

We threaded through the crowd, sweaty under the Colorado noonday sun, into a side door and down a warren of corridors strung with wires and empty boxes. Melanie caught sight of a shadowy figure in a doorway.

"Michael!" she cried.

We approached. Melanie hung back a respectful distance as a tanned old man in Florida casual wear—Michael, apparently—concluded a confidential consultation. Melanie introduced me as a writer. This displeased Michael.

"A writer, eh?" he said, sizing me up. "Whattaya writing about?" He shot Melanie an annoyed look.

"Marijuana," I said.

He nodded, taking this in as if I had suggested a new and devilishly clever angle.

We exchanged semi-cordial phrases. It became clear to me—I have a nose for these things—that Michael had no interest in being interviewed, quoted or identified with the magazine or the Cannabis Cup in any way. This despite the impression that Michael was the owner, or part-owner, or financial partner in some shell-corporation kind of way, of the magazine and the marijuana show. The guy radiated all the warmth and fuzziness of a Mafia don.

"What exactly is your role with the magazine and the show?" I asked.

He glared at me.

"I'm in . . ." He paused.

Construction? I thought. *Waste management?*

"Let's just say I'm an advocate for the magazine."

We parted in a *this never happened* kind of way, and I returned to ye merry cannabis faire.

The bloom of youth had long since abandoned the Denver Mart, a sad old barn stuck out by the Union Pacific rail yard. The walls wanted paint. The carpet shouted, "Go ahead! Stain me some more." The choice of venue puzzled me until someone mentioned that at the previous year's Cannabis Cup, attended by some 17,000 partakers, the organizers had neglected to properly clean up after the party. Word got around. Planners of the 2014 event didn't just need a space rugged enough to handle a surging and moderately sloppy crowd. They needed a venue desperate enough to take their money. Hello, Denver Mart!

It took me a while to get the lay of the land. According to the Cannabis Cup map, there was an indoor (nonsmoking) area and an outdoor (smoking) area. Inside featured a stage where leading cannabis industry figures engaged in panel discussions on issues of the day: Dabbing in Denver, Legal Cultivation, The Art of Edibles, The Future of Legalization. Indoor booths tended toward the industry's ancillary businesses. Potting soil. Grow lights. Synthetic urine.

Wait, what?

"The Whizzinator Touch!" featured a disturbingly lifelike schlong attached to a reservoir of drug-free pee. "#1 Synthetic Urine in the World!" boasted the company's banner. Which demanded the question: Had there been a judged competition? Obviously I had to know more. "Very quiet, fast acting, warm synthetic urine instantly," the company's literature promised. It was the adjective *warm* that turned my stomach.

The most popular booth inside the Mart was the one that offered a ticket to exit the Mart. By law, only those with proof of over-21 status could enter the outdoor smoking portion of the show. Cannabis Cup organizers employed three young women to stand behind a table. Their job was to individually verify the IDs of 37,000 people and band them with Tyvek bracelets. It's a shame the Guinness people weren't around, because I'm sure there was some sort of world record involved.

Once accessorized, Cannabis Cuppers streamed through a chain-link gate where security guards shouted, "Wristbands up!" and scanned to make sure everyone bore the plasticky-papery ring of approval. I stood and panopticonned the carnival around me. Clearly this was where the cool kids were hanging out. Across the warm blacktop stretched row upon row of vendors hawking product. There were glass pipe makers, botanical extraction machine manufacturers, cultivation soil sellers, mechanical trimmers, vape pen designers, cannabis-infused skin-care lines, grow room showrooms, T-shirt designers, seed sellers and dab stations. Many dab stations. The outdoor smoking area was essentially a dab tasting fair. Colorado law prohibited the unlicensed selling of marijuana and dab tokes, but it remained technically legal to freely share such things. So it was like attending an Oktoberfest where all the beer was free.

Here are more things that I saw: Neck tattoos. Electric-blue sneakers. Competitive beards. Flat-brim caps, often black. Blunts, vape pens, joints and more blunts. Young women in pot-leaf-patterned yoga pants. Tie-dyed knee socks. Old dudes with long, stringy hair and leather vests. Many young adult men wearing camouflage cargo shorts and extra-large T-shirts. Dogs: Pomeranians, Afghans and bull mastiffs. (Who brings a dog to a marijuana convention?) I saw a short person wearing a full-body reefer costume modeled on *Doonesbury's* Mr. Jay. T-shirts with half-clever dope references: a milkishly fonted GOT VAPE?, a Smokey the Bear logo, "The Cat and the Hash," Darth Vapor.

As I strolled the grounds, a curious realization came over me. Marijuana had become strangely absent from the marijuana scene. By marijuana I mean the plant itself. For the hard-core cannabist, the scene had shifted. Everywhere I turned, braceleted Cuppers queued up for their turn at the red-hot dabbing nail. Vegetable matter had become the wooden tennis racket of hard-core pot culture. It was all about carbon fiber now.

Nowhere was the line longer than at the dabbing tent sponsored by Mahatma Concentrates. I fell into talking with Shannon Wilson, co-founder of the company. She sat on a stool at the head of the line, checking IDs. "Of the first hundred people I've checked, only one was from Colorado," she told me. "How about that."

I asked why she saw the need to check IDs, given the bracelet system. She responded with a raised eyebrow. *You think I'm gonna trust my livelihood to 'Wristbands up'?* Shannon was a solidly built woman who wore a black hemp cadet cap. She was kind enough to walk me through her operation. "We've got four stations here," she said, indicating a bar with four stools and a budtender servicing each. At one station, a budtender named Nick waved his next customer in. Nick offered the young man, who had driven here from Atlanta, his choice of Kings Kush wax, Gucci OG wax, Trainwreck shatter or Hindu Kush shatter. (Shatter is a solid cannabis concentrate, named for the way it resembles shards of amber glass.) Atlanta chose the Kings Kush.

"Usually we like to check and see if they've done this before," Shannon told me. "If they haven't, we suggest they have a friend stand behind them in case they get a little lightheaded."

Nick loaded the rig with the Kings Kush wax. Instantly, a puff of smoke appeared in the glass chamber. Atlanta inhaled it all. He closed his eyes, allowed the molecules to sprint from lung to blood to brain and exhaled the satisfied *whoosh* of the blissed. He nodded in thanks, then pushed himself away from the bar.

Nick offered me the next dab. I politely declined. I would do a lot of polite declining over the course of the 4/20 weekend. This wasn't out of some sort of moral stance but because I knew enough about my "set" to know that a dab or even a hookah puff would close down the writerly portion of my brain.

After an hourlong meander down the outdoor pavilion, I aimed my compass at the Dixie Elixirs & Edibles booth. Or rather, the Dixie Tower. Tripp Keber had erected a three-story platform that reminded me of those scaffolding towers college football coaches use to oversee practice.

"Bruce!" he shouted from somewhere in the sky. "Come on up!"

I climbed to the second floor, which contained a DJ station and a wet bar. Up one more level I found the Trippster surveying the grounds from a black leather couch.

"How do you like our DJ deck?" he said. He slapped my palm with a cold Bud Light. "One of our new guys built it for us out of some shipping containers. We're going to start marketing them."

Of course they were. If Tripp Keber's business philosophy could be summed up in a phrase, it would be this: never stop expanding. Wants and desires came to him like hunger pangs, and when they struck he noted them and rationalized that others probably shared the same cravings. Voilà: a market. Just a few hours into the Cannabis Cup, Dixie Tower had become the envy of every merchant in the joint.

I emptied the beer and caught up with the edibles king. "We've started up an event-planning division," he said. "We usually have others produce shows for us, but I figured we could do just as well ourselves." He pressed a ticket on me. It was for a show the following evening at Denver's Fillmore Auditorium featuring Matisyahu, the Jewish reggae rapper. "Can you make it?" he said.

"I'll try," I said.

There were questions that needed putting to Mr. Keber. "We've got a kid who freaked out and fell off a balcony," I said. "And a man who murdered his wife. Both had reactions to infused edibles. How are you handling this?"

Keber nodded. After Levy Thamba's death, he and other Dixie executives addressed the issue with local reporters. "Our company was the only one that stepped up," he said, even though a Dixie product wasn't involved. "It's incredibly tragic. It makes me stop and think about a few things." Responsible consumption, he said, "has always been one of the foundations of Dixie." Had Levy Thamba or Richard Kirk purchased Dixie products, they would have seen an infograph on the label advising them on proper dosage. A toxicology report found that Thamba had 7.2 nanograms of active THC in his blood, slightly more than the legal limit for drugged driving in Colorado. "That's the equivalent of a couple glasses of wine," Keber said. "So I'm not sure what the story behind that is."

Both incidents, he told me, brought home the fact that during these early months of legalization, marijuana is being held to a standard of purity and scrutiny that few other products could withstand. "How many people died across the country last weekend under the influence of alcohol? How many overdosed on opiates?"

As Tripp left to attend to business, I spoke with Dixie's new marketing director, Joe Hodas. Hodas was a middle-aged father of three. Six months earlier he worked at a Denver ad agency. Dixie Elixirs was one of his accounts. Keber liked Hodas's work and offered him a job. After much discussion with his wife, Hodas accepted. Now his job involved meet-and-greets on the DJ deck at Cannabis Cup 2014. I asked him what he made of the scene.

"It's my first Cup," he said. "I come at this from the perspective of moderation. And from up here, I see a lot of excess." His arm swept over the crowd. "That concerns me."

"Tripp talks a lot about Dixie reaching the mainstream," I said, "but it seems like you've got to do it without losing this hard-core portion of the market."

He nodded. "That's the challenge we have. Ice Cube opened the show last night. And it made me think. He's a performer who's taken a unique path. He started out in hard-core gangsta rap. As he matured, he began to make more mainstream movies. Now he stars in family comedies like *Are We There Yet?* That's a long way from *Straight Outta Compton.* Yet somehow he hasn't lost his street cred. He can still come here and jump onstage and be accepted as the hard-core rapper." He turned and gazed at the hard-core cannabis crowd milling below him. "That balancing act is a tough one."

Since joining Dixie Elixirs as its chief marketing officer, Hodas had experienced a number of wild turns in the business. In early January the company's food and drink flew out the door faster than Dixie's chefs could cook. Then came April 14 and the murder of Kristine Kirk. The news hit Hodas hard.

"It's not just theoretical to me," he told me. His own children were acquainted with the Kirk children.

The Kirk tragedy forced him to take a hard look at his decision to join Dixie, he told me. "Am I doing the right thing?" he asked himself. Hodas told me he ultimately stuck with Dixie. More good could be done by leading the industry than by leaving it, he said. In fact, he said, Dixie was getting ready to launch a low-dose product line called Dixie One. The beverages and edibles would contain just a single dose, 10 milligrams of THC or less. Dixie One, Hodas believed, could revolutionize the market and make edibles safer.

"These incidents are wake-up calls," he told me. "We have to hammer the public education on edibles. If they don't work, wait. Don't eat more." As he spoke, though, I thought I detected the kind of concern that might not be allayed by a public education campaign. He was clearly troubled.

———

That night I sorted through data on alcohol, crime, overdose and death. I wanted perspective.

As much as the deaths of Levy Thamba and Kristine Kirk shocked me, I was wary of turning those tragedies into modern retellings of the Diane Linkletter myth. I wanted fathers to talk to their sons about marijuana and warn them about the real risks to the developing brain. I didn't want them to plant a vision of Levy Thamba tumbling off a hotel balcony in a psychotic panic.

In cognitive science there's a phenomenon known as confirmation bias. In many of us, there's a tendency to seek out and assign greater weight to evidence that confirms our preconceived notions—that's confirmation bias. For those who saw marijuana legalization as a foolish experiment bound to unleash harm on society, the Thamba and Kirk deaths exactly confirmed their suspicions.

Those were only two cases, though. Tens of thousands of people purchased and consumed state-legal cannabis in the first six months of 2014. There had been zero overdose deaths and two tragic fatalities linked to the use of legal pot.

Was my own confirmation bias a factor? I knew Tripp Keber. I enjoyed talking with him and watching him expand his business empire. Maybe my own bias was looking for a way to let him off the hook. Eighteen months into my marijuana explorations, I'd met countless marijuana researchers and members of the cannabis industry. Some of them were disingenuous, a few were outright fools, but for the most part I found them to be intellectually curious and undriven by political dogma. I couldn't say the same about those who were fighting to keep marijuana outlawed. I'd heard a few compelling arguments from leaders in the drug recovery community. But most of the anti-pot people I spoke with were either spin doctors like Kevin Sabet or uninterested in a genuine dialogue about the issues. So now and then I tried to remind myself: cordiality does not imply correctness.

In the 2000s the U.S. Department of Justice commissioned a number of studies to look into the influence of alcohol on crime. Here's what they found: More than one third of state prison inmates convicted of violent crimes were using alcohol at the time of the crime. One in four victims of violent crime reported that the perpetrator had been drinking prior to the act. More than one third of all victims of sexual assault reported that the offender was drinking around the time of the assault. Two thirds of domestic abuse victims reported that their abuser was using alcohol when the abuse occurred. The data on homicide is a little more varied. The Department of Justice estimated that alcohol was involved in one third to half of all murders in the U.S.

One third to half. There were 14,196 homicides in the U.S. in 2013. To be conservative, let's figure that booze was a major factor in one third of all murders that year. That means alcohol mixed into the murder of a Kristine Kirk somewhere in America every two hours of every day in 2013.

The Levy Thamba incident hit closer to home for me. I was once a 19-year-old who road-tripped over the border to indulge in a little recreational intoxication. It was the '80s. I lived in Seattle, where the drinking age was 21. In Canada it was 19. We piled into my roommate's '68 International Scout, talked our way across the 49th Parallel, and hit a Vancouver liquor store before crashing eight deep in a motel called The Sportsman.

College kids do that all the time. We returned home unscathed. Others are not so fortunate. According to the NIH's National Institute on Alcohol Abuse and Alcoholism, 1,825 college students between the ages of 18 and 24 die each year from alcohol-related unintentional injuries. That's five Levy Thambas every day. And though the circumstances of Thamba's death were ghastly, they're sadly common. From 1996 to 2008, students in six separate incidents suffered severe injuries after falling from college windows, balconies or roofs. All were drunk or had been drinking prior to the fall. Three of the six students died. Here's the thing. That data doesn't cover the United States. Or even one state. It's taken from *a single college*: my alma mater, the University of Washington.

Does that mean we should encourage college kids to get high instead of drunk? No. It means we need to consider marijuana within the context of other inebriating substances and their effects on society.

———————

At 4:18 on the afternoon of 4/20, hundreds of celebrants packed themselves like pickles in front of the DJ booth. A stack of speakers bumped the bass line to Afroman's stoner classic, "Because I Got High." Everyone was grooving. *"I was gonna clean my room, until I got high / I was gonna get up and find the broom, but then I got high . . ."* It's possibly the greatest anti-drug anthem ever written. By the end of the tune, Afroman is sleeping on the streets, lamenting having "messed up my entire life because I got high." I found myself smiling. It was a nice reminder that stoner culture wasn't just about the stupid. There were admirable parts to it, too. Like its eagerness to laugh, and laugh at itself.

"Thirty seconds!" the DJ announced.

More people pressed into the crowd.

At 4:19, I overheard a young woman behind me ask her friend, "How'd 4:20 start, anyway?" I didn't answer. It would have taken too long to explain.

Here's the deal. In 1971 a group of friends at San Rafael High School in Marin County, the affluent suburb north of San Francisco, began meeting at a statue of Louis Pasteur after school to light up. They'd gather around 4:20 in the afternoon. Before long, the meeting time became code; "4:20?" could mean anything from "Do you have any?" to "Shall we gather at the feet of *M. Pasteur* for weedly fellowship this afternoon?" The phrase was adopted by local Deadheads, who spread the custom nationwide as they followed the band on tour. Eventually the time became the date, and the date became a globally observed cannabis holiday.

The DJ counted down. "Ten! Nine! Eight!"

At exactly 4:20, everybody lit up, inhaled and blew a fog into the blue yonder. It was kind of anticlimactic, actually.

I made another spin of the outdoor smoking court. At a booth on the far side of the grounds, I spotted Ross Kirsch, the Stink Sack packaging king. "Ross!" I called out. "How's business?"

He smiled. "Very good, thank you."

In late 2013, he told me, an infusion of investment cash gave him the opportunity to develop a childproof package for the Colorado recreational market. Working with a manufacturing plant in Guangdong, China, he designed a zip-close bag that retailers were now ordering by the thousands. "We've even got a special design for Cannabis Cup," he said.

Across from Kirsch I spotted Andy and Pete Williams, the Medicine Man brothers. It took me a while to realize it was them, because they were all done up as characters from *Alice in Wonderland*. Pete was the Mad Hatter, and Andy was Tweedledee. Both wore the sunburned cheeks, permagrins and glazed eyes of men who had been hitting the company hookah all afternoon. They smiled and said hello, but I don't think they recognized me. Frankly, I'm not sure they would have recognized their own mother.

A curious thing happened around 4:40 that afternoon. Time slowed. Everybody at Cannabis Cup began moving in . . . slow . . . motion. Overbaked men found patches of shade and rested their bodies. Clumps of four to five friends, or new acquaintances, formed napping circles. As I moved through the grounds, I felt as though I had acquired the superpower of speed. I had, after all, spent the day not partaking.

That mind-space allowed me to make this observation. Here I was, hanging out with tens of thousands of testosterone-heavy young men in a hot, packed space, and I saw no violence. I saw no conflict. For two days I heard zero angry words and saw not a single clenched fist. At 4:20 nearly everybody at Cannabis Cup took long, strong draws of THC, CBD and a host of other cannabinoids. By 4:40 most of them were pleasingly high. Many adopted positions of repose. The scene made me think back to the La Guardia report, when researchers had the Rikers Island cons get high. The pot "produced a euphoric state with its feeling of well-being, contentment, sociability, mental and physical relaxation, which usually ended in a feeling of drowsiness." All across the Denver Mart, as the four o'clock hour gave way to five, bedtime beckoned. I stepped carefully between the supine Cuppers and caught a cab back to my hotel. Then I took a long, hot shower.

YOU ARE
NUMBER 121

Pete O'Neil and his C&C Cannabis company secured 502-legal storefronts in Seattle, Lynnwood and Bremerton. Chance would determine
whether he won licenses to operate one, two, all three—or none.

On May 1, 2014, the Washington State Liquor Control Board
announced the results of the marijuana license lottery to all those who
had applied. The email to Pete O'Neil began with a reminder that Seattle had been allotted 21 retail marijuana stores. The first 21 randomly
drawn applications would win the licenses. O'Neil's company had been
chosen number 121.

He opened other emails from the Board. Bremerton: no luck. O'Neil
got shut out of Lynnwood, too. Gene Wilder's Willy Wonka rejection
came into my head: *You get nothing! You lose! Good day, sir!*

I called O'Neil. "We didn't win anywhere," he told me. "Seattle, Lynnwood or Bremerton."

I didn't say a word. This was a disaster.

"In Bremerton there's too many numbers," he said. "And with our

Lynnwood application, they put us in the Seattle lottery." His voice didn't crack with defeat. He'd overcome longer odds in his life. He wasn't about to quit now.

"I'm on the other phone with my lawyer right now," he said. "I'll call you later."

He hung up.

———————

Pete O'Neil called back two days later.

"I just came from a meeting with my investors," he said. "They were a little uptight."

I could imagine. They'd invested upward of a quarter-million dollars with O'Neil. Everyone assumed he'd win at least one license. If O'Neil was a horse, his bettors would be tearing up their tickets.

"I got out my checkbook and told them, 'This is how much money is left in the account. I'll give it back today. Just say the word.'"

The investors demurred. *No, no, no,* they said. *Let's talk this through.*

"They want to keep fighting," O'Neil told me. "So we're going to explore some options. Maybe we do a deal with some of the lottery winners. Buy out their licenses. My lawyer is drawing up papers to incorporate a cannabis retail services operation."

"A what?"

"It's a management company. These sort of companies run half the gas stations in America. They hire the staff, run the books, do the marketing."

"So you'd be a marijuana store consultant," I said. "But you haven't ever run a marijuana store."

"I've got a thousand times the retail experience of most of these people who got the licenses," he said. "It's a way to establish the C&C brand, which is the main thing. Oh, and we're also thinking about opening a medical dispensary. It may be open for just a few months, but at least it would get us in the business. And get some cash flowing."

"So you're basically telling the Liquor Control Board to go fuck themselves."

"Why not?" he said. "They just did that to us. Listen, we're not getting out of the game. It's just going to be a little tougher than we thought."

A couple of days later, O'Neil sent out an email to his investors.

> FROM: Pete O'Neil   May 4, 2014
> TO: C&C Investors
>
> Dave Comeau reached out to me today by phone. He is with Better Buds Inc., #1 in the retail lottery in Bremerton. He wants to sell his license. He said his starting point is $100K for the license + extra part of income.
>
> I spoke to him just a hour ago. We are going to have lunch at Anthony's in Bremerton on Tuesday at noon.

I called him. "Pete, I'm not far from Bremerton," I said. "If you're going to buy Dave Comeau's license, I want to be there."

"OK," he said. "Where do I catch the ferry?"

Like O'Neil, Comeau had combed the countryside searching for a 502-legal storefront. "I called 25 realtors," he told me. "None would work with me." Finally he found an old two-story clapboard building in East Bremerton. Comeau was elated at winning the license. But it also put him in a bind.

"To build that space out into the kind of shop that people would feel comfortable walking into, to hire staff . . . well, that requires financing." He figured he'd need at least $100,000. That was a problem. No bank was going to offer a small business loan to an ex–restaurant manager stepping into the marijuana business.

That's where Pete O'Neil came in.

He could appear hyperactive and scattered at times. He talked too much. He drove his lawyers crazy by sharing his business plans with old friends, new acquaintances and untrustworthy writers like me. But the genius of O'Neil was the way his goofy M.O. attracted goodwill. Everywhere he went, people liked him and remembered him. They felt good about doing him a solid. O'Neil created his own karma.

Dave Comeau happened to know the property owner who had leased a Bremerton storefront to O'Neil. When Comeau mentioned his financing problem, the property owner said he should get in touch with the C&C owner. "I think he'd be interested in what you've got going on."

And of course he was.

O'Neil wanted the Bremerton license in the worst way. To get it, he needed cash. Fast. He called all the potential investors who had been waiting to jump in. *Now's the time*, he told them. He contacted Steve Alexander at CEO Space, a Seattle-based start-up financing group. "Steve: Know any WA-based investors who can cut checks this week? We are buying two retail licenses this week. Our deal is $25k per unit. We can pay finders fees. I'm four units short on covering LOI's I'm signing by Friday."

That evening, he ended an email message to David Kerr, his lawyer, with a kind of optimistic desperation. "David, let's make the Bremerton deal happen, the shop there is going to make lots of money!"

———

Comeau strolled into Anthony's restaurant wearing sneakers, jeans and a green T-shirt that read "Washington: The Green State," with a pot leaf dotting the *i*. He looked right at home in Bremerton. The Navy port town skewed young, male and working-class. That's what made the market so attractive to O'Neil.

O'Neil rushed in at 12:15, apologizing for his tardiness. "The guys on the ferry had to wake me up," he told Comeau. "They didn't seem too pleased about it, either."

They talked. Comeau told O'Neil his price had increased. Considering how many lottery losers there were, Comeau figured his license was worth $200,000.

O'Neil didn't respond directly. He told Comeau about C&C's nationwide plans. He talked about the investors he had on board. He talked about his branding deal with Tommy Chong. He laid out a scenario in which Dave Comeau ran the Bremerton store and became part of the rising C&C empire. O'Neil offered $150,000 and a slice of the earnings at the Bremerton shop. "I'll cut you a check for 10,000 right now as earnest money," he said.

Comeau agreed. If he could be a part of C&C *and* pocket the cash, so much the better. Comeau knew the limit of his skill set. He was a damn good store manager. Finance wasn't his thing.

An hour later, they signed the papers.

"We've got a storefront now on Callow Avenue that might work a little better than your place in East Bremerton," O'Neil told Comeau. "We've got a 7-11 on one side of us and a pizza chain on the other." A munchieville district.

Later that afternoon I watched as Dave Comeau pulled away from the parking garage underneath Anthony's. He was driving a black Chevy Astro van, a broke-ass machine with rust spots and a rumpled bumper. He was smoking a cigarette and smiling. A check for $10,000 sat on the seat beside him.

IN MY

BACKYARD

Legal marijuana unleashed a wave of NIMBYism in Washington and Colorado. The law in both states said that local counties and towns could allow marijuana farming and pot shops. It didn't say they must. That led to problems.

More than half of Washington's 100 biggest towns banned or temporarily halted the permitting of marijuana stores. In Colorado, eight of the 10 largest cities did the same. In Brush, Colo., a farm town near the Pawnee National Grassland, a businessman bought the former High Plains Correctional Facility, a mothballed state prison, and proposed turning it into an indoor-outdoor marijuana grow. The Brush City Council responded by enacting a citywide ban on marijuana grows.

A similar drama played out in my own town of Bainbridge Island. We're a semi-rural bedroom community, 24,000 people sharing a rock the size of Manhattan. About one in five adults commutes to Seattle on the ferry.

My neighbors voted 2-to-1 for legal pot. When it came time to issue permits to Bainbridge's lone pot shop and a handful of grows, however, a NIMBY pandemic swept the island. It was one thing to embrace the theory of legal cannabis. To welcome a pot shop into your own neighborhood—well, that turned out to be something else entirely.

———————

Bainbridge Island had been allotted a single marijuana store by the Liquor Control Board. A mysterious company called Evergreen won the license. Evergreen was located in Rolling Bay, an upscale neighborhood on the island's eastern shore. I drove over to check it out. It turned out to be an empty storefront between the Jiffy Mart and our friend Pino's Italian deli.

"Not a bad location," I told my friend Gordon. "Get yourself a meatball sub at Pino's place, Doritos at the Jiffy Mart. It's all right there. The Jiffy Mart owner must be psyched. I bet he's shopping for a new slushy machine right now."

Gordon reminded me that the island's one-room courthouse was right across the street from the pot store. "Sample some weed, hit the Jiffy Mart, drive erratically, get pulled over, go directly to court," he said. "It's all right there."

Not everyone was amused. When a Rolling Bay resident named Kristina Pujolar discovered the location of the pot lottery winner, she blasted an email to her neighbors. "Even though pornography shops and adult video stores are legal in WA State, we do not allow them on the Island," she wrote. "Why would we allow this type of commercial space in a small quaint community?" She urged her neighbors to rally against the pot shop at the next city council meeting.

At said meeting, most seats were taken half an hour before the Pledge of Allegiance. A group of Rolling Bay neighbors gathered near the back. By the window I spotted David, a local medical marijuana grower who kept his island operation on the down low. Just before the meeting started, an old bearded dude in a soiled skullcap plopped himself in the seat in front of me. His proximity offered a forensic view of the biohazard tattoo on his neck. About which—appropriate! Because the man reeked of the weed. I mean, like a Pigpen cloud, like a garbageman after a hard day of garbaging. He appeared as an apparition rubbed out of a genie's lamp to embody all the worst fears of every anxious mother in the room.

In filed our council members. Steve Bonkowski, a portly military contractor. Roger Townsend, a lawyer whose daughter was a friend of Lucy's. Wayne Roth, a grandfatherly gent who used to run Seattle's NPR station. Sarah Blossom, an attorney for the local water board. Val Tollefson, a maritime lawyer with a florid beard.

Mayor Anne Blair called the council to order. A regal woman with bobbed silver hair and owlish eyeglasses, Blair ran her meetings tickety-boo. Following a nod to National Police Week and a word from the Road Ends Shoreline Access Committee, we moved to the night's hot topic.

Kent Scott, a neighbor of mine, spoke first. Scott had secured a marijuana grow license for his small farm, but the island's current zoning law prevented him from growing pot. "This is our greenhouse," Scott said. He flashed a picture on the screen. "It's about the size of a double-car garage. No fences, lights, signs—nothing to draw attention to it." Most of his neighbors didn't have a problem with the pot grow. Scott couldn't understand why the city disallowed it. "I ask you to reconsider your current ordinance."

In front of me, Biohazard Bob nodded.

Chuck Beek, another neighbor, said he approved of the Scott grow. "If done right," he said, "it will be a straightforward farming operation." Those opposing it had "no evidence, just fear-based suppositions," he said.

Susan Wilmot, whose house sat across the street from the Scotts, disagreed. "There is no public benefit to this," she said. "It's a detriment to all the neighboring property values." If she wanted to sell her house, Wilmot said, "I will have to fill out a Form 17 to disclose the fact that I'm near a marijuana farm."

Another neighbor was certain that she did not like uncertainty. It really freaked her out. When marijuana sales begin in Washington State, what then? she asked. "Nobody knows!" she cried. "Nobody knows!"

By and by, attention turned to the proposed pot shop in Rolling Bay.

Rolling Bay was a place of expensive houses and long driveways. At its center was a four-block business district anchored by the Jiffy Mart, the Island Music Guild and Bay Hay & Feed, a plank-floor feed store.

Kristina Pujolar, the Rolling Bay resident who started the hue and cry, rose to speak. She painted a scene of idyllic summer days, of boys and girls pedaling their bikes to the Jiffy Mart to buy candy bars from the owner, Mr. Hong, of piano lessons at the Music Guild, of cocker spaniels wandering the aisles of Bay Hay & Feed. "What this neighborhood gives children," she said, "is the gift of being children." A pot shop, she said, would introduce an element of menace and worry. She wondered what kind of sinister outsiders would be drawn to the neighborhood. "What will it do to the children on this island?"

Another speaker mentioned the offensive smell he feared would waft out of the store. "I can smell it in here right now!" shouted a woman in the back.

I glanced at Biohazard Bob. *Tell me about it, sister.*

A Rolling Bay resident named Tom foresaw a 365-day-a-year stoner parade. "You're going to see all these people going by to get their dope, driving through the neighborhood. It's not acceptable."

In the back, Soon Hong rose from his chair. During the course of the evening, word spread through the gallery that the elderly Mr. Hong owned not just the Jiffy Mart but the entire shopping center complex, which contained the Jiffy Mart, Pino's Italian deli—and the proposed marijuana shop itself!

The room hushed as he padded to the microphone. He was a slip of a man with wire-rimmed glasses. He wore the wary, confused look of a man at an airport in a foreign country whose language he did not understand.

"Nineteen years over there," he said. "I like the neighborhood. We have 19 years—our life 19 years here. I don't want the marijuana. Everyone don't like the marijuana. The music guild. Children's Sunday school. I hope you stop the marijuana store."

I was confused. Didn't Mr. Hong own the building in which the marijuana store would operate? A man sitting nearby filled me in. A few years ago Mr. Hong leased the empty storefront to the Bainbridge Island Taxi Service, which used its tenancy to store idle cabs in the parking lot. The taxi company owner cut a deal with the pot license winner to sublet the storefront for a marijuana shop. Neither party informed Mr. Hong about the plan.

I tried to find the owners of the marijuana store license, but nobody seemed to know who they were or where they came from.

The council members found themselves in a pickle. Public opinion ran hard against the pot store. The council was split on whether to allow grows like Kent Scott's in rural areas. Mayor Blair called for a time-out. She needed to consider the council's options in a private and candid setting. So she took the council into executive session, "on the grounds that we are dealing now with an issue that could involve potential litigation."

The council members filed out.

During the break, a couple of neighbors advised Mr. Hong on his options. "If you don't want a marijuana shop on your property, you don't have to allow it," one man told him. "Do you have a copy of the lease?"

"The lease," said Mr. Hong. "Yes. I have a lease."

"Well, you need to have someone look at that lease and see if there's a section in there that covers illegal activities. Because this is still a federally illegal drug, and I'm betting you could stop the sublet with that clause."

Near the front door, I caught up with David, the medical marijuana grower. "Did you get a 502 grow license?" I asked.

"No," he said. "I'm helping out these guys, who are working to get their retail license."

He introduced me to Tim and Jana Wilkins, owners of the Bainbridge Island Taxi Service.

"The guy who's starting Evergreen couldn't make it tonight," Tim Wilkins told me.

That struck me as a colossal mistake. The fate of his business would be decided right here, right now. And he *couldn't make it*? Are you kidding me? (Later I learned the Evergreen entrepreneur had good reason to keep a low profile: he was a teacher at an off-island school.)

"Sounds like the Jiffy Mart owner doesn't want the shop in his building," I said.

"Nothing he can do about it," said Tim Wilkins. He fanned a manila folder stuffed with legal documents. "We've got a six-year lease with the option to sublet. Had our lawyers go over it. It's ironclad."

———————

The council returned. Their stiff body language indicated that an imperfect decision had been reached.

"I move that we approve Ordinance 2014-06 as amended, and that it shall expire on November 12, 2014," said council member Steve Bonkowski.

"Second," said Sarah Blossom.

"Oh my God," said somebody behind me. Mass confusion in the gallery.

"Val, will you explain what we're doing here?" said Mayor Blair.

Val Tollefson nodded. "Our intent is to revisit and reorganize the ordinance dealing with marijuana," he said. "This is what we have to do to gain more time to deal with it."

In other words, the city council froze the issue. No pot shop, no pot growing—for now. Thanks for coming out, folks! See you again in a few weeks.

———————

Roger Townsend, the council member whose daughter went to school with mine, met me a few days later for coffee. Townsend wanted to find a way to allow Kent Scott to grow pot on his farm. But by the time we sat down, it had become clear that he didn't have the votes to allow marijuana grows in rural residential zones. The council, he said, was going to relegate marijuana grows to a six-acre business-industrial zone off Day Road.

The problem was zoning. For Kent Scott to grow marijuana, the council would have to allow licensed pot growing on all land zoned rural residential like Scott's. And there was a hell of a lot of rural residential land on Bainbridge Island.

Townsend found it frustrating. "The fact is, marijuana is already grown on the island," he told me. "It has been for years. People have come up to me and said, 'I know X and Y are growing a hundred plants over here.' The whole idea of tax and regulate is to tax and *regulate*. To bring the growing under a regulatory structure that forces the black market to wither away."

"I voted for legalization," he said. "I saw prosecutors use it to manipulate cases. I saw it play out as a race issue, ruining lives, exerting tremendous financial costs on society. It didn't make sense.

"But I didn't for one minute think of it as a zoning issue. Back then I think we all kind of figured we'd just turn the old state liquor stores into retail marijuana shops."

That still kind of made the most sense, I said. But the federal insistence on a 1,000-foot buffer zone between schools and marijuana operations made that impossible.

Roger nodded. He still thought we ought to try, though. He was troubled by the idea that he and his fellow council members were heading toward an ordinance that made it appear as though marijuana operations were legal on the island—when in fact the new zoning ordinance would make it nearly impossible. "If you use technicalities to make it impossible to grow or sell legally here," he said, "you're not really following the spirit of Initiative 502."

———

Six weeks later the Bainbridge Island City Council returned to the subject of marijuana.

It was a balmy June evening, so warm and lovely that they opened the building's barn door and let the crowd spill out onto the sidewalk. The residents of Rolling Bay turned out in force.

"I sent around a post online," said Mayor Blair, "about how we might amend our ordinance of May 15th. The first change I'd like to suggest is that we limit marijuana sales to the business-industrial zone."

Blair's suggestion would eliminate the Rolling Bay pot shop. The island's business-industrial zone was so small that the zoning law made it extremely unlikely that a pot shop would ever open on Bainbridge. Cheers erupted in the gallery.

Deputy Mayor Tollefson frowned. "This council is trying to treat these issues with respect," he said. He eyed the crowd like a vice principal. "This is not a high school gymnasium. We would appreciate you holding your applause."

When it came time for public comment, Tollefson explained that the council had amended the marijuana ordinance to kill the pot shop in Rolling Bay. "So if that's what you came here to speak on," he said, you may want to hold your fire.

"Have you voted on it?" somebody shouted.

"What?" said Tollefson.

"Have you voted on it?"

"No," Tollefson said. "We'll do that in a couple weeks when the ordinance has been drawn up to reflect what we've just discussed."

If the gallery could have risen as one and responded, it would have said, respectfully, *Fuck that noise. We're firing both barrels.*

A crowd rushed the podium. Six weeks earlier the council had come within minutes of approving a marijuana store next to the Jiffy Mart. Tonight they claimed to be against it. Who was to say they wouldn't change their minds again? The people of Rolling Bay had come to lay some wood on the city council. And wood would be laid.

Ted, a Rolling Bay resident, took the first swing. "Why approve a retail outlet, period?" he demanded. "My request is, just say no!"

A line of people repeated variations on the same theme.

Jeff, of Sunrise Road: "Why should we be the guinea pigs for others? Why experiment on our own citizens? Let others go first and learn from their data."

Doug, who ran the Island Music Guild: "Whoever's trying to push these things, don't push it down the public's throat."

Charles, from Rolling Bay: "We don't have the resources to handle this. It's not appropriate in any neighborhood service center. What's happened in Colorado—that's daunting. Walk slowly and carefully."

Laura, from Rolling Bay: "This conversation is about where we don't want it. How about talking about where we *do* want it? One young man I spoke with suggested we put it next to police headquarters. I'd rather it be out in the open, where everyone can see it."

Mike, from Rolling Bay: "Think about how this will affect property values! I just don't see a real estate agent bragging that a house is within short driving distance of a retail pot shop."

An emergency room doctor at a nearby clinic: "I'm here to tell you that Bainbridge Island already has a drug problem. In the past year, I've seen octogenarians try marijuana for the first time. That's not good. We don't need easier access to it. If people want it, let them drive off-island to get the stuff."

Off-island. The phrase was local code for a host of issues having to do with race, class, socioeconomic status, crime, children and schools. The fear in Rolling Bay had nothing to do with Bainbridge Islanders shopping there. It was the specter of *off-islanders* coming on-island to buy weed. Off-islanders were working-class; they were loud and rude; they shopped at Walmart; they stole our mail. We didn't want that class of people crossing the moat.

———————

In late June the Bainbridge Island City Council voted to restrict marijuana growing, processing and retail sales to the island's tiny business-industrial zone. The vote was unanimous. Because of the U.S. Attorney's insistence on 1,000-foot buffer zones, this effectively limited marijuana businesses on Bainbridge Island to an area about the size of five football fields.

More than two thirds of my neighbors approved the legalization of marijuana in November 2012. Eighteen months later, we all but ran it off the island. We wanted legal pot, but we wanted it kept in somebody else's backyard.

23

DOCTORS WITHOUT

DATA

By the summer of 2014, Denver's marijuana boom was attracting a wave of immigrants in their 20s and early 30s. You could see these hopefuls every day in the waiting room of the Colorado Marijuana Enforcement Division (MED) office on Sherman Street, a few blocks south of the state capitol. Workers in the marijuana industry had to have a MED occupational license. To get one you had to prove you were over 21, lived in Colorado and hadn't been convicted of a felony drug charge within that past five years. So the MED office turned into a kind of Ellis Island for Colorado's cannabis boomers.

Meanwhile, in the city of Colorado Springs, cannabis attracted a different kind of migrant. Families with children suffering from Dravet syndrome, a severe form of pediatric epilepsy, began moving to Colorado Springs to treat their kids with low-THC, high-CBD cannabis oil. Colorado Springs was the home of the Stanley brothers, the family of pot growers who had cultivated the low-THC, high-CBD strain Charlotte's Web. By the spring of 2014, Dr. Margaret Gedde and her

Clinicians' Institute for Cannabis Medicine in Colorado Springs were treating more than 200 children, many of whom had recently moved with their families to Colorado.

Officials at Children's Hospital in Denver, which is associated with the University of Colorado's School of Medicine, began fielding more and more calls from out-of-state doctors and parents desperate for information about high-CBD cannabis. The staff at Children's found themselves frustrated and hamstrung. They didn't know much about marijuana and weren't sure it was legal to even offer an opinion. With or without that advice, though, desperate parents were dosing their own kids. The federal suppression of medical marijuana research had reached its predictable denouement. Since 1944, when Harry Anslinger vowed to arrest any researcher who touched cannabis without his approval, the government had quashed almost all studies into marijuana as a healing agent. Now, at the moment when pediatricians needed hard data, none existed.

In an effort to gain traction on the issue, the CU Medical School held a lunchtime discussion on cannabis and pediatrics during a weekday in June. I sat in at the invitation of Kari Franson, associate dean of CU's Department of Clinical Pharmacy.

Franson kicked off the discussion by presenting a hypothetical case involving "Tommy," a 14-year-old boy experiencing seizures. Tommy hadn't responded well to conventional medications. The first drug failed. Now his doctor was trying a second drug, to little effect. "His parents have heard about the reputed effects of the high-CBD marijuana strain Charlotte's Web," Franson told her colleagues. "They think it might work, they want something more natural, and they'd like to try it. What are your thoughts?"

Wary silence. Finally a pharmacist raised her hand. "They want something 'natural,'" she said. "But high-CBD cannabis is still a chemical. A chemical that hasn't been tested." (I wanted the participants to speak candidly, so I didn't take names during the discussion.)

A doctor across the room took a run at it. "We haven't given a full course of the second drug, which may work. Do we want to pull marijuana onboard before giving the second drug a full try?"

A woman on the far side of the room raised her hand. "I'm a big fan of the movie *Dallas Buyers Club*," she said. "I can't help but comparing that situation to the one we're talking about here. When we look back 30 years from now, I'd like to think that CU and Children's will be the heroes of that movie—that we had the courage to take the risk and push the research."

A man from across the room responded. "The thing about that movie was that the substances they used in the buyers club *didn't work*," he said. "Researchers and advocates working together—that's what brought about significant breakthroughs."

"I treat patients with HIV," he continued. "I see this kind of situation when a patient comes in with something he found at the local GNC store. We make up a protocol and keep a close watch. Because he's going to try it whether I approve or not. The one thing I would caution about is the use of the word *natural*. When that word comes up, it's often a sign of miracle-drug thinking. Most drugs, even the best drugs, are not miracle drugs. Miracle-drug thinking is liable to lead you down a bad path."

The hour passed. The seminar ended. The doctors, nurses, researchers and administrators returned to their offices, labs and exam rooms. I overheard one of them comment to a colleague on the way out. "The only thing I know for sure," she said, "is that we need more research on this stuff."

One day after the CU ethics discussion, I met up with Suzanne Sisley, the University of Arizona PTSD researcher, who was in Colorado to meet with colleagues at CU-Boulder and the local VA hospital. "They're interested in collaborating on the study," she told me. "They're not sure if it's legally possible."

She brought me up to speed. "I got approval from the Public Health Service a couple months ago," she said. But now there were problems with the university. Sisley couldn't carry out the study without a secure lab in which to store and administer the pot. She'd been waiting two years for lab access.

Across the room: "I have a child with Type 1 diabetes, and if that kind of drug was available, I would probably try it. I know about a case with a child suffering 300 grand mal seizures a week. If it was called anything other than marijuana, would we have such a problem giving it a try?"

If the doctor refuses to discuss marijuana, another person asked, are we simply sending the patient away to try it on their own, with no input from the physician? "We see this in dealing with stem cells. Patients become medical tourists, seeking a miracle cure in some other country, and then they return home, where the local physician has to deal with the fallout, good or bad."

"And what if we do engage?" said a physician. "Are providers at fault if something goes awry? What if the marijuana has an unforeseen outcome, or a poor drug interaction?"

A Children's Hospital doctor spoke up. "My neurology colleagues get calls on this every week," she said. "Parents of these patients are desperate to know if this CBD phenomenon is real. And there are legal issues here. We're not allowed to prescribe marijuana. At Children's we have had patients admitted with drug interactions between marijuana and anti-epilepsy drugs."

Another doctor said colleagues in other clinics were starting to work with a "don't ask, don't tell" policy when it came to medical marijuana.

"Please tell me we're not doing that," said a Children's administrator.

Across the room: "Are professional ethics and compassion mutually exclusive?"

That rankled a doctor on the other side of the room. "The word *compassionate* gets thrown around too much in these discussions," he said. "There's not even an ICD code for high-CBD marijuana," he added, referring to the International Classification of Diseases codes used to record patient histories. "Without ICD codes we can't chart and document what's going on. And by the way, it's still federally illegal. So we're putting our DEA licenses at risk—and possibly the institution's license as well."

Nearby, a response: "Maybe the most compassionate thing is to say, 'I don't know.' Because how compassionate is false hope?"

"Why so long?" I asked.

"They're fearful."

There was more to the story. A few months earlier, a Republican state senator killed a bill that would have used some of the taxes generated by Arizona's medical marijuana dispensaries to fund Sisley's PTSD research. A group of MMJ advocates responded with a recall campaign against the senator. (Sisley was not part of the effort, and didn't approve of the tactic.) That angered Republican legislators, whose support the U of A needed to pass its annual budget. That didn't sit well with university administrators, who felt Sisley's pot study had jeopardized the entire university's funding package. True or not, the optics weren't favorable.

That wasn't the only hurdle.

"I heard back from Dr. ElSohly in Mississippi," she said. "He doesn't have the high-CBD strains I need for the study."

When Carlton Turner left NIDA's marijuana nursery to join the Reagan administration, he was replaced by a biochemist named Mahmoud ElSohly. Over the past 30 years, as marijuana growers carried out a hybrid-and-hydroponic revolution, ElSohly and his University of Mississippi team continued to grow the same old low-THC brickweed. In 2014, dispensaries throughout the West offered high-CBD strains and hybrids with 22 percent THC. NIDA's highest-THC strain topped out at 12 percent. ElSohly didn't manage a research station. He curated a time capsule.

"The stuff they have is years old, dried up, and they have none of the high-CBD strains that are common out here in Colorado Springs," Sisley told me. "The whole point of the study is to look at high-CBD strains, which we think might be better for the vets."

"It's frustrating," she said. NIDA's research pot growers were so out of touch with the real-world marijuana market that they asked Sisley if *she* knew how to find any high-CBD clones. "The people in Mississippi say that if they plant now, they could have something ready for us in six months. You talk to the growers here in Colorado, they could have it done in six weeks."

That would be federally illegal, though.

———

One week later, the University of Arizona fired Suzanne Sisley.

Universities prefer not to use rude verbs like *fired*. Technically the U of A "declined to renew" Sisley's annual contract, which had been re-upped as a matter of formality over the past seven years. Sisley's teaching record brimmed with positive comments from students and colleagues. She was doing cutting-edge research—indeed, research that could have a profound impact on the lives of thousands of American war veterans. Campus officials gave no explanation for Sisley's firing. The university, a spokesperson said, could not speak on personnel matters. He did say that the university remained committed to conducting research on marijuana. How that would happen without Suzanne Sisley, he did not say.

24

EDIBLES ARE
A PROBLEM

During 2014 the marijuana industry grew so fast that weeks felt like years. Companies rose and fell overnight. Rules underwent constant change as regulators struggled to keep up with unforeseen events. Investments flourished here, failed there. It was like watching evolution happen in time-lapse speed.

The crazy velocity of the build-out was brought home to me at a National Cannabis Industry Association (NCIA) business expo held in Denver in late June 2014, nearly six months into full legalization. The expo gave me a chance to check in with people I'd last seen on opening day.

Toni Savage, owner of Denver's 3D Cannabis Center, told me her business had exploded since Jan. 1. "It's crazy growth," she said. "I'm exhausted." At the end of 2013 she had six employees. Five months later she had 40 and was looking to hire more. Not that she was complaining. Since opening 3D as a medical dispensary in 2011, Savage had never turned a profit. Full legalization changed that. "In our first three months as a recreational store, I did more sales than in three years as a medical center," she said.

Others were also prospering. At a Friday night industry event in Denver, Jan Cole, owner of The Farm, Boulder's premier pot shop, told me she'd just dropped off $150,000 in taxes at the state Department of Revenue office that afternoon.

"Yourself?" I asked.

"No," she said. "I used to take in the cash myself. But now I have a guy who does it for me."

People in the industry evolved quickly too. At the NCIA show I chatted with Jane West, the woman I'd bumped into outside O.penVape on New Year's Day. In just four months she'd become one of the industry's most influential cultural impresarios.

Jane West was her *nom de cannabis*. At home she was 37-year-old Amy Dannemiller. Until recently Dannemiller had been an event planner for *Fortune* 500 companies. In 2013 she started a side business: Edible Events, a marijuana-themed event company. She started hosting a monthly bring-your-own-cannabis party series. For 4/20 she planned a Wake-N-Bacon Brunch featuring medicated chocolates and cakes. Soon she became a minor industry celebrity, appearing on TV shows and magazines as the face of marijuana's mainstream moment.

The double life worked right up until the moment it didn't. In February 2014, West appeared in the CNBC documentary *Marijuana in America: Denver Pot Rush*. In one scene she was shown taking a sip from a vape pen. "I use marijuana, and that's OK," West told correspondent Harry Smith. "We're really starting to change the face of what a cannabis consumer looks like. I guess I'd say I'm one part Martha Stewart and one part Walter White."

The next day Dannemiller's boss asked for her resignation.

"After that," she told me, "I went all in as Jane West."

On the day we spoke, West had just finished the first of three cannabis-friendly fundraisers to benefit the Colorado Symphony Orchestra. "Classically Cannabis: The High Note Series" marked the first time a major American arts organization hosted an event at which patrons were overtly allowed the freedom to smoke marijuana.

Looking to bolster a shrinking budget and find young new subscribers,

Symphony officials wondered if there was something they could do to connect with Denver's cannabis entrepreneurs.

A mutual friend put CSO officials in touch with Jane West. "I thought it would make a great event," West told me. "We set the price at $75 a ticket and told people bring their own cannabis."

"Like the Colorado Symphony, the cannabis industry is entrepreneurial, innovative and responsive to the people of Colorado," CSO chairman Jerome Kern told the *Denver Post*. "These businesses have expressed a willingness to support the Colorado Symphony's mission. Our doors are open to any legal, legitimate business that wants to help."

Denver mayor Michael Hancock didn't like the sound of that. Kern and West received a cease-and-desist letter from the city.

West and her attorney, Christian Sederberg, met with City Attorney Scott Martinez. Martinez told them the city considered the CSO evening to be a public event. Marijuana could not be consumed at public events.

"What if it were a private event?" Sederberg asked.

Amendment 64 allowed consumption in private, Martinez said.

"Let's talk about defining a 'private event,'" West said.

That afternoon Sederberg, West and Martinez negotiated the boundaries around private, legal cannabis events. The model they came up with was a wedding reception: big party, lots of people, each individually invited. The general public can't buy tickets to a wedding reception.

The following week West and the CSO refunded every one of the 250 tickets purchased. That effectively canceled the "public event" portion of Classically Cannabis. Next, West personally invited, via email, each of the previous ticket holders to make a donation of $75 or more to the Colorado Symphony Orchestra. The CSO then invited each contributor to a private donor appreciation event. Classically Cannabis was back on.

The first evening had been a smash hit, West said. "We've got one event in July and another in August," she said. "You should come."

I told her I'd think about it.

"Let me ask you something," she said. "Do you use cannabis?"

I stammered. When in doubt, choose honesty. "Yes," I said. "I bought a vape pen a while ago. I use it now and then. If I'm writing about it, I figure I need to know what I'm writing about."

"OK," she said. "Good. Because most of the media people I talk to are happy to write up these stories about the experience, but they don't really know the experience."

I nodded. "It's still not something I can talk about outside gatherings like this," I said. "It's like there are two different lands and an ocean between. There are plenty of people out there who are curious, who are interested, but they have no access point. They have no safe, comfortable and socially acceptable way to try this stuff."

West listened intently. "You know what we need?" she said. "We need something like Mary Kay parties for cannabis."

"No," I said. "You need something more like those Passion Parties suburban moms hosted 10 years ago. The ones where they'd bring out the sex toys, pass the wine, and make the products fun and silly, not creepy and embarrassing."

She laughed. "Yes! That's it!"

Many people said many flattering things about marijuana during the NCIA business expo. But the most honest and urgent conversation was one I overheard while walking out for lunch. A young dispensary owner was talking with an edibles manufacturer. (Not Tripp Keber.) The dispensary owner said, "Dude, I love your products. I want to keep carrying them. But right now edibles are a *problem*."

He spoke the truth. By the summer of 2014, marijuana-infused edibles had become a problem for the industry and the entire legalization movement. I expected the death of Levy Thamba and the murder of Kristine Kirk to go viral. But they hadn't. Instead the two incidents seeped slowly into the national consciousness, week by week. Then Maureen Dowd published an article that crashed edibles into the national conversation.

Weeks earlier, the *New York Times* columnist had eaten a cannabis-infused candy bar in her Denver hotel room. Nothing happened for an hour. Then the THC kicked in.

> I barely made it from the desk to the bed, where I lay curled up in a hallucinatory state for the next eight hours. I was thirsty but couldn't move to get water. Or even turn off the lights. I was panting and paranoid, sure that when the room-service waiter knocked and I didn't answer, he'd call the police and have me arrested for being unable to handle my candy.

At her lowest point, Dowd became convinced that she had died and no one was telling her.

A portion of America recoiled in Nancy Graceian horror. (And give Grace her due—with the murder of Kristine Kirk, she had a bona fide freak-out crime to display the next time she encountered Mason Tvert.) Others mocked the newb's inability to handle her liquor. "Jesus Christ, Dowd. That's what I call breakfast," novelist Neal Pollack posted on Facebook. For about a week, Dowd became the favorite joke-butt of the American chattering class.

For all the ridicule she endured, the *Times* columnist did the cannabis industry an enormous service. She forced it to confront a crisis that too many pot people wanted to ignore. "Why should the whole industry suffer just because less than 5 percent of people are having problems with the correct dosing?" Bob Eschino told Dowd. Eschino was the owner of Incredibles, a leading Colorado edible maker (and, I recalled, sponsor of the chocolate fountain at the New Year's Eve party at Casselman's). "My kids put rocks and batteries in their mouths. If I put a marijuana leaf on a piece of chocolate, they'll still put it in their mouths."

As a response to a developing industrial crisis, Eschino's quote wasn't merely politically obtuse. It smacked of arrogance and willful blindness.

Edibles were a problem because when humans are given a choice between eating delicious sweets and inhaling hot smoke, most will choose the sweets. A large percentage of customers at Colorado's recreational pot shops were out-of-state tourists and Coloradans who hadn't gotten high for years. (Most regular partakers had previously obtained their medical marijuana cards. They continued to patronize Colorado's MMJ dispensaries, which offered lower prices and shorter lines.) Those newcomers and returning users often opted for edibles over smokeable leaf. And that was a problem.

It was a problem because industry and state officials miscalculated their dosing rules. A single package of recreational edibles in Colorado could contain no more than 100 milligrams of THC. That meant one cookie, in its own package, might max out at 100 milligrams. But the state considered a "serving size" to be 10 milligrams. So a single cookie might constitute 10 servings. Who looks at a single cookie and thinks, *Ten servings?* Nobody, that's who.

Among people who don't use marijuana, there's a lot of worry about the higher THC potency of today's bud. "It's so much stronger than it was in the '70s," people say. That is true. 1970s marijuana contained 2 to 3 percent THC. Pot in West Coast dispensaries typically runs 18 to 22 percent. But here's the thing about stronger pot: It's like stronger alcohol. It hits you immediately, so when you've had enough, you stop ingesting. You'll smoke half a joint to get the same high that would have required two full joints in the '70s. But you'll stop after half a joint because you'll realize you've had enough. This is known as self-titration. We do it with beer all the time. Craft beers can contain twice as much alcohol as light beers. So we don't pound Third Coast Old Ale like Bud Light at a Fourth of July barbecue.

That's not the case with edibles. Because edibles take a while to digest, their THC may not hit the brain until an hour after eating. Users can get frustrated at the delay and eat two or three more cookies in an effort to get high. Once the THC finally kicks in, the user has overserved himself and is in for a long, strange and uncomfortable trip.

Budtenders in the best shops scrupulously explained the "many servings" concept to their customers. I can tell you, having been a customer in some of those shops, that the advice of the budtender flew over my head like so much Charlie Brown teacher talk. You know why? Because mainstream adults in a marijuana store are nervous. We are Methodist ministers in sex-toy shops. We want to purchase our goods and bolt.

Edibles were a problem because chocolate bars are not rocks and they are not batteries. When I brought those chocolate-covered gummy bears home from my first trip to The Joint, I secured them in a locked strongbox I picked up at the local hardware store. I knew that if I hid them somewhere "safe," I'd forget about them for a few months. Then somebody else would find them. And eat them. There was a two in four chance that the person who found them would be one of my children. If my children were to find loose weed in the house, the chances of them popping it in their mouths, or making the effort to smoke it, paled by comparison (especially given their long-standing boycott of all foods green).

Edibles were a problem because eating marijuana is a less than ideal way to ingest it. I went back to an interview I'd done with Kari Franson, the University of Colorado medical school dean and former THC researcher, weeks earlier. A lot of people don't like to smoke marijuana because running hot smoke into the lungs "can be unpleasant," she told me. And we've built up a cultural aversion to the practice based on our experience with tobacco and cancer. "So people say, 'It's better to eat it.'" In the case of cannabis, though, oral ingestion is just about the worst way to take it.

"When we were working with THC in the Netherlands, our subjects always preferred to take it orally," Franson told me. "But oral doses were too inconsistent." The THC in smoked marijuana is absorbed into the bloodstream through the lungs. In edibles, the THC is absorbed as the food is broken down in the small intestine. That requires time. "For some people, the peak effects happened fairly quickly," Franson told me. "For others, it took hours. There was huge inter- and intra-patient variability. What I mean by that is this: If I needed one aspirin to achieve a certain effect, whereas you needed 10, that's a tenfold difference. With THC, we found there could be a fourfold difference between patients. There was also *intra*-patient variability. In other words, one day I might need a single aspirin to get pain relief; the next day I might need four aspirins for that same relief."

In the end, Franson said, she and her Dutch colleagues ended up dosing their test subjects by heating cannabis in a Volcano, a $400 vaporizer that looks like a cone-shaped kitchen blender. "That's what gave us the most consistent administration."

Franson's comments shed some light on the strange case of Levy Thamba. His mind freaked out with only 7.2 nanograms of active THC in his blood. Given Franson's findings regarding intra-patient variability, it's possible that Thamba might have eaten the same cookie one week later and not experienced any psychotic reaction at all. *Set and setting*: that was the old hippie rule of marijuana etiquette. "Set" is a person's experience, personality, body type and mood. "Setting" refers to the physical and social circumstances. If you're going to smoke up, do it in a safe, comfortable place in the right frame of mind and with an appropriate dose.

———————

In the conference hall at the NCIA business expo, Tripp Keber asked me if I'd seen Dixie Elixir's newest product line. "Dixie One," he said. "It's a low-dose cannabis-infused beverage. They just hit the shelves two days ago."

The original Dixie Elixir, a drink that tasted kind of like a wine cooler, contained 75 milligrams of THC. A budtender at a pot shop near Colfax Avenue once warned me about its potency. "My usual advice is to share one bottle among three people," he said. Dixie's new product line came in at 5 milligrams, one fifteenth the regular dose.

Joe Hodas, the Dixie marketing director, told me he'd been meeting with the Colorado governor's panel on edible dosage. Gov. Hickenlooper had convened a group of state officials and industry insiders to come up with a better way to regulate edible dosage. Mason Tvert and the Marijuana Policy Project were cooking up a "Start Low and Go Slow" campaign; one of their first billboards would feature a very Dowd-ish woman and the tagline, "Don't let a candy bar ruin your vacation." In the meantime, Dixie was testing the low-dose drink to see if the market would respond.

Later that afternoon, I stopped by Natural Remedies, a recreational pot shop just off Denver's 16th Street Mall. A bottle of Dixie One ran me about seven bucks. I smuggled it into a nearby Panera Bread and accompanied it with a turkey sandwich. Five milligrams? I wondered if I'd feel it at all.

The strawberry-watermelon-flavored beverage went to work within about seven minutes. Worry and anxiety lifted from my mind. A very light fog moved in. I closed my MacBook. The day's work was done. I strolled back to my hotel room, about 12 blocks away, noticing and enjoying sounds and smells along the way. By the time I reached my room, the light buzz was dissipating. An hour after my first sip, it was gone completely. Five milligrams—not bad. Relaxing. Enjoyable. Fun. It seemed just right.

A few days later, back at home, I took Lucy and Willie out for pizza at the Treehouse. Claire was in Seattle teaching a memoir workshop. The kids asked me about my trip. I told them about the ethics discussion, the business expo and the trouble with edibles. I let slip the fact that I'd purchased a bottle of strawberry-watermelon Dixie One.

"What did you do with it?" Willie asked.

"With what?"

"The bottle of pot pop."

"What do you mean, what'd I do with it?"

"Did you drink it?"

My heart stopped. I'd spent more than a year in the world of legal marijuana but still hadn't directly addressed the issue of my own use with the kids. I was determined not to lie to them about marijuana. That was the point, goddammit. Yet here I was, feeling like I was about to admit to hooking up with a call girl.

"Well, Willie," I said, "I drank it."

"What was it like?"

"Tasted like Snapple with kind of a sour aftertaste. And I felt like I feel after drinking a couple glasses of wine. But a little different. A little foggier."

"Oh," he said. I could hear the gears turning in his head. *Processing . . . processing . . . processing.*

We moved on with our evening.

25

WHAT CAN HAPPEN IF
WE DO IT RIGHT

Pete O'Neil called me on an overcast day in June.

"We're getting offers from all over the state," he said.

When news of Dave Comeau's windfall leaked, O'Neil became every-body's new best friend. In theory, Washington's license lottery gave everyone a fair shake. In practice, it created a retail pot industry crippled at birth. Comeau wasn't an exception. He was the rule. Many of those who won licenses had zero retail experience. Some had never seen a cannabis plant. Others couldn't scrape together enough cash to build out and stock a marijuana store.

By early summer, O'Neil was negotiating to buy licenses in Olympia, Seattle, Ellensburg, Bellingham and Longview.

"Oh, and the Bremerton deal might fall through," he said.

"Dave Comeau?"

"Yeah. Turns out his location is near a senior center. The Liquor Control Board considers that a 'sensitive area,' which could disqualify his application."

"So you're out the hundred-fifty thou?" I asked.

"No, just the 10,000," he said. "Lesson learned. All these people want option money, but I can't go around just tossing out $10,000 checks. The kid in Longview, I agreed to a $1,000 option. He called back 10 minutes later and demanded six. I told him to get fucked."

Later that week I joined O'Neil for a meeting with John Davis, the state's dean of dispensaries. Davis was a 50-something businessman who could have passed for a banker. He owned the Northwest Patient Resource Center, a Seattle dispensary with two locations and more than 3,000 patients. As a longtime organizer of Hempfest, he had street cred. As a man comfortable in a suit and tie, he often played the role of diplomat, working behind the scenes with state legislators and city officials. John Davis was the adult in the room.

"I want to talk with John about opening a dispensary," O'Neil told me as we walked to Davis's shop. He was still thinking about bucking the 502 system and turning C&C's empty Lake City Way storefront into an MMJ. "We're bleeding money and I haven't sold a single joint," he said.

John Davis's message to O'Neil was clear: if you run a dispensary, retail politics are your job. Davis's main dispensary was on an arterial in West Seattle. Signage was minimal. "We talked with our neighbors to find out what their concerns were," Davis explained. The locals wanted no green crosses, no pot leaves on windows. Davis talked about getting to know everyone, from his state legislators to the local cop on the beat. "Operate openly," he said.

Toward the end of their meeting, O'Neil asked Davis the obvious question. "How do you make sure the feds don't raid your dispensary?"

He worked at that every day, Davis said. "The thing you've got to understand," he told O'Neil, "is that there's federal law, and then there's policy. The law is the law. Policy is a decision about which laws to enforce, when, and how." Congress made law. Jenny Durkan, the U.S. Attorney for Western Washington, set policy. West of the Cascade divide she decided how marijuana laws were enforced. "You have to listen very carefully to what comes out of her office," Davis said. "And follow the changes in her policy to the letter."

After his meeting with Davis, O'Neil's mind was set. Licenses be damned. He was going full medical on Lake City Way and would operate until the city or Jenny Durkan shut him down.

———————

A couple of weeks later, O'Neil called again.

"Can you believe this?" he said. "They're about to open the 502 shops and there's not going to be enough weed!"

It was June 30, 2014. Washington state's first retail pot shops were scheduled to open the following week. But most 502-legal crops hadn't matured to harvest.

"Them's the breaks," I said.

I often felt compelled to remind O'Neil that at the end of the day, he was in the business of selling legal marijuana. So maybe he should shut up and roll with the punches. "Prices will spike," I said, "but things will settle down in a few months. Supply will catch up with demand."

I asked how his businesses were doing. "Have you got a retail license yet?"

"Our latest tip is on a store in Olympia," he said. An older couple there won the license lottery. "I think we can get the license. I don't know if my investors will put up the money to close the deal, though."

He was meeting with the Olympia license owners the next day. I told him I'd be there.

———————

The next morning I showed up a few minutes before 11 at C&C's Lake City Way storefront, which was becoming a medical dispensary. "We're not officially open yet," O'Neil said, holding the door for me. "Patricia's stocking the case now."

Patricia Barker, C&C's merchandise manager, showed me the wares. "We've got two strains of our Tommy Chong–brand medical cannabis," she said. "And four other strains. All grown by local organic farmers."

There was a rattle at the door. "That's them!" O'Neil said.

The Sultons were an African-American couple in their 60s. Mr. Sulton wore a light summer business suit; Mrs. Sulton led with a silk Chinese shortcoat. She wore her hair swept up in a bun like my grandmother used to do. Accompanying the Sultons was their daughter, a lawyer in her 30s.

I was surprised that they were not white. That said something about my own prejudiced assumptions, but it also spoke to a problem pervading the marijuana industry: it was overwhelmingly male and pale. Women were making inroads. Jan Cole and Toni Savage were two of Colorado's leading cannabis retailers. Tonia Winchester was becoming an executive force at Privateer Holdings. Women Grow, an industry networking group founded by Jane West, doubled its membership every month. But for the most part the business was dudes, dudes, dudes. People of color were even harder to find. I was reminded of Ethan Nadelmann's warning that "the people who may come to dominate this industry are not the people who are a part" of the drug reform movement. It troubled Michelle Alexander, too. "Here are white men poised to run big marijuana businesses, dreaming of cashing in," the *New Jim Crow* author said in an interview, "after 40 years of impoverished black kids getting prison time for selling weed, their families and futures destroyed."

People of color had less access to start-up capital. Some were wary of identifying themselves to the police as drug sellers, even if the drug was legal. Past drug convictions prevented some from passing the state-required background check. In many cases, the people of color caught up in the drug war couldn't enter the new legal marijuana industry because they were still serving time in prison for selling marijuana.

The Sultons enjoyed notable careers prior to entering the cannabis business. Jim Sulton had been the executive director of the Washington State Higher Education Coordinating Board, which oversaw the state's public colleges. Anne Sulton was a well-known civil rights attorney in Denver who fought some of the city's most contentious race discrimination cases in the 1990s.

Adam Girton, C&C's operations manager, walked the Sultons through the store's wares. He pointed out the rack of edible candies: lemon drops, gummy bears and candy orange slices, 10 to 25 milligrams of THC per piece. The package warned, "Medical Use Only—Keep From Children." Mr. Sulton's face expressed curiosity. "This is the stuff that woman from the newspaper ate," he said.

O'Neil moved some chairs into a circle. The negotiations began.

The Sultons' daughter paged through a copy of the contract. "We like much of the original language here," she said. "One thing we would like to do is move up the payments, from installments over 36 months to 24." She offered her mother a loving glance. "My parents, as you see, are old."

O'Neil nodded. "We can do that."

Then began one of Pete O'Neil's monologues, this one about the onerous nature of Washington's pot regulations, or some such, which he was unfortunately wont to do. I thought of that old rule about negotiating: *He who is explaining is losing.* Girton, standing behind the counter, gently steered O'Neil back to the contract at hand.

"Do you have a photo of your location?" O'Neil said.

Mr. Sulton whipped out his smartphone. "I feel like I'm showing off pictures of my grandchildren," he said.

The location was typically cannabis-shabby: a humble midcentury rambler, too much moss and too little paint, on the outskirts of town. But it was legal and it was leased.

Mrs. Sulton glanced at her watch. "I hate to rush this, but I have got to catch a flight," she said.

Though Mrs. Sulton had been quiet during the early negotiations, it soon became clear that she was a force with which to be reckoned. "The location is a few minutes from I-5, very easy to get to," she said.

Pete asked what she thought of C&C's business plan.

"I like it," she said. "I want to see this industry succeed."

Then Mrs. Sulton pulled something out of her heart and laid it bare.

"I am a criminologist," she said. "I wrote about the problem of drug laws 20 years ago. I want this to be successful not just because of the money but because of the model. I want to be certain anything my name is connected to is something that is socially responsible."

She looked squarely at O'Neil. "Understand," she said. "I want to make money. But that is secondary to my desire to make certain it is responsible. If we are successful, we will be able to show people across the nation that we don't need to arrest all these people."

She glanced at the rack of edible candy.

"When I read that story about that 19-year-old college kid—"

"The one who fell out the window," said O'Neil.

"The one who *jumped* from the *balcony* of a hotel in Denver," Mrs. Sulton corrected. "That is not the kind of story you want."

"I know this field," she said. "I've worked with police and the addiction recovery community for over 35 years. I know what it can do if we do it right. I also know what it can do if it's *not* done right. They will shut it down so fast it will take your breath away."

Mrs. Sulton, her husband and their daughter exchanged pleasantries with O'Neil and made their exit. A few days later a signed contract arrived in the mail. O'Neil and the Sultons figured it would take them a few months to renovate the house. They planned to open in November 2014.

DAY ONE IN
WASHINGTON STATE

At 1:20 a.m. on July 7, 2014, the Washington State Liquor Control Board alerted 24 marijuana shop owners that retail sales could commence at 8 a.m. the following day.

Finally! By the hammer of Thor have we waited! As Colorado racked up millions in first-month sales, Washingtonians endured delay after delay. We ate patience three meals a day.

Frankly, by the time legal Day One arrived, I was a little embarrassed by my state's wobbly performance. Only a handful of stores would open on July 8. Because growers had only recently put in their crops, the state expected a product shortage through the end of the year.

Oh well. At least the doors were opening.

———————

I drove up to Bellingham the next morning. Rumor had it that a shop there would open at 8. I found Top Shelf Cannabis across from a lumberyard on Hannegan Road. At 7:30 a.m., more than 100 customers formed a line that stretched around the corner of the store.

An old graybeard folded his arms and leaned against the building. A tie-dyed bandana encircled his head. "Not gonna stand in line?" somebody asked him.

"No, man, I got plenty of weed," he said.

"How long you been smoking?"

"Since '63."

The queue included a surprising mix of ages and backgrounds: old hippies, young women, stoner bros, housewives, househusbands, matrons and patrons and marrieds and singles. Ellen McCauley and Lori Bradford, a middle-aged married couple from California, told a reporter they'd recently moved to Washington because of the new marijuana law. They showed up at Top Shelf, McCauley said, because they were running low on supply.

Inside the shop, co-owners Tom Beckley and John Evich ran last-minute checks on their product-tracking software.

At 7:58 Beckley invited the media into the shop. A TV reporter with a coiled wire running up the back of his neck went all Ron Burgundy on his colleague back at the anchor desk. ". . . THE DOOR IS OPENING RIGHT NOW. WE'LL BE INSIDE LIVE WHEN THAT FIRST SALE HAPPENS . . . UNTIL THEN, BACK TO YOU, LISA."

There are moments when I am ashamed of my trade, situations in which, were God to grant me a single wish, I would ask only that all civilians in the room understand that *I am not with this assclown troupe.* For a second I considered clipping the cord on Burgundy's neck.

At 8:00 the first customer strolled through the door. Cameras whirled and clicked.

Cale Holdsworth, a 29-year-old man from Abilene, Kans., perused the merchandise. Holdsworth ran the parts department at an RV dealership. "My girlfriend and I are out here visiting family, and we thought we'd come out and get in line," he told me. Holdsworth and Sarah Gorton arrived at 4:30 that morning. "We had no idea we'd be first."

Holdsworth selected two grams of OG Pearl. The budtender retrieved a sealed package of the strain from a drawer.

"CALE, HOW DOES IT SMELL?"

The studio had apparently returned to a live shot from Burgundy.

"Um, it smells amazing. Very good quality."

"SMELLS AMAZING, HE SAYS!"

Holdsworth strolled to the cash register. Another reporter asked what he selected.

"This is a strain known as OG Pearl."

"OG PEARL IS THE 'STRAIN' OR 'TYPE' OF MARIJUANA HE BOUGHT!"

At 8:03, Tom Beckley rang him up. Holdsworth held up a small brown paper bag and his receipt above his head like a trophy. Claps and cheers.

"CALE, HOW EXCITED ARE YOU RIGHT NOW?"

"I'm thrilled," he said.

———

In Seattle, only a single shop managed to open on day one. That was Cannabis City.

Store owner James Lathrop delayed his opening until noon. He wanted to give his staff extra time to prepare. The media attention would be intense. He didn't want to rush things and screw up.

Lathrop's tiny store was located between a florist and a Subway about half a mile south of Safeco Field, home of the Mariners. Lathrop had been paying rent on the place since the previous November—the price of admission to the license lottery.

By the time I arrived around 11 a.m., the block around Cannabis City was a nuthouse riot. Orange cones claimed half of 4th Avenue for the crowd. A feeding pack of tripods noshed at the shop's front door. Under a banner that proclaimed "Seattle's First Cannabis Store," a fervid crew in top hats, orange blazers and Heatmiser wigs blustered about. I turned to Bob Young, the sharp old pro who covered the pot beat for the *Seattle Times*. "Who are these guys?" I asked.

Bob rolled his eyes. "They're with Magical Butter, the jokers who run the edibles food truck," he said. "Every radio and TV reporter who comes to Seattle does a story on them." Bob expressed a strong opinion about the, ahem, legality of their operation.

A young woman standing next to us was taken aback. "Actually, they have a medical license."

Bob spun. "There's no such thing!" he said. "There's no such thing as a medical marijuana license, so it's impossible for them to have one." Bob had been covering marijuana for nearly two years. He and Ricardo Baca of the *Denver Post* were the only reporters dedicated to the cannabis space. Pushing back against a tide of misinformation and magical thinking was something they did on a daily basis.

"These 'Butter' guys plan to sell God knows what out of a food truck that's a converted school bus," Bob said. "The whole point of regulating and cleaning this industry up is to get it out of the hands of kids."

I Googled an image of the bus. Bob had a point. The company's name appeared in balloon lettering next to its corporate mascot, "Mr. Butter," a green cube with a fun-lovin' Kool-Aid Man smile. The whole setup reminded me of *The Magic School Bus*, a cartoon my kids loved when they were little.

Bob turned back to the young woman. "I'm sorry," he told her. "I don't mean to be rude. But they're trying to sling unlicensed pot-infused food to *patients*, people who may really have medical conditions. It's irresponsible."

First in line at Cannabis City was Deb Greene, a 65-year-old grandmother and retired insurance agent from Seattle's Ballard neighborhood. She arrived on Monday afternoon with a folding chair, a sleeping bag, a roast beef sandwich and an iced tea lemonade from Starbucks. "My old supplier just texted me," she told one reporter as she waited. The text said, "I saw you on TV. Now I know why you're not calling me."

At 11:45, Initiative 502 author Alison Holcomb and Seattle City Attorney Pete Holmes appeared. Holcomb wore a bright-red blazer that matched her lipstick. Holmes was the only man in a five-block area to don a well-fitted suit and tie.

"Today is an amazing day," Holcomb told the gathered crowd. "We're moving marijuana out of the shadows, regulating it for consumer and community safety, dedicating new tax revenues for keeping kids healthy and keeping them in school. We're finally taking marijuana out of the criminal justice system and treating it as a public health issue."

A news helicopter buzzed overhead. Traffic crawled along 4th Avenue South. A jackass passing in a dented Nissan hollered, "You're all a bunch of tools, paying 25 bucks a gram!"

A gentleman standing next to me whirled in defense. "Hey, shut up, motherfucker! It's finally legal!"

Holmes, looking fatherly and responsible, stepped forward. He recalled standing with Holcomb three years earlier at the official filing of Initiative 502. "I'm honored and pleased to be standing with her again as we witness the opening of Seattle's first cannabis store," he said. "It's important to recognize that we're in short supply. There's only one store. And there are going to be other bumps in the road as we veer away from the failed war on drugs toward a regulated system."

"The most important takeaway is that today, marijuana sales became legal," Holmes said. "And I am here to personally exercise this new freedom."

Cannabis City owner James Lathrop didn't have a lot to say. But he made it memorable.

"On this beautiful Seattle day, July 8, 2014, I declare this war *over!*" he said. "It's time to free the weed!"

Grandma Greene stepped over the threshold and made her purchase. She didn't smoke pot often, she said, but she intended to consume the purchase at home while watching *Game of Thrones*.

"It's the dream of every retiree," she said. "Sleep in and smoke a bowl."

Not far behind her was Holmes. The 58-year-old city attorney bought two $40 two-gram packages—one for posterity and one "for personal enjoyment, when appropriate." Which, he added, was in the privacy of his own home when he wasn't working in any legal capacity.

"It's been a long time," Holmes said. "Since college."

As he exited the store, he held the brown paper bag up high for everyone to see.

Of the 24 stores licensed on July 7, only five were able to obtain enough dried, cured and legally packaged marijuana to open on July 8.

A check of receipts confirmed that Cale Holdsworth, the 29-year-old Kansan, made the first legal purchase of marijuana in Washington State at 8:03 a.m. in Bellingham. In Spokane, the state's second largest city, a man named Mike Boyer lined up at 7 p.m. on Monday night to make the first purchase at Spokane Green Leaf. The next day, clad in a tie-dyed T-shirt, Boyer bought two grams of Sour Kush. "Go Washington!" he cried.

Boyer invited a TV crew to film him enjoying the product that afternoon at home, in private, legally. Which they did.

Within hours Boyer saw his triumphant score broadcast on news outlets all over Washington. So did his boss.

On July 9, Boyer returned to work. He was asked to take a drug test. He complied. He failed.

Later that day, this post appeared on Craigslist:

> LOST MY JOB! still #1 tho!! (spokane)
> I lost my job due to the news coverage of me being the FIRST PERSON TO BUY MARIJUANA LEGALLY IN SPOKANE! I regret nothing. But now I'm jobless and have decided to post my resume here. Thanks for reviewing it.
> MICHAEL KELLY BOYER

The next day, officials at TrueBlue Labor Ready, Boyer's employer, reconsidered their decision. Boyer had gone through proper channels to take the day off on July 8. He had shown up for work sober, on time and competent on July 9. A spokesperson for TrueBlue told NBC News: "When we realized that he was not on assignment, we reinstated him."

"Pot is legal," she said.

27

EARLY

DATA

As the warmth of summer settled in, a calm came over America's marijuana industry. In Washington State, demand still ran far ahead of supply. At Seattle's Cannabis City the crop arrived once every couple of weeks and sold out within a day or two. The phone never seemed to stop ringing.

Ring.

"Do you guys have pot?"

"No."

Ring.

"Any pot yet?"

"No."

Eventually Lathrop devised a semaphore system. When he had pot to sell, Lathrop flew the Washington State flag atop his store. When he ran dry, the flag came down.

Medical dispensaries continued to operate even though they were technically illegal. Or at least operating in a very gray area. This led to confusion. Out-of-state tourists barged into medical dispensaries looking to exercise this exotic new freedom. They'd heard all about Washington's adult-legal pot. Here they were with cash in hand. And they *still* couldn't purchase weed. Exasperated employees at The Source, a dispensary in Pioneer Square, taped a handwritten sign to their door. "We are a medical marijuana facility," it read. "Not a retail store. A medical card is required to purchase here."

Washington continued to have supply problems. Only a fraction of the awarded retail licenses actually turned into pot shops. The rest became ghost licenses, haunting the slots denied to more able shopkeepers. Meanwhile, many of the shops that launched had only enough marijuana to stay open two days a week. There simply weren't enough 502-licensed farmers growing at capacity.

As a result, the state's black market showed no signs of imminent demise. When a friend of mine named Emily happened to mention her weed dealer, I expressed surprise.

"You still have a weed dealer?" I said.

"Sure," she said. "It's convenient. The legal shops are expensive and don't have any pot."

"At least get a medical card," I said. "The stuff in the dispensaries is so much better. You can comparison shop."

A few weeks later Emily sent me an email. She'd gotten her green card and found a dispensary she loved. "It's a little place on Rainier Ave.," she wrote. "Very good pot bartender. I told him to steer me away from 'anxious weed,' and he knew just what I needed."

It was a half step in the right direction. Emily had moved from the black market to the gray. Now she was telling her friends with weed dealers to get their own green cards. And she mentioned an unexpected side benefit of legalization. "One thing that's really nice," she wrote, "is being able to finally talk about pot use honestly with my family doctor."

In Colorado, meanwhile, legal sales boomed. Government regulators and industry officials seemed to be containing the edibles crisis. The emergency task force that Dixie executive Joe Hodas served on came up with a number of sensible reforms. New rules required manufacturers to seal their products in child-safe packaging. Previously that responsibility had been left up to the retail stores. In medical dispensaries in Seattle, pot-infused edibles came in clear cellophane candy bags. In the retail shops of Denver, they were secured in plastic pharmaceutical bottles. The dosing issue was a tougher nut to crack. Somebody on the task force came up with the idea of rating dosages like ski runs: a green circle for low dose, blue square for intermediate, black diamond for high dose. I thought that was a brilliant solution. Colorado's powerful ski industry did not. It caught wind of the idea and put an end to it.

Beyond the edibles trouble, Colorado's rollout met with nothing but success. Customers purchased $20 million of marijuana per month. During the first six months of 2014, the state of Colorado realized nearly $30 million in tax revenue from pot sales. The most surprising data came in the area of crime, though.

Let me open this discussion with a strong caveat. Correlation does not imply causation. It's a drum I keep beating, I know. But it's worth keeping in mind when you see the crime stats from the city of Denver. Because they're kind of shocking.

During the first six months of retail marijuana sales, crime in Denver dropped significantly. Murder: down 32 percent. Rape: down 15 percent. Robbery: down 7 percent. Aggravated assault: about even. Burglary: down 8 percent. Auto break-ins: down 31 percent. The one crime on the increase: arson, up 55 percent.

Any number of factors might figure into the city's crime drop. If we assume it's unlikely that marijuana played a role in the arson spike, we've also got to discount marijuana's role in halving the city's homicide rate. Still, those were statistics worth thinking about. Nearly 60 percent of Colorado's retail marijuana outlets were in Denver. Had the crime rate increased, I imagine Kevin Sabet and his allies would have run screaming to Nancy Grace about the cannabis-powered crime wave.

Six months in, this was the bottom line: Revenue up, crime down.

28

TRUE

COMPASSION

There's a relationship I've been avoiding. It's the connection between gay marriage and marijuana. *Connection* isn't quite the word. It's more like gay marriage and marijuana are neighbors. Neither sought each other out. They just happened to end up living next to each other.

In 2012 I voted for gay marriage and legal pot on the same ballot. One month later, I witnessed the marriage of my cousin and his long-time partner. It was one of the proudest and most emotionally charged moments of my life. On the first day of marriage equality in Washington, Seattle mayor Mike McGinn turned City Hall into a wedding chapel, and 138 couples said their vows before justices of the peace. It was a cold morning with intermittent sprinkles. As each newlywed couple paraded down the stairs fronting 4th Avenue, well-wishers they'd never met showered them with rice, flowers and cheers. When it was time for my cousin's ceremony, Lucy and I joined our family band inside. The vows were sweet and short. Lucy had just turned 14. It was hard to convey to her the depth of the change she was witnessing.

A little more than a year later, I purchased legal marijuana in a Denver pot store. The moment was similarly profound, if marked by a bit less pride and emotion.

I've been avoiding a comparison of these historic turning points because I find something disrespectful about the lumping. Marijuana users have suffered arrest and imprisonment for enjoying an illicit substance of intoxication. Gay men and lesbians have suffered arrest, imprisonment, job loss, housing discrimination, ridicule, family and community ostracization, oppression, assault and death for who they are. These are not moral equivalents.

Yet they kept turning up together. What bound them was the path of acceptance that both movements traveled. For most of the 20th century, America's moral authorities portrayed homosexuality and marijuana as malignant forces threatening to destroy society. They passed laws to isolate and punish anyone caught loving incorrectly or getting high. As a child I was taught to fear, hate, ridicule and report gay people and pot smokers. That message didn't come from my parents. It came from schoolteachers, baseball coaches, church leaders, newspapers, magazines, television shows, first ladies and presidents. Resist the temptation of pot. Shun and ridicule the gay people. You're a kid. You don't know. A few years earlier, you didn't know the difference between real animals and imaginary monsters. You're trying to figure out the world. Adults are telling you not to play with guns or fire. Keep the fork out of the electrical socket. They tell you gay men are evil predators and marijuana will turn you into a heroin addict, you figure OK. The fork-in-socket info was solid. I guess the gay stuff and the pot warnings must be too.

Then the days pile up. Experience accumulates. If you're lucky, you meet new people. They're different than you. Some of them turn out to be gay. And honestly, they don't strike you as evil or predatory at all. In fact, the ones you know are kind and smart and seem to have their shit together. This evidence runs counter to what you've been taught.

As I grew older, more evidence appeared. During my first year of college, I slipped out alone to see a documentary at the Grand Illusion, a rep house in the University District. *The Times of Harvey Milk* chronicled the life of San Francisco's first openly gay city supervisor. At that point in my life I'd never met an openly gay person. I had suspicions about some of my teachers, but it was a small town and that sort of thing wasn't discussed. Watching the film, I could feel a sense of sadness and outrage grow within me. It wasn't just anger over the murder of Harvey Milk. I was furious at all the adults who had subtly instructed me to fear and hate gay people.

More information came to me. I spent a summer as an intern at the *Village Voice*. The *Voice* was one of the first papers to publish an annual Gay Pride issue. That year they ran a cover photo of two gay men with their child in a stroller. A gay family. In 1986, that was a shocking image. Back in Everett, Wash., my grandparents, bless them, subscribed to the *Voice* to support their grandson. They displayed each new issue on their coffee table. When the gay-dads cover came out, they tossed it right on top, like no big thing. I loved them for that. I also liked that the photo made us all consider the question: Well, why not?

When new evidence contradicts belief, each of us must choose. Dismiss the evidence or change the belief. My belief changed.

Something else changed too. The moral authorities lost some of their authority. Their warnings had been knit from the cloth of their own fears and reinforced with outright lies. They had encouraged children to engage in a kind of florid cruelty. They were eventually revealed to be wrong, but it took such a long damn time. With each half step of progress—to live openly without fear of arrest; to retain custody of their own children and adopt others; to teach schoolchildren; to serve in the military—the pillars of civilization failed to wobble and fall. When the idea of gay marriage was raised, a majority of Americans resisted it. Too much, said the moral authorities. Too far. So we tried pilot projects in a few states. Gay men and lesbians were allowed to register as domestic partners. Roommates with benefits. As if they needed a trial period.

Again, society withstood the challenge. Seemed better for it, actually. So the fearful were reassured. They took the next step and voted for full gay marriage. And my cousin was finally allowed the same civil right that all his other cousins had taken for granted our entire lives.

Medical marijuana is the domestic partnership of the marijuana legalization movement. As each state passes an MMJ law, it opens a pilot project. Dispensaries appear. Patients purchase marijuana under controlled conditions. Madness fails to go viral in the streets. Evidence and experience accumulate. The fearful are reassured.

Though they moved down similar paths to acceptance, I still hesitated to intertwine gay rights and marijuana legalization. And then something fairly remarkable happened. It may not be remarkable to you, but it became so to me. In the course of investigating the history of marijuana, I always felt there was a missing piece. Articles about medical marijuana tended to begin in 1996, when California passed the nation's first MMJ law. But how did California get there? I didn't have a clue. When I began looking into it, I discovered that the roots of today's medical marijuana movement could be traced back to the AIDS crisis that devastated San Francisco in the 1980s. It turned out that marijuana and gay marriage were more than just neighbors.

In the depths of the plague years, there was a kindly Irish Catholic woman named Mary Jane Rathbun who volunteered at Ward 86, San Francisco General Hospital's HIV/AIDS clinic. Rathbun was known as Brownie Mary. Rathbun baked marijuana brownies in her house in the Castro and offered them to Ward 86 patients suffering from AIDS wasting, a horrible syndrome that shuts down the appetite while depleting the body with fever and diarrhea. The munchies, long a staple of pothead jokes, proved to be no joke on Ward 86. Marijuana's appetite-stimulating properties helped patients stay alive.

Around that same time, a gay activist and pot seller named Dennis Peron was also becoming aware of the drug's medicinal benefits. It was 1990. Peron's partner, Jonathan West, was dying of AIDS. West's drug regimen made him so nauseous he couldn't eat. Marijuana eased his pain and restored his appetite. Shortly after West died, Peron hatched the

idea for a cannabis buyers club modeled after experimental AIDS medicine co-ops. He opened his first club in the Castro.

Peron and Brownie Mary joined together in 1991 to push San Francisco's Proposition P, a citywide initiative that called on the state of California to allow cannabis use for medicinal purposes. With the AIDS
crisis ravaging the city, the measure passed with 79 percent of the vote.
In terms of the modern legalization movement, this was Initiative Zero.

Brownie Mary died in 1999, but I was pleased to discover that Dennis
Peron still ran a guest house in the Castro. I sent an email asking if he
would be willing to talk. He replied within a couple of hours. "Any time
really," he wrote. "I'm not as mobile as I was."

A couple of weeks later, I rang the bell at the Castro Castle, a funky
three-story Victorian on the western edge of the city's world-famous gay
district. It was a gorgeous San Francisco summer afternoon. A breeze
played lightly through the hills and hollows. Across the street, the slant-
ing afternoon light wrapped shadows around Mission Dolores, the old
Friar Serra church founded in 1776.

"Come on up!" somebody yelled.

I climbed a narrow staircase.

"Dennis will be out in a minute. Let me show you your room." John
Entwistle, Peron's husband, guided me through a series of hallways,
stairways and plankboard footbridges that led to a backyard cottage
faced in Day-Glo dots, swirls and stars. "We're very into color here,"
Entwistle told me.

Peron appeared a few minutes later. He was thin, with white spun-
cotton hair and a devilish smile. There was a trace of New York in his
voice. "Where's that come from?" I asked.

"Long Island," he said. A gay kid raised in the conformity of the '50s
suburbs, Peron lugged a rifle in Vietnam before settling stateside in the
Bay Area. "In San Francisco I didn't have to hide," he told me. Peron
ran a popular Castro restaurant called The Island and campaigned for

his friend Harvey Milk. He also dealt a lot of weed. "I got busted for pot about once a year," he told me. "But I had a good lawyer. So I'd usually only end up spending a few days in jail."

AIDS arrived in 1980. "Twenty people died in this house," Peron told me. He drew on a cigarette. "We were right in the center of it. Around us, in this neighborhood, 5,000 people died." Most of his weed buyers were gay men. "One after another, people would come in and sit down and say, 'I got it too,'" recalled Entwistle, who at the time was a young gay activist fresh off the plane from New York. "Everyone had it."

West, Peron's partner, contracted AIDS wasting syndrome, which is like a stomach flu that never ends. "We were all blind, searching for any drug that might work," Peron recalled. "They gave him Marinol for the nausea, but he'd just vomit that up," Peron continued. By smoking marijuana, the drug went straight into his bloodstream. "It's not a miracle cure. But it gave him some moments of dignity in that last year."

The pot eased West's suffering, but it also attracted attention from the SFPD. One night a narcotics squad showed up at the Castro Castle around midnight. They rushed the door and threw an emaciated West to the floor. One cop kept a boot on his neck as others searched the house. "Know what AIDS stands for?" the cop taunted. "Asshole In Deep Shit."

The police turned up a quarter pound of marijuana and arrested both men. The district attorney declined to charge West, but he brought the full weight of his office down on Peron. At Peron's trial, West testified that he used the drug to treat his disease. The judge dismissed the charges against Peron. West died two weeks later. He was 29.

———

It was around this time that Robert Randall, the glaucoma patient, re-entered the story. In the early 1990s Randall began encouraging AIDS patients to join the Public Health Service's Compassionate IND program, the protocol that allowed him to receive joints from the federal farm in Mississippi. He sent application packets to AIDS organizations around the country.

By the summer of 1991, the George H.W. Bush administration faced the prospect of having to admit hundreds of AIDS patients to the IND program. The federal government would be issuing as medicine a drug that by its Schedule I definition had "no currently accepted medical use." Bush responded by killing the IND program. "If it's perceived that the Public Health Service is going around giving marijuana to folks, there would be a perception that this stuff can't be so bad," explained Public Health Service Chief James Mason. Mason later inserted a grandfather clause that allowed Randall and seven others already enrolled in the IND to continue receiving their federal joints. "Everyone else," Martin Lee wrote in *Smoke Signals*, "was told to drop dead."

After burying his partner, Peron spent restless nights pacing the floors of the Castro Castle. "All my friends were dead," he recalled. "What was I going to do with my life?"

He decided to turn his pot business into a patient business. The first step was to get the city behind him. In the fall of 1991, he put a simple memorial before the citizens of San Francisco. Proposition P asked the state legislature to "restore hemp medical preparations" to the list of available medicines in California. The measure passed.

A few days later, Peron opened America's first medical marijuana dispensary. The San Francisco Cannabis Buyers Club operated out of a storefront on Church Street a few blocks from the Castle.

"We invited the media in," he recalled. "We knew we had a great story. These were old women, people with AIDS, with glaucoma, non-Hodgkin's lymphoma, all types of cancer. People who were dying. They were coming to us for marijuana. You want to bust them? Go ahead. The cameras are waiting."

On the morning of the second day, a line formed down the block. John Entwistle rushed over to calm the crowd.

"Look, we haven't vetted most of you," Entwistle told the throng, "and we expect the cops any minute now. So if you want to go elsewhere, we understand."

Nobody left. The cops never came.

Over time, even the SFPD began to soften. "The cops hated Dennis, but even they lost guys to the AIDS crisis," Entwistle told me. "They saw what was happening. In fact, they started referring people. We had patients come up and say, 'You'll never believe who sent me here. I got busted in the park, and when the cop heard my story he gave me this address.' "

Peron smiled at the memory. "In the middle of the War on Drugs, in the eye of the hurricane, I started a club to help the sick."

Inspired by Peron's success, marijuana clubs catering to AIDS patients began popping up around the country: New York; Washington, D.C.; Pittsburgh; Little Rock; Key West; Seattle. When cancer patients heard about AIDS patients using marijuana, the cancer patients began using it too. Or rather, they began to use it more openly. As a retired oncology nurse once told me, "Honey, we were doing that in the '70s. A nurse would stand in front of the closed door while the patient smoked. Nobody said anything about it, but everyone knew what was going on."

In the mid-'90s that interest grew into a political movement. Twice the California legislature passed bills legalizing the medical use of marijuana. Twice Republican Gov. Pete Wilson vetoed them. In 1996, Peron and his allies took the issue directly to the voters. Getting an initiative on the ballot in California isn't easy. First you've got to gather 433,000 signatures. As the deadline drew near, the organizers of Proposition 215 had nowhere near that many. Then they got lucky. Billionaire financier George Soros, an outspoken opponent of the war on drugs, happened to read a *New York Times* article about Prop. 215. Sitting next to him was Ethan Nadelmann, the economist and then head of the Lindesmith Center, a Soros-funded drug policy institute. "Soros basically passed the article over to Nadelmann and told him to get on the line to California, hire a pro and get those signatures," Peron recalled. Almost overnight, petitioners appeared in front of supermarkets in California. Prop. 215 made the ballot.

———————

As the summer of 1996 wore on, opinion polls tracked a steady rise of support for Prop. 215. California attorney general Dan Lungren, a conservative Republican with a rising national profile, grew alarmed at the prospect of his state turning into a stoner's paradise.

A plan was hatched. Working with the DEA, the state narcotics bureau and the SFPD, Lungren launched an operation to infiltrate and destroy Dennis Peron and the San Francisco Cannabis Buyers Club. Peron, the face of Prop. 215, would be arrested and exposed as nothing but a dirty drug dealer.

On Aug. 4, a Sunday, more than 100 cops swarmed the Buyers Club at 8 in the morning. Armored personnel vehicles blocked Market Street. The cops arrived in heavy black body armor. They brandished pistols, shotguns and assault weapons. They took a battering ram to the front door. By the end of the day, the cops had hauled away 150 pounds of marijuana, 11,000 patient records and tens of thousands of dollars in cash.

The raid backfired on Lungren.

"Overnight, the media came to life," Peron recalled. TV cameras exposed the damage. Editorials condemned Lungren's jackbooted tactics. "Mainstream California was hit with a tsunami of sympathetic stories," Peron later wrote, "all urging the electorate to vote for Proposition 215 to end this madness."

The final push came from Zonker Harris.

Two editors at *High Times* bumped into *Doonesbury* cartoonist Garry Trudeau at a Manhattan party a couple of weeks after the Cannabis Buyers Club bust. They told him the story. Trudeau knew good material when he heard it. Two weeks later, Dan Lungren found himself lampooned in the nation's newspapers as the man who "would raid a sanctuary for dying AIDS and cancer patients." Zonker, the beloved pot-smoking baby boomer, was depicted handing out pot brownies to

AIDS patients.

Lungren flipped out. At a press conference he lashed out at Trudeau, *Doonesbury* and Zonker Harris. Lungren accused them of corrupting the nation's youth. Reporters at the presser swapped glances. *Is he putting us on?* He was not. Brian Lungren, the attorney general's brother and political adviser, capped the episode with a quote that effectively ended the anti-215 campaign. "Zonker's a real person," he said. "He is not fictitious. And we should put Zonker behind bars where he belongs."

California Proposition 215 passed on Nov. 5, 1996, with 56 percent of the vote.

———

It was late afternoon. I called an Uber car and had the driver drop me at the corner of Market and Castro. The setting sun sprayed the scene with that golden California glow where the cars and the people and the storefronts turn all warm and groovy and it's so beautiful you wonder why the whole world hasn't moved there already. Though I'd never been there before, there was something familiar about the spot. It was . . .

It was the candlelight vigil. The night after the murders of George Moscone and Harvey Milk, thousands of San Franciscans poured into the Castro. They lit candles here at Market and Castro and marched to City Hall, together in silence. To mourn. To express their outrage. To come together and say, *Enough.* Enough with the cruelty and the oppression and the gay bashing, and enough with hiding in the closet and taking it. That part is over. The place seemed familiar because it had been seared into memory by the final devastating scene in *The Times of Harvey Milk*, the scene of that candlelight march and those people, all those people, each one holding a spot of light and there seemed to be no end to them.

I thought about that scene, and I became less bothered by the intertwining of gay marriage and marijuana. Dennis Peron did that for me. In his story I found a maddening consistency of theme. When confronted with new evidence that challenged the beliefs of those in power, those in power dismissed the evidence. Time and again, they balked at the tiniest change in course because of concern about "the perception." In the White House, President Reagan and his advisers refused to address the AIDS crisis out of fear that doing so might lead to the perception that being gay was OK. George H.W. Bush refused medical marijuana to dying AIDS patients because, as his Public Health Service director explained, "there would be a perception that this stuff can't be so bad." President Clinton's drug czar rejected the findings of his own experts on marijuana.

The common thread here is the idea that the American people can't handle the truth. That we must be saved from our own weak character and lack of willpower. For decades we've heard worries about perception and "the signal we're sending to kids" about marijuana. The signal we've been sending to kids about marijuana is a lie. Every kid who's ever smoked a joint knows it. If you overhype marijuana as some sort of irresistible crazy-making drug, you reveal yourself as a liar the first time someone lights up, gets high, enjoys it and goes on to live a happy and productive life.

Perception and deception are not working. The catastrophe that is the war on marijuana started with the lies of Harry Anslinger, but it found its truest voice in Richard Nixon. "Educate them, shit," Nixon told Bob Haldeman. Kids can't be educated about marijuana. "You've got to scare them."

Enough with the scary lies, I thought. Enough. It's time to try something else.

I turned and walked back toward Mission Dolores and the Castro Castle. When I came upon Peron and Entwistle, they were standing over some shrubs in a planter on the sidewalk. "We're in the middle of a drought, and this is not a drought-tolerant species!" Entwistle told Peron. "We need to replace it with something else."

Peron shrugged. "Yeah, but I like it," he said.

Entwistle had already cut one shrub and was threatening to cut another. I wished them luck and stepped away. When I closed the door to my room I could still hear them going at it, an old married couple bickering.

29

CLASSICALLY

CANNABIS

Jane West sent me a reminder about her Colorado Symphony Orchestra series. The next Classically Cannabis event was coming up on a Friday night in late July. It was at a gallery in Denver's arts district. She had me on the guest list. BYOC: Bring Your Own Cannabis.

Sure. Why not. I'd seen plenty of unappealing marijuana consumption over the previous two years. The CSO gig seemed like an opportunity to enjoy it in a more sophisticated setting. I bought a cheap ticket on Frontier and flew out to Denver.

If you discounted the open use of a federally illegal drug, the scene inside the Space Gallery was completely unexceptional. Men in business casual shirts and snooty jeans chatted up women in cocktail dresses with daring necklines. An open bar served cheap wine, local craft beer and San Pellegrino. On the walls: abstract paintings of middling interest. The CSO's brass quintet struck up an old jazz standard. I made my way to the outdoor patio.

The place was lousy with pot industry insiders. In one corner I spotted

Mahatma Concentrates co-founder Shannon Wilson; in another, The Farm owner Jan Cole. Marijuana Policy Project point man Mason Tvert shared a laugh with his Amendment 64 comrade Christian Sederberg. Jane West held court in a billowing maxidress. Here and there a joint was shared, a pen vaped. It reminded me of art openings back in the day when people smoked cigarettes. The only difference was that people here were acting extra friendly to one another.

I folded myself into an Adirondack chair and fumbled in my pocket. I'd arrived fortified: two joints and half a gram of crumbly concentrate from a pot shop a couple of blocks from the Ramada on Colfax. The concentrate was Matanuska Thunder Fuck, a legendary strain nurtured in Alaska during that state's brief moment of cannabis decriminalization in the '70s. No sooner had I popped the lid on the joint container, though, than my neighbor made a friendly gesture. "Like a taste?" he said.

"Well . . . sure. Tell me what you've got there."

"This is my own concentrate. Made with CO_2. Good pure stuff. None of that hydrocarbon filth."

So—not a fan of the BHO extraction process.

Eric told me he had been making concentrates for the local MMJ market for the past few years, but now it was time for him to leave. "It's getting too hard to find product," he said. Back in the day, the raw materials for his concentrate—the plant's less-potent trim leaves—were given away for free. Pot growers were only too happy to have somebody else haul away the trash. With the opening of the retail market and the growing popularity of concentrates, trim leaves had become a valuable commodity. It was becoming tougher for a guy like Eric to turn a buck.

"Where you moving to?" I asked.

"I'd rather not say."

He pressed a button on his vape pen. A foggy vapor formed in a bulbous glass chamber. I wrapped my lips around the mouthpiece and inhaled.

Not bad. Fairly smooth. Stress and anxiety flowed out of my body like air from an untied balloon. "Thank you," I said.

The brass quintet moved on to Gershwin's "Summertime." I quite fancied the idea of listening to classical music with a light cannabis buzz. If pot could turn *Dark Side of the Moon* into an epic aural experience, imagine what it might do for *The Magic Flute* or Beethoven's Ninth. Sadly, the combination of five brass instruments and the high-and-hard acoustics of the art gallery turned the concert into a crashing mess. *Dear merciful Lord, shut it off!* The sound bounced around my skull like a misfired slug.

Todd Mitchem, the O.penVape executive, caught my eye. Mitchem had recently exited O.penVape after a disagreement with the company's founder. "I've got a new venture," he told me. "I'm Kickstarting a brand campaign called 'I Choose Cannabis.'" The idea was to positively re-brand the industry. He introduced me to his project partners, Olivia Mannix and Jennifer DeFalco. Mannix and DeFalco ran a marijuana-focused marketing agency called Cannabrand.

"As a mainstream person who's used cannabis for 20 years, it's always frustrated me that I couldn't say to people, *I do this because it's a choice*," Mitchem said. He gave me a sticker with the slogan written over a green checkmark. "I'm not a devil. It's not a disgusting habit. It's a choice. I enjoy it. I'm tired of hiding it. If you don't like it, I actually don't care anymore."

Mannix nodded. "Weed is the new wine," she said. "I choose it because I can have a little cannabis at night, instead of a couple glasses of wine, and I will be ready to go to the gym the next morning at 6 a.m."

"Denver is the inception point," DeFalco added. "We're the ones building the norms for the rest of the world. The media tends to focus on the extreme subcultures, but we know there are a lot of mainstream people using cannabis. We want to make it safe to talk about, openly, as an adult choice."

I mingled, seeking non-industry folk. Rachel, a young woman wearing a red dress and henna tattoo stockings, struck up a conversation with me. She was an aspiring writer, mid-20s. "I'm always looking for ways to connect with the arts scene here," she told me. "So I figured I'd give this a try." Rachel used to write for Ask.com, a notorious piecework mill, "but it was so soul-sucking I had to quit." Now she works for a law firm that specializes in asbestos litigation. "It's not exciting, but I leave it behind when I walk out the door," she said. "And it leaves me time to write fiction."

The brass quintet took five. *Allah be praised.* Jan Cole waved me over. "I've been thinking about something the past couple weeks," she told me. "Since the opening of retail, I'm seeing a lot of big players moving in. And I'm worried. They've got money. They could crush smaller independents like The Farm." The notion of "big players" was always a vague fear of people both inside and outside the industry. People outside the industry heard "big players" and thought R.J. Reynolds Tobacco. But inside the industry, "big" could mean a local grower who had hooked a couple of deep-pocketed investors. "I'm thinking of starting up a consortium of independent organic growers," Cole said. "Something that might help us survive."

Survive? Colorado was only six months into the legal adult-use retail era. And here was Cole talking like an independent bookstore owner worried about getting crushed by Barnes & Noble and Amazon.com.

Past 11, the last stragglers drifted away. I wandered north, Santa Fe Drive asleep but for a couple of taverns drawing night owls with neon. There was talk of an afterparty at a place called Point Gallery, so I stopped in. Mannix and DeFalco met me at the door. "Do you want to consume?" Mannix asked.

"Sure," I said.

"Where should we go?" she wondered. "Can we light up in here?"

I looked around. Large paintings of lumpy white people hung on the walls. I imagined the gallery owner frowning on us.

"Probably not here," I said. "Let's find a place outside."

The three of us wandered like Scooby-Doo sleuths through the gallery's maze of hallways and white cubes. Once again I found myself forced to solve the place-of-consumption puzzle. It was illegal to light up on a public sidewalk. We couldn't smoke anything indoors. In Colorado, marijuana always felt legal right up until the moment you wanted to smoke it.

Finally we came upon a door that led to a secret alley.

"Sativa or hybrid?" Mannix asked.

"Sativa," I said.

She presented a joint. Its wrapper had a beautiful rice-paper opacity, like a tiny Vietnamese spring roll.

Mannix put fire to the doob. Matt Nager, a portrait photographer, popped his head around the corner. "Mind if I shoot?" he said. Nager was there on assignment for *Marie Claire*.

Mannix and DeFalco gave each other a look. They passed the joint. "I don't know . . ."

I put the filter to my lips and inhaled. I had learned to draw in the smoke slowly so as not to burn my windpipe. Mannix's weed was smooth, with a mild flavor. Not like that trachea-torching crap I smoked back in January. I held the smoke for a count of three, then exhaled.

The Cannabrand founders debated the photo question. "This is the point, right?" DeFalco said. The point being, to bring cannabis use out of the closet. To show no shame in smoking pot in America's first legal state. And yet . . .

"I don't know if an alley is the right place to be seen consuming," Mannix said.

Probably not, but that was the reality of consumption here and now. And truthfully, it was a pretty romantic alley. Tea lights and lanterns gave the scene a soft Parisian glow. Someone had painted a crude rendition of Picasso's Blue Period guitarist on a brick wall. Two pigeons cooed near a nest.

They came to an agreement. Photos were OK as long as the women weren't depicted actively inhaling. "Nobody looks good pulling on a cigarette," I said. "Except maybe Keith Richards."

I took another drag.

"Go ahead and kill it," said Mannix.

I hesitated. I found myself struggling to work through the pleasure-to-comportment ratio. The remainder of the joint held enough cannabis to take me to a place where conversations with hotel drapes were held. That seemed undesirable. Because *What I really want to see is a stoned middle-aged man stumbling through an art gallery*, said nobody ever.

"Thank you, no."

I swanned through the gallery, letting the newly magnificent artwork play on my brain. The skin textures of the white-people portraits felt like landscapes to explore. A painting of a big round Cheerio in gold leaf caught my fancy. But it was the work of Gary Bibb that truly seduced me. Bibb had created a mixed-media piece of 12 soda cans crushed in the street. He painted them flat black and arranged them like pinned beetles. I found it extraordinary. It spoke of death and the body, each can unique in its folds and creases yet each destined for the same fate of black decomposition. Had I the means, I would have purchased it on the spot. My wife would've killed me.

A woman appeared with a silver tray of candies.

"Would you like a chocolate?"

The goodies were medicated. "They're low-dose, five to 10 milligrams," said their creator, Denver chef Melissa Parks.

I savored a piece of chocolate bark. "That's pink Himalayan sea salt with cranberry," she said. Mmm. Delish.

Somebody introduced me to Heidi Keyes, a local artist. "Ask her about her glasses," I was told.

"What's this about your glasses?" I said.

"Classes," she said. "I have a series I call 'Puff, Pass, and Paint.' People come, use a little cannabis, and it makes them feel more comfortable about making art."

"People are doing this?"

"I have so many classes that I quit my day job," she said. "Last week a woman came in with her 80-year-old grandmother. The grandmother smoked for the first time in 40 years. She said, 'Pass me that pipe.' And she painted, and it was amazing—not just the work she created, but to see someone in her 80s connect with people in their 20s. I think it really says something about the way people can connect through cannabis."

Keyes's friend joined us. She too was in the business. "I'm opening a 420-friendly spa next month," she said. Her name was Jordan Person. She'd been a nurse for 14 years, a massage therapist for eight. A few years ago an illness forced her to undergo six surgeries over three years. "I used cannabis to help my recovery," she told me. "I smoked it, I ate it, I drank it, I rubbed it on my body. My healing time was probably cut in half."

Person's spa was called Primal Therapeutics. She planned to offer massage therapy with cannabis-infused oils.

"What exactly does it do?" I asked.

"I'm a deep-tissue therapist," she said. By the time she gets done with her clients, they often require ice packs to reduce tissue swelling. When she uses cannabis oil, though, she sees far less swelling. "I've never used a product as effective."

My brain floated pleasantly. I found myself enjoying an exceptional openness to new people and ideas. Would I have met so many interesting characters at a wine-and-cheese gallery? Hard to say. At the very least, I might not have been as receptive to the opportunity. Sober Bruce might have written them off as annoying, unscientific, delusional. Maybe sober Bruce could learn a thing or two from high Bruce.

At 1:35 in the morning, I shuffled down the alley to Santa Fe Drive. Two young men were talking excitedly about fracking, the smart grid and the future of wind energy. An Uber car pulled up. A woman in a blue dress climbed inside. I spotted a Car2Go parked across the street. I checked my head. *Not a bright idea.* I punched the taxi numbers into my phone and called it a good night.

THE WORLD

CHANGED

So this is what the new world looks like.

Two years after legalizing marijuana, my home state of Washington is thriving. Colorado is also booming. None of the fears of 2012 have come to pass.

Neither Colorado nor Washington has reported an increase in stoned workers, stoned managers, stoned drivers, stoned mothers, stoned fathers, stoned baristas, stoned IT guys, stoned HR managers, stoned CEOs, stoned CFOs, stoned grocery clerks, stoned ferry captains, stoned ferry passengers, stoned doctors, stoned lawyers, stoned cable guys, stoned electricians, stoned farmers or stoned stoners.

Legal pot seemed to have little effect on crime. Wrongdoing fell in some places and rose in others. In Denver, violent crime and property crime dropped in 2014. In Seattle, they ticked up. By mid-2014, drunk and drugged driving arrests in both Washington and Colorado were at all-time lows. Through the first seven months of 2014, Colorado highway deaths were also near their all-time low.

Illegal pot growers were moving their operations elsewhere. In 2009, Washington State Patrol eradication teams destroyed 609,000 plants in illegal grow operations on public land. In 2013, with the same level of enforcement, those teams eradicated only 39,000 plants. That's a 94 percent decrease in dangerous and environmentally disastrous grows.

Cities and counties saved tens of millions of dollars by not chasing marijuana users. In Washington State, 6,879 people were arrested on low-level marijuana charges in 2011. In 2013 that number was 120—a drop of 98 percent. More important, nearly 7,000 people enjoyed lives undisrupted by the trauma of arrest and jail time. The mass incarceration of African-American men continued throughout the rest of the nation. But not in Colorado and Washington.

Those arrests will soon stop in Alaska and Oregon, too. Encouraged by the success of Colorado and Washington, the two states voted to legalize marijuana in November 2014. Washington, D.C., also voted to legalize, but Congress's control over the nation's capital may delay implementation in D.C. indefinitely.

The day after those elections, talk turned to 2016 and the expected legalization of marijuana in California. In 2010, California voters narrowly rejected a poorly conceived and underfunded legalization measure. With a well-written law and a fat campaign chest in place, most pundits predicted a Golden State landslide in favor of legal pot in 2016. By Jan. 1, 2017, the entire West Coast of America could very well be marijuana-legal.

———

Though public life in the legalized states changed little, my own private life underwent profound adjustments. By the close of 2014, I was a different person. My two-year expedition into the marijuana world left me more suspicious of government authority and more hopeful about the common sense of most Americans. It made me a more open, tolerant and forgiving person. I believe the continued expansion of cannabis legalization will do the same for others across the nation.

Anyone familiar with the history of slavery, Indian treaties, race relations and civil rights in America cannot be shocked by displays of dishonesty and raw cruelty by those carrying out the nation's business. Still, I found myself gobsmacked by the magnitude of deception practiced in the name of keeping marijuana illegal. Let me be clear: marijuana is not a safe drug. No drug is safe. Not caffeine, not alcohol, not morphine. Each contains a universe of possibility and risk. The idea that marijuana is, as I explained to my young son, less akin to heroin and more like alcohol— this is not a new idea. It was documented by the Indian Hemp Drugs Commission in 1893. It was confirmed by the U.S. Army's Panama Canal Zone investigation in 1925. The La Guardia report discovered the same truth in 1944. The Shafer Commission came to the same conclusion in 1972. Ten years later, the National Academy of Sciences confirmed the Shafer Commission's findings. The White House drug czar asked the Institute of Medicine to reopen the question in 1999. The institute's researchers came back with the same answer. In every instance, those in power were forced to adjust their belief about marijuana or reject the evidence. In every instance, they rejected the evidence. The belief was too great to overcome. It was as entrenched and politically powerful as racial prejudice because the demonization of marijuana was itself a form of racial prejudice. There was no upside to bucking it, because those arrested, imprisoned and ruined by the belief were the disenfranchised. They were first called Negroes and Mexicans, then hippies and Hispanics and blacks, then African Americans and Latinos. They often couldn't vote and were rarely seen writing checks to political campaigns. The more of them put away in prison, the fewer of them showed up to vote. By the turn of the 21st century, when the War on Drugs had grown to grotesque proportions and marijuana laws had become nothing but trawl nets to catch and hoist dark-skinned men into the hold of the world's largest prison system—well, then a lot of us looked up and realized things had gone too far. We cast a vote and said, *Enough*.

Not just enough with the outrageous laws. Enough with the stigma and prejudice. As much as Perry Parks, Dennis Peron and Bernard Noble changed my perspective, I have to say that unreconstructed capitalists like Tripp Keber and Todd Mitchem did as well. "I am choosing to use cannabis," Mitchem told me. "I'm not a devil."

He's right. The shaming and stigmatization of pot users has gone hand in hand with draconian sentencing laws and mass incarceration. How could the outrageous prison terms be justified if not by the shameful character and nefarious choices of the marijuana smoker? Two years ago, pot use by my friends disappointed me. Now I look back on myself in disappointment.

I tried for the longest time to find words and metaphors to convey what I was feeling. I finally found them in late summer at, of all places, Hempfest. Seattle's annual cannabis festival is a free, three-day, open-to-all-ages event. There are music stages and booths and food and all sorts of carryings-on. The police generally smile and look the other way. In 2013 the cops passed out free bags of Doritos as a kind of peace offering and acknowledgment of the new legal era. Over the years, I've done my best to avoid the event. This year I stopped by for a couple of hours on a Friday afternoon prior to meeting Claire and the kids at Green Lake.

To my disappointment, the scene was everything I'd imagined. Unshowered dreadlocked men walked about as if on profound quests. (For their missing shirts, one assumed.) Women in long skirts practiced the circus arts. Bald men with beards paraded their head tattoos. Bros in flat-brimmed snapbacks wore those Dr. Seuss T-shirts with marijuana puns. Along the fringes clumped friends and families who knew one another from the West Coast street fair circuit.

As I stood before a stage where a comedian made jokes about smoking weed while playing golf (not the worst idea, actually), my phone buzzed with an incoming call. It was my daughter. I turned the ringer off; I wouldn't be able to hear her in this din. She texted, "Where are you?"

Onstage: "... *and you know I love gettin' high. You know it!*"

My thumbs went to work. "Can't answer," I texted. "Hempfest speaker too embarrassing."

She wrote back. "How's it goin over there?"

"Too much hippie funk," I wrote. "Leaving soon."

And I did.

Later that night, it occurred to me that my problem with Hempfest was the issue Mason Tvert raised with Nancy Grace. *The fact is, you don't like people who use marijuana.* It wasn't that I didn't like people who used marijuana. I didn't like *these* people who used marijuana. Then I had one of those thoughts that in retrospect seem so obvious, you're ashamed of yourself for admitting it came to you afresh. If I didn't like the people who attended Hempfest, I thought, maybe I shouldn't go to Hempfest.

Look, I like all kinds of music. But I'm not a big fan of electronic dance music. It's not my thing. Given that, it's probably not a good idea for me to spend a day at the Electric Daisy Carnival. My lack of appreciation for the genre—some might call it a loathing—does not, however, lead to the conclusion that electronic dance music should be outlawed. Let others enjoy it. They don't care that I hate it. I don't care that they love it.

This is where I've ended up with marijuana. I like all kinds of people who enjoy marijuana. I'm not so fond of the circus-panted freaks who attend Hempfest. That's OK. It doesn't mean they should be arrested. I can enjoy a conversation with Todd Mitchem or Jan Cole without thinking any worse of them for enjoying a little marijuana. (Or vice versa.) Knowing what I now know about pot, I still haven't become a connoisseur or aficionado. But I no longer disdain it. I have my vape pen and I use it a couple of times a month, usually late at night. When I catch a whiff of pot in public these days, I'm not annoyed. I have a different association with the scent now. It reminds me that the community in which I live took a brave step toward progress and justice. It makes me smile and enjoy the fact that I can talk honestly and laugh with my kids about pot and alcohol and sometimes even sex. It makes me think about the fact that we who make the rules are adults. We can handle this. And by doing so, we will create a better and more just world.

I left Hempfest and walked toward Dexter Avenue, happy to be on my way to see my family. It was a gorgeous August afternoon, filled with that glorious Seattle sunshine that feels like a kiss meant to apologize for all the suffering and pain of the previous winter. The sidewalk floated hazily with the scent of marijuana. It felt like summer and it smelled like freedom.

ACKNOWLEDGMENTS

Many people generously gave me their time, thoughts, opinions and insight, and for that I am grateful. This book wouldn't exist without them. The still-controversial nature of marijuana prevents me from naming them all, but someday that will change. I want to thank Dr. Donald Abrams, Jan Cole, Henry Wykowski, Allen St. Pierre, Dennis Peron, John Entwistle, Pete O'Neil, Jane West, Olivia Mannix, Jennifer DeFalco, Christie Lunsford, Troy Dayton, Steve DeAngelo, Gaynell Rogers, Jane West, Sean Azzariti, Toni Fox, Alison Holcomb, Todd Mitchem, Max Montrose, Otsie Stowell, Andy and Pete Williams, Kevin Sabet, Jeff Gilmore, Brendan Kennedy, Michael Blue, Christian Groh, Tonia Winchester, Patrick Moen, Jeff Guillot, Marjorie Esman, Gary Wainwright, Bill Rittenberg, Roger Townsend and Kari Franson.

There were friends, colleagues and editors who made me think, laugh, reconsider and keep moving forward. Thanks to Christopher Solomon, Jim Thomsen, Dan Glick, Leslie Dodson, Christine Aschwanden, George Meyer, Wendy Redal, Skip Card, Mike Gauthier, Erika Schickel, Dave Howard, Bryan Monroe, Craig Welch, Florence Williams, Elizabeth Hightower, Ilena Silverman, Will Dana, George Black and Doug Barasch. Tracy Ross provided the key link in the chain. Thuy Nguyen and her wonderful staff at Roosters were friendly and kind at the right moments, which means always. A dear group of friends helped more than they know: Scott and T, Linda and Steve, Gordon and Dawn, Brett and Dee, Christine and Leonard, Chris and Diana, Heidi and Johnny, Anne Phyfe and Bez. Mary Barcott, Jim Barcott, Mike Dederer, Donna Dederer and Larry Jay provided support in generous and often unexpected ways.

I owe a special thanks and a note of support to Bernard Noble. He remains trapped in the Kafkaesque institution known as the Louisiana prison system. In late 2014 the Louisiana State Supreme Court declined to hear his appeal. He is currently scheduled for release in the year 2023, with no possibility of parole.

Todd Shuster at Zachary Shuster Harmsworth believed in the book from the beginning, and Steve Koepp at Time Books made it a reality. I am profoundly grateful to my children, who encouraged me with their curiosity, sophistication, humor and their ability to handle the subject. And finally: I am blessed to share this life of adventure with Claire, who told me I should write it and she was right, as always.

SOURCE NOTES

Most of the narrative in *Weed the People* was drawn from interviews and my own experience. Any writer who touches on history, though, stands on a mountain of evidence discovered, collected and recorded by others. This list is by no means exhaustive, but it contains many of the sources from which I drew. For readers interested in a deeper dive into America's marijuana history, any of the books listed here would be an excellent place to start.

Alexander, Michelle. *The New Jim Crow: Mass Incarceration in the Age of Colorblindness*. The New Press, 2010.

Anderson, Patrick. *High in America: The True Story Behind NORML and the Politics of Marijuana*. Viking, 1981.

Baum, Dan. *Smoke and Mirrors: The War on Drugs and the Politics of Failure*. Little, Brown, 1996.

Bourne, Peter. " 'Just Say No': Drug Abuse Policy in the Reagan Administration," in *Ronald Reagan and the 1980s: Perceptions, Policies, Legacies*. Cheryl Hudson and Gareth Davies, editors. Palgrave Macmillan, 2008.

Brown, Peter. *The Love You Make: An Insider's Story of the Beatles*. Macmillan, 1983.

Bonnie, Richard J.; Whitebread, Charles H., *The Marijuana Conviction: A History of Marijuana Prohibition in the United States*. Lindesmith Center, 1999.

Booth, Martin. *Cannabis: A History*. Doubleday, 2003.

De Quincey, Thomas. *Confessions of an English Opium-Eater*. Oxford World's Classics paperback. Oxford University Press, 1998.

Goldman, Albert. *Grass Roots: Marijuana in America Today*. Warner Books, 1980.

Gray, Mike. *Drug Crazy: How We Got into This Mess and How We Can Get Out*. Random House,

1998.

Grinspoon, Lester. *Marihuana Reconsidered*. Harvard University Press, 1971.

Herer, Jack. *The Emperor Wears No Clothes*. Ah Ha Publishing, 11th edition, 2000.

Holland, Julie, ed. *The Pot Book: A Complete Guide to Cannabis*. Park Street Press, 2010.

Hudson, Cheryl, and Davies, Gareth, eds. *Ronald Reagan and the 1980s: Perceptions, Policies, Legacies*. Palgrave Macmillan, 2008.

Joy, Janet E., Watson, Stanley J., Benson, John A., eds. *Marijuana and Medicine: Assessing the Science Base*. National Academies Press, 1999.

Lee, Martin A. *Smoke Signals: A Social History of Marijuana—Medical, Recreational, and Scientific*. Scribner, 2012.

Linden, David J. *The Compass of Pleasure*. Viking Penguin, 2011.

Ludlow, Fitz Hugh. *The Hasheesh Eater*. Level Press, 1975.

Malott, Michael. *Medical Marijuana: The Story of Dennis Peron, the San Francisco Cannabis Buyers Club and the Ensuing Road to Decriminalization*. CreateSpace Publishing, 2009.

Manatt, Marsha. *Parents, Peers, and Pot*. National Institute on Drug Abuse, 1979.

Martin, Alyson, and Rashidian, Nushin. *A New Leaf: The End of Cannabis Prohibition*. The New Press, 2014.

Massing, Michael. *The Fix*. University of California Press, 1998.

Matthews, Patrick. *Cannabis Culture*. Bloomsbury, 1999.

Mezzrow, Milton, and Wolfe, Bernard. *Really the Blues*. Random House, 1946.

Miles, Barry. *Ginsberg: A Biography*. Virgin Publishing, 2007.

Morgan, Bill. *I Celebrate Myself: The Somewhat Private Life of Allen Ginsberg*. Viking Penguin, 2006.

Musto, David. *The American Disease: Origins of Narcotic Control*. Oxford University Press, 1999.

National Commission on Marihuana and Drug Abuse. *Marihuana: A Signal of Misunderstanding*. Signet/New American Library, 1972.

Nicosia, Gerald. *Memory Babe: A Critical Biography of Jack Kerouac*. University of California Press, 1994.

Peron, Dennis, and Entwistle, John. *Memoirs of Dennis Peron*. Medical Use Publishing House, 2012.

Roffman, Roger. *Marijuana Nation: One Man's Chronicle of America Getting High: From Vietnam to Legalization*. Pegasus Books, 2014.

Sloman, Larry. *Reefer Madness: A History of Marijuana*. Bobbs-Merrill, 1979.

Torgoff, Martin. *Can't Find My Way Home: America in the Great Stoned Age, 1945–2000*. Simon & Schuster, 2004.

Vyhnanek, Louis. *Unorganized Crime: New Orleans in the 1920s*. Center for Louisiana Studies, University of Southwestern Louisiana, 1998.

Walton, Stuart. *Out of It: A Cultural History of Intoxication*. Three Rivers Press, 2001.

Wilentz, Sean. *Bob Dylan in America*. Knopf, 2010.

ABOUT THE AUTHOR

BRUCE BARCOTT, a Guggenheim Fellow in nonfiction, is a contributor to the *New York Times, Rolling Stone, National Geographic,* the *Atlantic Monthly, Outside* magazine, and many other publications. *The Last Flight of the Scarlet Macaw,* his critically praised nonfiction book, was reviewed on the front cover of the *New York Times Book Review,* and has been adopted as a "One Book" choice by a number of cities and colleges across the United States. His previous book, *The Measure of a Mountain,* earned the Washington State Governor's Award. He lives on an island near Seattle with his wife, the memoirist Claire Dederer, and their two children.